The Choose to Lose Diet

Also by Dr. Ron Goor and Nancy Goor

*Eater's Choice: A Food Lover's
Guide to Lower Cholesterol*

== THE
Choose to Lose
DIET ==

A Food Lover's Guide to Permanent Weight Loss

Dr. Ron Goor, Nancy Goor
and Katherine Boyd, R.D.

HOUGHTON MIFFLIN COMPANY
Boston 1990

For information about permission to reproduce
selections from this book, write to Permissions,
Houghton Mifflin Company, 2 Park Street, Boston,
Massachusetts 02108.

Library of Congress Cataloging-in-Publication Data
Goor, Ron.
    The choose to lose diet : a food lover's guide to
permanent weight loss / Ron Goor, Nancy Goor,
and Katherine Boyd.
        p.   cm.
    Includes bibliographical references.
    ISBN 0-395-49336-6
    1. Low-fat diet.   2. Food — Fat content —
Tables.   I. Goor, Nancy.   II. Boyd, Katherine.
III. Title.
RM237.7.G66   1990   89-24467
613.2'5 — dc20   CIP

Printed in the United States of America

V 10 9 8 7 6 5 4 3 2 1

Book design by Joyce C. Weston

Before beginning this or any diet, you should
consult your physician to be sure it is safe for you.

Acknowledgments

Ron and Nancy Goor wish to thank the many people who have contributed to the development of this book: Robert R. Betting, Dr. J. P. Flatt, Alex Goor, Dan Goor, Jeanette Goor, Anita Hamel, Genevieve Kazdin, Suzanne Lieblich, Roland Lippoldt, Helen Miller, Martin Miller, and Isabelle Schoenfeld.

Katherine Boyd wishes to thank Fran Gillen, Mark Litke, Marcia Pruzan, and Estelle Schwalb.

Contents

Food Tables 191

Introduction

THE *Choose to Lose Diet* is an outgrowth of our book, *Eater's Choice: A Food Lover's Guide to Lower Cholesterol.* Soon after *Eater's Choice* was published we began receiving letters from ecstatic readers. Not only were they lowering their cholesterol, they were losing weight — typically 10 to 15 pounds and some up to 40 or more pounds. This was not the intention of the cholesterol-lowering plan, but it was a side effect that was appreciated as much (or more!).

Readers tell us that they find the *Eater's Choice* method simple, direct, and flexible. It gives them the tools and knowledge to take control of their diet for the first time. And it is positive. All foods are allowed. No exchanges, no two-week meal plans to follow for the rest of your life. *You* determine which foods you eat.

Choose to Lose uses essentially the same approach that was successfully utilized in *Eater's Choice.* But while *Eater's Choice* limits only saturated fat intake, *Choose to Lose* limits *total* fat consumption. Saturated fat is the chief culprit in the diet that raises blood cholesterol, but all three types of fat — saturated, monounsaturated, and polyunsaturated — in the foods you eat make you gain weight. In recent years scientific research has shown that dietary fat, not carbohydrates or total calories, is the primary cause of weight gain. Furthermore, the researchers note that weight loss can be achieved simply by limiting fat intake. That is why *Choose to Lose* uses a fat budget and the total fat content of foods to help you make food choices that satisfy your palate and help you to lose weight.

Like *Eater's Choice, Choose to Lose* helps you adopt a new eating lifestyle. After all, permanent weight loss, like permanent cholesterol lowering, requires a new lifelong eating pattern, not just a two-week crash diet. Whatever changes are made to lower cholesterol and weight must be continued. The diet plan must therefore be palatable and practical.

Not only is *Choose to Lose* easy to follow, it is also enjoyable. Most people eat a limited number of foods and are probably bored with their diet. This new low-fat way of eating will broaden your culinary horizons and add spice and variety to your life. You will explore new foods and new food preparations. To discover a world of new taste treats, try the 58 mouth-watering recipes in *Choose to Lose* — as well as 180 more in *Eater's Choice* — recipes for real foods, such as *Tortilla Soup, Cajun Chicken, Broiled Ginger Fish, Cinnamon Sweet Cakes, Honey Whole-Wheat Bread, Calzone, Divine Buttermilk Pound Cake,* and *Deep-Dish Pear Pie,* to mention just a few favorites.

Any change in eating patterns takes commitment and motivation. *Choose to Lose* provides you with the tools and knowledge to make food choices to keep you lean for a lifetime. You will find you are eating more food and enjoying it more. And most important, you will also lose weight.

Good luck and good health.

The Choose to Lose Diet

1. Fat's the One

TAKE A LOOK in the mirror — a good look. Is the person staring out at you a little pudgier than you would like? Has the muscle turned to flab? Are the seams and buttons on the verge of splitting and popping? Don't turn away in disappointment. Give yourself a smile. Already you are making a big change in *you*. You are starting on the *Choose to Lose* diet. Soon you will be seeing a trim version of what you see now. The trim version will be beaming. No suffering made the pounds melt away. Only good, abundant food, including your all-time favorites. *Choose to Lose* is not a miracle diet. In fact, it's not even a diet. It's a new way of eating that is easy, healthy, and delicious. And it works.

The key to *Choose to Lose* is FAT.

FAT MAKES FAT

The word is FAT. FAT is what you don't want to be and FAT is what you ate to become FAT. So, the way to become NOT FAT is to reduce fat in your diet. Don't focus on total calories . . . or sugar . . . or starch. Focus on FAT.

Until recently, most diet formulators based their weight loss methods on reducing *total calories*. Sugar and starch were always forbidden. These approaches pinpointed the wrong culprit. The reason that foods containing sugar make you gain weight is not because they contain sugar. It is because they contain *fat* and sugar. It is the fat in the cheesecake, not the sugar, that puts dimples in your knees. It is the fat in the sour cream, not the starch in the potato, that rounds your belly. It is your fat tooth, not your sweet tooth, that gets you into trouble.

1

CARBOHYDRATES: WEIGHT LOSS FOOD

Carbohydrates are the good guys. They increase your energy without increasing your girth. You can eat them with gusto and, as you will see below, you should eat lots of carbohydrates to keep up your metabolism. *Choose to Lose* encourages you to eat complex carbohydrates — fruits, vegetables, whole grains, even some simple sugars — without counting carbohydrate calories. *Choose to Lose* focuses on reducing the nutrient that is making you fat — FAT.

You may find this recommendation hard to accept. After all, you have probably been trying to cut *total calories* and limit carbohydrates for years. Please. Don't just accept this advice on faith. Read the following section, which explains simply how the fats and carbohydrates you eat affect your weight. The science behind *Choose to Lose* is fascinating, illuminating — and motivating!

FOOD — MORE THAN JUST PLEASURE

This is a book about fat, food, and you. Ice cream sundaes, chicken soup, T-bone steaks, potato chips — for most people food offers more than just gustatory satisfaction. Food may represent love (you want to please those you love; therefore you feed them); status (with your raise you can afford to eat filet mignon and caviar); nostalgia (the aroma of hot dogs conjures up visions of baseball games and family picnics); or something just plain wonderful to eat. Food fulfills a different need in each person, but for everyone — no matter how thin, fat, young, old, rich, poor — food is energy.

ENERGY EXPENDITURE

BMR. Your body needs a certain amount of energy to function. The amount of energy you use when you are completely at rest is called your basal metabolic rate (BMR). This is the energy needed to power your heart, lungs, brain, kidneys, and other organs and keep them in good repair, and for children, the energy to grow.

Physical Activity

You also need energy for physical activity — walking, running, moving. This is an expandable amount depending on how active you are.

So, the total amount of energy you expend is equal to the sum of your BMR and your physical activity.

ENERGY INTAKE

Food — Source of Energy

Where does your body get this energy? Energy is stored in fats, proteins, and carbohydrates in the foods you eat. More calories are stored in fat than in carbohydrates. One gram of fat has 9 calories (some scientists say 11!). One gram of carbohydrate or protein has 4 calories. Fat is so densely caloric that when you eat a little, you've eaten a lot of calories. For example, when you eat 1½ ounces of fat-laden potato chips you are consuming the same number of calories as when you eat 12 ounces of potatoes (two medium-large potatoes).

To release energy stored in fats, carbohydrates, and protein they must be burned. Picture a stack of logs blazing in a fireplace. The burning of nutrients and the burning of wood in a fireplace are similar chemical processes. In both cases the chemicals are combined with oxygen (burned or oxidized) and the energy stored in them is released. In the case of wood, the energy is released all in one step as heat. In the body, the oxidation goes on at a lower temperature (98.6°F) in small steps controlled by enzymes. In this way, most of the energy stored in the food is captured for growth, maintenance, repair, and physical activity, and less is wasted as heat.

All Calories Are Not Equal

You may have thought that everything you ate ended up as those rolls of fat rippling down your belly. You may even have been avoiding carbohydrates in the belief that they are fattening. But you were misguided.

In the past it was believed that calories from all foods contributed equally to weight gain. Recent scientific evidence has shown that fats, carbohydrates, and proteins are metabolized (burned and stored) differently. Fat calories are fattening while carbohydrate and protein calories (consumed in reasonable amounts) are not. In fact, eating carbohydrates can help you lose weight. To understand why, read on.

CARBOHYDRATES

The body has a limited capacity to store carbohydrates (about 800 calories or approximately one day's intake). Consequently, when you eat a meal, the carbohydrates are either burned immediately (for quick energy) or temporarily stored and then burned within a few hours to make room for the next day's intake. A small amount of carbohydrate always remains stored as glycogen* in muscle and other tissue as a source of quick energy.

How does this need to dispose of carbohydrates affect your weight? Under normal circumstances, *the carbohydrate you eat is never stored as fat* — that soft padding that currently covers too much of your frame.

Controlling Your Carbohydrate Appetite

As an additional safeguard against overloading the body with too much carbohydrate, eating carbohydrate triggers a feeling of satiety. You feel full so you stop eating, thus limiting the amount of carbohydrate you consume.

Thermogenesis

To prevent overloading the body's limited storage capacity for carbohydrates, much of the carbohydrate you eat is quickly burned off. The body can't capture all the energy that is released. The important factor here is that the energy that is not captured to power your BMR plus physical activity is converted to heat and is not used to satisfy your

---

Won't I Gain Weight If I Overeat Carbohydrates?

It is almost impossible to overeat carbohydrates because the body has developed mechanisms to prevent it.

1. Within normal limits the body burns off almost all the carbohydrate you eat. You can even occasionally eat up to 2000 calories of carbohydrate in addition to your normal diet and not gain weight.
2. Eating carbohydrates makes you feel full, so you stop eating them.
3. If you overeat carbohydrates one day, you tend to undereat them the next.
4. In addition, carbohydrates provide so much bulk, it is difficult to overeat them. Imagine eating 990 calories of air-popped popcorn: that amounts to 33 cups! Compare this with a Dairy Queen large chocolate shake, which also has 990 calories.

---

* Carbohydrate is stored in the body as glycogen, long chains of the simple sugar glucose.

energy needs nor is it stored as fat. This process of producing heat from burning carbohydrate is called the thermogenic effect of food. When you feel warm during or after a meal you're feeling the thermogenic effect.

Why *Choose to Lose* Encourages You to Eat Carbohydrates

To recap: *Because your body has limited capacity to store them, much of the carbohydrate you eat is burned.* Some of the energy released is used to power the body's needs, and much of the rest is converted to heat (except for a small amount stored for quick energy).

Low-Carbohydrate Diets = Short-Term Weight Loss

It takes 2 to 4 grams of water to store 1 gram (4 calories) of glycogen, the storage form of carbohydrate. Low-carbohydrate weight loss diets rely on depleting your glycogen stores. You may lose weight quickly, but what you are losing is the water used to store the glycogen and not fat. This weight loss may be fast, but it is not permanent.

WHY *CHOOSE TO LOSE* IS BASED ON REDUCING FAT

In contrast to carbohydrates, the fats that you eat are not burned right away but are immediately and completely stored in the adipose tissue, where they promptly become the soft, squishy blubber that pads your body. The adipose tissue contains enormous stores of fat (140,000 calories or more) and has an essentially unlimited capacity to store additional amounts of fat.

Eating fat neither causes the body to burn it quickly — or burn it at all, for that matter — nor does it trigger satiety. You can eat and eat fat without feeling full, and since all the fat is stored, overeating fat makes you fatter and fatter. When you overeat fat one day, your body has no mechanisms for limiting your fat consumption the next. You feel just as hungry for fat as you did the day before.

Burning Fat

Now you know why the carbohydrates you eat don't become fat on your body and the fats you eat do. Now you have a scientific reason to reduce your fat intake in the future. But what can you do about the fat that already rounds your edges? How can you make your body mobilize the fat out of the fat stores so you can lose weight?

Under normal conditions, the carbohydrate and protein you eat do not supply enough energy to meet all your energy needs (BMR + physical activity). The rest of the energy is supplied by burning fat removed from the fat stores.

The Secret to Weight Loss: Raiding the Fat Stores

Each day fat from the foods you eat is added to the fat stores. Some is removed for burning to furnish energy not supplied by the carbohydrate and protein you eat. Your weight is determined by how much fat you add to the fat depots versus how much you remove.

If you eat just the amount of fat needed to furnish the energy not supplied by the carbohydrate and protein, your weight will remain the same. If you eat more fat than is needed, the excess will go into the fat stores and you will gain weight. If you eat less fat than is required to satisfy your energy needs, then the body will have to make up the deficit by burning additional fat. And where does this fat come from? It is removed from the fat stores and you **lose weight.**

It all makes sense. You became fat because you ate *more* fat than you burned. To lose weight, you have to eat *less* fat than you burn so that your body will use up lots of fat in your adipose tissues to help supply your energy needs.

Now you understand why fat is the key to *Choose to Lose. Choose to Lose* focuses on fat because it is the major culprit in the diet that has made you fat, and reducing it is the solution to making you thin.

MAXIMIZING YOUR WEIGHT LOSS

Before you start on the *Choose to Lose Diet* and learn how to take control of fat and lose weight, here are two extremely important energy issues that affect the amount of fat you burn and thus your weight loss. Both are under your control.

BMR Is Variable

Eating Too Little Can Be Hazardous to Your Diet. You may think that a nifty way to force your body to burn fat from its fat stores is to drastically reduce your total energy intake. How about a 500-calorie-a-day crash diet for three weeks to turn you into a stringbean? The problem is that not only are 500-calorie-a-day diets dangerous and sometimes even fatal, deficient in vital nutrients, and impossible to follow for more than a few weeks, but starvation diets also depress your basal metabolic rate. If you eat fewer than 1000 to 1200 total calories a day, you will find that your weight loss will *slow down*. Your body doesn't know that you are starving just to lose weight. It reacts to the intake of too few calories by burning food more slowly, by lowering the BMR to conserve stored energy. That's a great help if food is really scarce, but if you are trying to lose weight, burning food more slowly means losing weight more slowly.

Yo-Yoing. People who go on starvation diets invariably gain back the weight they lose. The immediate response to a week or two of deprivation is to overeat. After all, so much suffering deserves a reward. But now, because of a lowered BMR, the reward sits on hips and thighs instead of being burned off. And since the dieters haven't learned new low-fat eating habits, the combination of a lower BMR and their old high-fat diet results in new pounds of fat being added back at a faster rate. This is the famous yo-yo effect. With each cycle of weight loss and gain, weight is lost more slowly and regained more quickly, and the dieter's preference for high-fat foods increases. Starvation is a system destined to fail.

Breaking the Cycle

If you are a former yo-yoer, don't be discouraged. You don't have to be trapped in the cycle. By eating a diet low in fat and high in complex carbohydrates and doing a moderate amount of exercise, you will be able to get your metabolism going again.

Eating a Lot Can Help You Lose Weight. The great news is that eating an abundance of food is a system destined to succeed. You need to eat enough calories to keep up your BMR and thus also your energy expenditure. Of course, you must eat a lot of the right foods. This does not mean a bag of fat-laden potato chips. It does mean replacing much of the fat in your diet with carbohydrates — lots of complex carbohydrates. Don't fear that those potatoes and bread and carrots and tangerines and nonfat yogurt will end up as double chins. Remember, the body is great at burning up carbohydrates, but quite inefficient at storing them.

Physical Activity: More Than Just Burning Calories

More great news: physical activity or exercise (don't groan), such as plain old-fashioned walking, also helps you lose weight because it causes you to lose fat instead of muscle.

Preferred Fuel: Protein. You think of your muscles as being permanent. But the protein that makes up your muscle is constantly being broken down and built up. When you use your muscles, some of the protein you eat is utilized to build them up again. When you don't use your muscles, the protein breaks down and is not restored. (If you have ever had a leg or an arm in a cast, you know how shriveled it gets without use.)

When you follow *Choose to Lose*, you reduce your fat intake so that your body will make up the deficit by burning fat from the fat stores. However, when the body is in energy deficit — that is, it needs more energy than is supplied by the food you eat — it prefers to burn protein from the muscle instead of fat from the fat stores. YOU DO NOT WANT YOUR BODY TO BURN PROTEIN INSTEAD OF FAT. To protect your muscle and make sure you are burning fat, you must exercise (not in bursts and spurts but continuously). **Aerobic exercise*** protects muscle from being broken down and burned for energy and forces the body to burn stored fat instead.

In addition, since muscle is more metabolically active (burns energy at a higher rate) than fat, protecting your muscle by aerobic exercise also increases the rate at which you burn calories. Not only will aerobic exercise help you lose weight, it will help you keep it off.

Telling It Like It Is

That's it. You are overweight

not because you eat too much food, but because you eat too much fat (more than you are burning) and the excess is going directly into your fat stores.

not because you eat too much carbohydrate, but because you eat too little.

---

*Aerobic exercise is exercise which is steady, repetitive, uses large muscle masses, and requires a steady supply of oxygen. Example: walking.

not because you are not a marathon runner, but because you are not exercising regularly to protect your muscle and force your body to burn fat from the fat stores.

So, to lose weight, you must eat less fat and more carbohydrates, and also exercise aerobically, which includes walking.

WHY *CHOOSE TO LOSE* WORKS AND KEEPS ON WORKING

Focus on Fat and YOU

You now know that *fat* is the culprit that is making you fat. But do you know the sources of fat in your diet? You know that cheesecake and ice cream sundaes are full of fat, but how about whole milk and granola bars? Are steaks high-fat or high-protein? You want to reduce the fat in your diet but by how much? *Choose to Lose* has the answers.

Choose to Lose provides insight, so you know where fat lurks in your diet and what changes you need to make to lose weight.

Choose to Lose helps you determine a FAT BUDGET, so you know how much fat you should eat to lose weight.

Choose to Lose shows you how to keep track of the fat you eat, so you know that you are making enough changes to reach your goal.

Choose to Lose puts you in control.

Freedom to Say No

Choose to Lose is not restrictive. It is an eating plan you can follow for a lifetime because it is palatable, practical, and flexible. You can choose to eat anything you want as long as it fits into your fat budget.

You're the boss. No one can tell you that you can or cannot eat something. But knowing that you can eat high-fat favorites gives you the freedom not to eat them. When you see a piece of cheesecake, do you regard it as the last cheesecake on earth? You know you shouldn't eat it, but it's your last chance to eat it — so you eat it. This reasoning is not logical; it is a gut reaction. Knowing that the cheesecake has 160 fat calories and that you can fit it into your fat budget (albeit you will have to eat a low, low-fat diet for a few days to compensate) frees you. Maybe you'll have it another day. Knowing you can eat the way others do relieves the pressure to gorge yourself whenever enticing food appears.

A Healthier You

Not only will shedding pounds improve your appearance, it will make you feel better and improve your health. Overweight people have all sorts of problems: increased risk of diabetes, heart disease, stroke, kidney disease, cancer of the breast and colon, bone and joint disorders, female sterility, pregnancy problems, and premature death. If you are obese now, after losing weight you will find that such simple activities as walking are a lot easier. No more huffing and puffing. No more embarrassment at stuffing yourself into chairs or navigating through narrow passages. What's more, you'll feel good about yourself.

Low-fat/high-carbohydrate eating will also make you more energetic. No more dragging yourself around from hour to hour after a heavy high-fat breakfast, lunch, and dinner. You may have to make a new set of friends twenty years younger who are able to keep up with the new you.

Expanding Your Horizons, Not Your Size

Changing the way you eat gives you a new lease on life. You will be introduced to a whole new variety of delicious, tasty low-fat foods. And when you do eat high-fat foods, you will really appreciate them. (Or you may be like some Choosers to Lose who lose their taste for high-fat foods entirely.)

Fitting In the Fat

Read the next chapter to see how you can fit that piece of chocolate cheesecake into your fat budget.

Remember:
1. Not all calories contribute equally to weight gain or loss.
2. Fat calories are fattening because
   a. all the fat you eat is immediately stored.
   b. the capacity to store fats is essentially unlimited.
   c. fat has more calories per gram than carbohydrates or protein.
3. Carbohydrates are not fattening because
   a. since you have a limited capacity to store carbohydrates, almost all the carbohydrates you eat are burned within a few hours.
   b. the more carbohydrates you eat, the faster they are burned and the more energy is wasted as heat (thermogenic effect).
   c. under normal conditions, carbohydrate is never converted to fat and thus never leads to weight gain.

4. To lose weight you must eat less fat than you burn.
5. Things you can do to maximize the amount of fat you burn:
    a. eat enough carbohydrates and total calories to keep your BMR at a maximal level.
    b. engage in regular aerobic exercise to
        (1) protect muscle protein.
        (2) force the body to burn fat.
        (3) maintain your BMR.
6. *Choose to Lose* is a simple, practical, and flexible weight loss plan based on these scientific findings. *Choose to Lose* helps you lose weight by reducing the main culprit in your diet that has made you fat — FAT.
7. *Choose to Lose* puts you in control and teaches you to make food choices that will keep you thin for life.

2. The *Choose to Lose* Plan

THE *Choose to Lose* plan is simple.

* First, you determine your personal **fat budget** (the maximum number of fat calories you can eat each day). This is yours alone. It is based on the total number of calories you need to eat to maintain your desirable weight.
* Next, you need to know the **number of fat calories in foods.**

Knowing your fat budget and the calories of fat in different foods, **you can choose to eat any combination of foods** — even your high-fat favorites — **as long as you stay within your fat budget.**

Knowing your fat budget also gives you a frame of reference to evaluate how fattening food is. A Hardee's Big Country breakfast at 630 fat calories means little to you now, but wait until you figure out your own fat budget.

Calories, Not Grams

Choose to Lose uses calories rather than grams for two reasons. First, calories are familiar. You have lived with them all your life. You probably even know approximately how many total calories you should be eating. If you see that a chocolate bar contains 99 calories of fat, familiarity helps you judge how fattening it is. What does the same amount of fat in grams (11 grams) mean to you? Second, grams are so much smaller than calories (one-ninth the size), their numbers have little impact. A microwave dinner labeled 20 grams of fat seems a lot less fattening than one labeled 180 fat calories.

YOUR VERY OWN FAT BUDGET

Choose to Lose is based on a fat budget that is tailored to you. It is based on your height, desirable weight, and frame size. You probably know what your desirable weight is without looking at the following tables. Skip to Step 2 if you know what you should weigh. Otherwise, if you want to determine your desirable weight or just want to see if the weight table agrees with your evaluation of perfection, consult Table 1.

Step 1: Determine Your Desirable Weight. Table 1 lists weights according to sex, height, and frame size — small, medium, or large. (To determine your frame size, see the box below.) Find your height along the left-hand column of Table 1 under the heading Men or Women. Look across to the weight range listed under your frame size and choose the weight within the range which is right for you. Take a few moments to imagine yourself as a gorgeous creature at this weight. Then fill in Step 1 of the worksheet on page 20.

How to Determine Your Frame Size

Place your left thumb and middle finger around your right wrist and squeeze your fingers together. If the thumb and finger overlap, you have a small frame. If they just touch, your frame size is medium. If they do not touch, you have a large frame. This method is crude, but adequate for our purposes. (If you know you have a smaller or larger frame than this method shows, use your actual frame size and ignore the results of the wrist test.)

Step 2: Determine Your Daily Total Caloric Intake. Table 2 lists daily total caloric intakes for various desirable weights. You may wonder why we ask you to determine total calories when *Choose to Lose* is based on a fat budget. Knowing your total caloric intake is important for three reasons. (See the box on page 16.)

To determine your total daily caloric intake, first find your desirable weight along the left-hand column of Table 2 under the heading Men or Women. Look across to the column labeled Total Daily Caloric Intake to find your number. Fill in Step 2 of your worksheet.

Table 1: Desirable Weights for Adults Age 25 and Over (weight in pounds without clothing)

HEIGHT WITHOUT SHOES		FRAME		
(FEET)	(INCHES)	SMALL	MEDIUM	LARGE
Men				
5	1	112–120	118–129	126–141
5	2	115–123	121–133	129–144
5	3	118–126	124–136	132–148
5	4	121–129	127–139	135–152
5	5	124–133	130–143	138–156
5	6	128–137	134–147	142–161
5	7	132–141	138–152	147–166
5	8	136–145	142–156	151–170
5	9	140–150	146–160	155–174
5	10	144–154	150–165	159–179
5	11	148–158	154–170	164–184
6	0	152–162	158–175	168–189
6	1	156–167	162–180	173–194
6	2	160–171	167–185	178–199
6	3	164–175	172–190	182–204
Women				
4	8	92–98	96–107	104–119
4	9	94–101	98–110	106–122
4	10	96–104	101–113	109–125
4	11	99–107	104–116	112–128
5	0	102–110	107–119	115–131
5	1	105–113	110–122	118–134
5	2	108–116	113–126	121–138
5	3	111–119	116–130	125–142
5	4	114–123	120–135	129–146
5	5	118–127	124–139	133–150
5	6	122–131	128–143	137–154
5	7	126–135	132–147	141–158
5	8	130–140	136–151	145–163
5	9	134–144	140–155	149–168
5	10	138–148	144–159	153–173

Courtesy of Metropolitan Life Insurance Company, New York, N.Y., 1959
For persons between 18 and 25 years of age, subtract 1 pound for each year under 25.

Table 2. Total Caloric Intake and Fat Budget Based on Goal Weight and Sex

DESIRABLE WEIGHT	TOTAL DAILY CALORIC INTAKE*	FAT CALORIES		
		20% BUDGET	17% BUDGET	15% BUDGET
Men				
110	1430	286	243	215
115	1495	299	254	224
120	1560	312	265	234
125	1625	325	276	244
130	1690	338	287	254
135	1755	351	298	263
140	1820	364	309	273
145	1885	377	320	283
150	1950	390	332	292
155	2015	403	343	302
160	2080	416	354	312
165	2145	429	365	322
170	2210	442	376	332
175	2275	455	387	341
180	2340	468	398	351
185	2405	481	409	361
190	2470	494	420	370
195	2535	507	431	380
200	2600	520	442	390
205	2665	533	453	400
Women				
90	1053	211	179	158
95	1111	222	189	167
100	1170	234	199	176
105	1228	246	209	184
110	1287	257	219	193
115	1345	269	229	202
120	1404	281	239	211
125	1462	292	248	219
130	1521	304	258	228
135	1579	315	268	237
140	1638	328	278	246
145	1696	339	288	254
150	1755	351	298	263
155	1813	363	308	272
160	1872	374	318	281
165	1930	386	328	290
170	1989	398	338	298
175	2047	409	348	307

*From *The DINE System* by Dr. Darwin Dennison

Three Reasons to Know Your Total Caloric Intake

1. When most people reduce their fat intake, they automatically reduce their total caloric intake to the ideal level for their desired weight. However, it is possible that when you reduce the fat in your diet, your total caloric intake may fall too low, thus decreasing your basal metabolic rate, the rate at which you burn calories. (Keeping a periodic food record will alert you that your total caloric intake is too low — or, possibly, too great.)
2. If your total daily caloric intake falls below 1000 calories a day, it is difficult to get enough vitamins and minerals for long-term health. You need to monitor your total daily caloric intake to ensure that you are getting adequate nutrition.
3. Table 2 lists three fat budgets — 20 percent, 17 percent, and 15 percent. Since fat budgets are based on a percentage of your total caloric intake, you will need to know your total caloric intake if you wish to determine a different fat budget (say, 13 percent).

YOUR FAT BUDGET: THE KEY TO PERFECTION

You will notice that three fat budgets are listed under the column Fat Calories: 20 percent, 17 percent, and 15 percent. You may want to start your fat budget at 20 percent, meaning that you will eat no more than 20 percent of your total calories as fat. If you are now consuming a typical American diet (about 35 to 40 percent of calories from fat), 20 percent will represent a substantial change in your diet. And for many, reducing fat intake to 20 percent of calories will create Marilyn Monroe or Robert Redford look-alikes.

After three or four weeks, you may find that a 20 percent fat budget allows you more fat than you need to achieve your ideal weight. Lower your fat budget to 17 percent. A 17 percent fat budget may be perfect for getting you into shape. If you want a stricter diet, follow the 15 percent budget. You're the boss. You want to choose a budget which you can follow without suffering pangs of martyrdom.

Losing by Stages

On the other hand, you may feel that the fat budget for your goal weight is too restrictive. For example, if you weigh 190 pounds and want to weigh 130, the 20 percent fat budget for 130 pounds is 304 fat calories. If a limit of 304 fat calories a day seems impossible to achieve, pick an attainable weight somewhere between 190 and 130 pounds — perhaps 160 pounds. Determine a 20 percent fat budget for the intermediate weight (374 fat calories) and adhere to it until you weigh 160 pounds. When you attain that weight, adopt the fat budget for your next goal, 130 pounds. Your weight loss may be somewhat slower this way, but if you feel more comfortable working in stages, you are more likely to follow *Choose to Lose* until you reach your final goal. After all, a diet plan works only if it fits your individual needs and you stick with it.

What's in a Number?

Choose a percentage and fill in Step 3 of your worksheet. Whatever percentage you choose, stick with it for at least three or four weeks. If you are uncertain, start with 20 percent of your recommended total daily caloric intake. You can always change the percentage if it's not a good fit. You need to choose a specific number for two reasons. First, knowing your personal fat budget number puts the fat content of all foods into perspective. Knowing that your budget is 300, you will be able to judge a Rachel's double chocolate brownie with walnuts at 153 fat calories. You might ask, "Is half my daily budget worth a few moments of bliss? Should I fit it in? Is it really *that* good?"

Second, you need a specific fat budget so you can make daily food choices to fit within that budget. "My budget is 240. . . . Let's see . . . zero fat calories for *Cucumber Soup* and 38 fat calories for *Grilled Apricot-Ginger Chicken* . . . or should I make *Chicken Nuggets Chez Goor** at 73 fat calories?"

A CASE STUDY

Meet Ellen. Ellen is trying to lose weight. Her example will clarify each step of the *Choose to Lose* system.

Here's how Ellen figures out her fat budget. Ellen is 5 feet 5 inches tall and weighs 160 pounds. She determines by the wrist test that she has a small frame. To find her desirable weight, she locates her height

---

*All italicized recipes can be found in *Eater's Choice: A Food Lover's Guide to Lower Cholesterol* by Dr. Ron Goor and Nancy Goor, revised edition, 1989, Houghton Mifflin.

Table 1				
HEIGHT WITHOUT SHOES		FRAME		
(FEET)	(INCHES)	SMALL	MEDIUM	LARGE
Women				
5	4	114–123	120–135	129–146
5	**5**	**118–127**	124–139	133–150
5	6	122–131	128–143	137–154

(5′5″) in the left-hand column of Table 1 under the heading Women. Reading across to the Frame column labeled Small, she finds that her weight range is 118–127. Ellen knows that she will look and feel great at 120 pounds.

Next, Ellen needs to determine her total daily caloric intake. She locates her desirable weight (120) on Table 2 under the heading Women. Looking across to the column labeled Total Daily Caloric Intake she finds her number — 1404. Ellen could choose any of the three budgets but she decides to start with 20 percent. Looking across to the column labeled 20% Budget, Ellen finds her daily fat budget — 281 calories of fat (20 percent of 1404 calories).

Table 2				
DESIRABLE WEIGHT	TOTAL DAILY CALORIC INTAKE	FAT CALORIES		
		20% BUDGET	**17% BUDGET**	**15% BUDGET**
Women				
115	1345	269	229	202
120	**1404**	**281**	**239**	**211**
125	1462	292	248	219

Use the blank worksheet on page 20 to figure out your fat budget. You may find Ellen's worksheet helpful as a guide.

Worksheet to Determine Your Daily Fat Budget

Name _____ELLEN_____ Date __5/31/89_____

STEP 1: DETERMINE YOUR DESIRABLE WEIGHT.

    A. Sex: Male _____ Female ___X_____

    B. Height: ___5_____ feet ___5_____ inches

    C. Frame (wrist method):

       Small ___X_____ Medium _____ Large _____

    D. Weight Range (Table 1): ___118-127_____

    E. Desirable Weight: _____120_____

STEP 2: DETERMINE YOUR DAILY TOTAL CALORIC INTAKE.

    Daily total caloric intake (use Table 2): ___1404_____

STEP 3: DETERMINE YOUR DAILY FAT BUDGET.

    DAILY FAT BUDGET (use Table 2): (*choose one*)

    20% of ____1404_____ = ____281_____
           your daily caloric intake   your fat budget

    17% of _____ = _____
           your daily caloric intake   your fat budget

    15% of _____ = _____
           your daily caloric intake   your fat budget

Worksheet to Determine Your Daily Fat Budget

Name _____ Date _____

STEP 1: DETERMINE YOUR DESIRABLE WEIGHT.

    A. Sex: Male _____ Female _____

    B. Height: _____ feet _____ inches

    C. Frame (wrist method):

        Small _____ Medium _____ Large _____

    D. Weight Range (Table 1): _____

    E. Desirable Weight: _____

STEP 2: DETERMINE YOUR DAILY TOTAL CALORIC INTAKE.

    Daily total caloric intake (use Table 2): _____

STEP 3: DETERMINE YOUR DAILY FAT BUDGET.

    DAILY FAT BUDGET (use Table 2): (*choose one*)

    20% of _____ = _____
           your daily caloric intake   your fat budget

    17% of _____ = _____
           your daily caloric intake   your fat budget

    15% of _____ = _____
           your daily caloric intake   your fat budget

WHAT DOES YOUR FAT BUDGET MEAN IN TERMS OF FOOD?

What does Ellen's budget of 281 calories of fat mean? How does this translate into food choices? Here are some foods and the calories of fat they contain. As you read, keep your own fat budget in mind.

FOOD	FAT CALORIES
Potato chips (1 cup)	75
Peanut butter (1 tablespoon)	74
Baked potato with skin	trace
Wendy's potato with cheese	306
Russian dressing (2 tablespoons)	140
Swiss cheese (1 ounce)	70
Broiled lamb loin chop with fat (3 ounces)	225
Chicken breast half, baked, without skin	28
Chicken breast half, batter-dipped and fried, with skin	166
Plain white rice (1 cup), no fat added	0
Whole milk (1 cup)	73
2% milk (1 cup)	42
Skim milk (1 cup)	4
Kit Kat candy bar	117
Weight Watchers Cheese Enchiladas Ranchero dinner	189
Margarine (1 tablespoon)	100

Are any of these foods familiar? Can you understand now why you haven't been mistaken for a stick recently?

Using Your Fat Budget to Make Choices

Knowing your fat budget, you will look at food in a totally new way. No longer will you perceive a piece of Swiss cheese as a delicious-tasting yellow square with holes; you will see 72 calories of fat. And then you will judge how much, if any, you can fit into your eating plan. Instead of gulping down a cup of cream of mushroom soup at 155 fat calories, you might choose to start dinner with 8 large boiled shrimp dipped in cocktail sauce (2 fat calories). You might decide that Kellogg's Nutri·Grain Wheat and Raisins cereal at zero fat calories is a better choice than Quaker 100% Natural cereal at 54 fat calories per quarter cup.

Here's Looking at You, Kid

But what about the fat calories in the food *you* have been eating? Aren't you curious to know how many fat calories you ate yesterday? Last weekend? By how much did you exceed your fat budget?

The Past Helps Determine the Future

Perhaps you don't even want to think about the past. You want to start afresh and discard your old eating habits. Fine. But do you really know your old habits? Before you opened this book, you didn't know your fat budget or the number of fat calories in foods. You just ate. You chose certain foods. For some foods you would gladly have sold your soul. Some foods you ate without thought. You probably knew that some of the foods were fattening, but you didn't know how fattening. You might even have avoided some low-fat foods because you thought they would make you gain weight.

To make changes that will last, you need to know what to change. You need to evaluate what you were eating to discover the sources of fat in your diet. The best way to find exactly how much fat is in the foods you were eating or which foods were loaded with fat is to keep a three-day food record, writing down *everything* you eat — honestly.

A Strong Recommendation!

We strongly recommend that you keep a food record for three days. We know you will find it invaluable. Detailed directions for keeping a baseline food record appear in Appendix A. But first, have a look at how Ellen keeps her food record.

ELLEN'S FOOD RECORD: AN ILLUMINATING EXAMPLE

Here's Ellen again. Ellen is supposed to be at work by 8:30 A.M., which means getting out of the house by 7:45. Ellen hates to get up in the morning, but she hates missing breakfast even more. She allows herself time to grab a muffin and a cup of coffee in the coffee shop in her building.

She records her muffin and coffee on her food record as she sits down to eat them. For the first time, Ellen questions her choice. It is a very large muffin and tastes a lot like pound cake. Perhaps she'll skip it this morning. A little voice inside her whispers, "This food record is for you alone. You are not keeping it to impress anyone with how little you eat. You need a baseline record so you can make changes — and lose weight. *Eat the muffin!''* By being honest with herself, Ellen has already made a step toward being a thin person.

Ellen's first entry in her food record looks like this:

TIME	FOOD	AMOUNT
8:15 A.M.	blueberry muffin	1 large
	coffee	1 cup
	half-and-half	1 tbsp

At about 10:30, Ellen's friend Sylvia often stops by with a treat. By this time, Ellen is already famished. Sylvia reaches into a small white bag and, with a flourish, pulls out a glazed doughnut. Normally Ellen eats the doughnut with gusto, considering it her splurge for the day. But today Ellen regards the doughnut with suspicion. She *knows* it's not going to look good on her food record. "How bad is it?" she wonders as she adds her midmorning snack to her food record.

TIME	FOOD	AMOUNT
10:30 A.M.	glazed doughnut	1 large
	coffee	1 cup
	half-and-half	1 tbsp

Ellen looks forward to lunch. She knows she's always "good" at lunchtime. A salad should balance out the doughnut. Ellen has second thoughts about her restaurant choice — a fast-food restaurant — but knows she must eat normally during this record-taking period. Anyway, her selections from the salad bar are bound to look good on her record. Ellen tops her salad with two ladles of Russian dressing and 1 tablespoon of sunflower seeds. Ellen notices that the ladle handle is marked 1 oz. A biscuit — it's so little and dry, it must be fat-free — with a pat of butter provides a nice contrast to the greens.

TIME	FOOD	AMOUNT
Noon	mixed salad	
	lettuce	2 cups
	tomato	½
	cucumber	¼
	carrot	¼
	Russian dressing	2 ladles (2 oz)
	sunflower seeds	1 tbsp
	biscuit	1
	butter	1 pat (tsp)

Ellen is so busy all afternoon that she has no time to take a coffee break. By the time she leaves work she is ready to eat her handbag. On her way home she runs into the grocery store to pick up a frozen dinner. She chooses a Weight Watchers dinner, Chicken Enchiladas Suiza. She always chooses Weight Watchers or some other lean or light frozen dinner. Ellen doesn't actually like the taste of frozen dinners, but she generally cooks only on weekends. She cuts up half a cucumber and eats it with her enchiladas. For dessert Ellen eats a carton of yogurt. She adds her dinner to her record.

TIME	FOOD	AMOUNT
6:15 P.M.	Chicken Enchiladas Suiza (Weight Watchers)	1 dinner
	cucumber	½
	coffee	1 cup
	half-and-half	1 tbsp
	yogurt (Whitney's 100% Natural), vanilla	6 oz

The evening stretches before Ellen. She has made no plans. She settles comfortably into her favorite chair, turns on the television, and proceeds to devour the peanuts in the bowl beside her. "Aha!" she thinks. "I'll measure the amount of peanuts in the bowl before I eat them and then I'll measure the amount left when I go to bed." Good idea, Ellen. The bowl originally held half a cup of peanuts. Ellen finds nothing in the bowl when she goes to bed. Where could all the nuts have gone? Ellen feels a bit foolish that she has devoured half a cup of peanuts, but she adds the item to her food record. She knows this record is for her.

TIME	FOOD	AMOUNT
7–11 P.M.	oil-roasted salted peanuts	½ cup

IT'S YOUR TURN

Please take three days to record your food diary. (See Appendix A.) This exercise is extremely important. You will be glad you did it, even if it means buying a new wardrobe because you become so thin as a result.

NOTE: Recording what you eat is your key to success. Significant changes can be made only if you know what to change.

Important:
- Record *everything* you eat and drink.
- Eat normally. *Do not change* your diet for the record — it's for you! Do not refrain from eating something just because you have to record it.
- Record food *when* you eat it. It is difficult to remember later.
- Record the time you eat each food item.
- *Measure* (if necessary, estimate) amounts as accurately as possible.
- *List components* of sandwiches, salads, stews, etc., separately.
- *Ask* questions at restaurants. (See Chapter 8.)
- Read Appendix A before you begin.

Remember:
1. *Choose to Lose* is a simple method for losing weight that limits the amount of fat you eat while still allowing you to fit in your high-fat favorites.

2. Use the step-by-step guide to *Choose to Lose* to:
    a. Determine your desirable weight (Table 1).
    b. Determine your daily total caloric intake (Table 2).
    c. Determine your fat budget (Table 2).
3. To gain insight into the sources of fat in your diet, keep a three-day food record. Be accurate and honest. This record is for *you*.

3. Where's the Fat?

THE POWER of *Choose to Lose* is knowing your fat budget and the number of fat calories in foods. Before we look at Ellen's food diary — and you evaluate your own — here's a chapter devoted totally to foods — literally from soup to nuts, even including fast foods and frozen dinners — and the fat they contain.

This chapter asks the question, "Where's the Fat?" The answer is simple: *everywhere!* As a result, the percentage of Americans who are overweight has grown to epic proportions. The first National Health and Nutrition Examination Survey, conducted between 1971 and 1974, found that 28.8 million American adults were obese (20 percent above their desirable weight); and, of these, 8.4 million were severely obese (40 percent above their desirable weight). Only five years later the second NHANES survey found that 34 million American adults were obese and, of these, 11 million were severely obese. In 1980 one out of every five adults was obese.

Fat . . . Fatter . . . Fattest

Why are we such a fat nation? Over the last eighty years our eating habits have been changing, most dramatically since the 1950s. Our total caloric intake is slightly lower than it was in 1910, but our intake of fat is vastly higher. Fat intake is currently 40 percent of calories versus 27 percent in 1910.

Fast . . . Faster . . . Fattest

Just look at our supermarkets. The old-time grocery store stocked primarily fresh produce, meats, and dairy products and a few shelves of staples — flour, sugar, coffee, and tea. Today these foods have been pushed to the outer walls. The ever-expanding inner rows of shelves and freezer cabinets are chock-full of high-fat convenience foods.

What's Our Hurry?

We no longer cook. We pop a frozen dinner (invariably high-fat) into our microwave or buy a prepared dish from the gourmet section of our grocery store. We feel too rushed to buy and prepare fresh vegetables. In fact, French fries and ketchup are the only vegetables many people ever eat and Froot Loops and fruit rolls are the only fruits.

Fast Foods Growing Fast

We eat out more often — but where? At high-fat fast-food restaurants. While rare in the fifties, fast-food restaurants are the only food services available in many areas today. If you travel on toll roads and interstates across the country, don't look for family-style restaurants. Fast-food chains have taken their place. And with the change, low-fat food choices have gone the way of the horse and buggy.

TV-Time Temptation

We are even victims within our homes. Every TV show is accompanied by a bombardment of ads for luscious, mouth-watering high-fat convenience foods and snacks. It's not only the visual onslaught — melted cheese sweetly hugging a big, juicy hamburger, creamy chocolate flowing over a nougat center, and cheese joyfully bubbling atop a pizza crust — but we have to suffer the psychological impact. People eating high-fat foods have so much fun. If you want to be one of the gang, eat the way we do.

You *Can* Resist

Yes, TV ads and fast-food restaurants and convenience foods may try to lure you into their fatty grips, but once you know where the fat lurks, you will have the power to overcome their grasp. Read the rest of this chapter to discover how much fat is in the foods you eat. Use these new discoveries to make the choices that will lead directly to thinness.

Where's the Fat?

Fat is everywhere. Some is visible, like the layer of fat on a sirloin steak. But much is hidden, like the fat added to processed frozen dinners. We Americans eat entirely too much of it. And there you are in the midst of it. To root it out of your diet you must know where it exists. You must dispel old notions. Do you consider beef a high-protein food or a high-fat food? Do you view whole milk and cheese as calcium-rich and wholesome rather than fat-laden? Do you consider skinny, little dried-out crackers good diet snacks or high-fat foods? The following discussion should start you down the road to a new, lean body.

NOTE: This is an extremely important chapter for you to read and reread. You may be disheartened to discover that fat lurks in so many of the foods you love, but don't lose hope. You'll learn how often and in what amounts you can comfortably fit them into your fat budget. True, you won't be eating your favorite high-fat foods in as large quantities or as often as before, but is this so bad? You won't just inhale that piece of apple pie, you'll *really* taste it. You will also learn to like foods you once scoffed at — vegetables and fruit, for example. Just relax. You're going to love being thin and eating healthfully. And, in just a few pages you'll find a whole chapter devoted to great weight loss food choices you once thought were forbidden fruit.

MEATS

Beef: A Dieter's Undoing

If you think of beef as a high-protein food that builds bulging biceps and triceps, scratch the thought. Beef is a high-fat food that creates bulging hips, tummies, and thighs. Removing the strip of fat that hugs the edge of a piece of beef will not eliminate all the fat. Invisible fat is marbled through. The better the quality of beef (the higher the grade), the more fat it contains. Even meats that appear to be lean contain a lot of fat. For instance, braised flank steak trimmed of fat has 35 fat calories *per ounce.* That's 140 fat calories per 4 ounces. The leanest beef is broiled top round trimmed of fat, which has 16 fat calories per ounce.

Take a look at the Meats category of the food tables for an eye opener. The entries are listed in *1-ounce* portion size for easy comparison. Of course, no one eats just 1 ounce of meat. Be sure to multiply the fat calories by the number of ounces you might eat. For instance, braised shortribs have 107 calories of fat per ounce. If you eat 4 ounces of spareribs, multiply 4 by 107 for a total of 428 fat calories. How does that compare with your fat budget?

Hamburger Dreams

The image of a big, juicy hamburger often ravages the subconscious of a dieter. Until that need is satisfied, the dieter can think of nothing else, often stuffing himself or herself with everything else around to satisfy that craving. Good news: you *can* fit the hamburger into your fat budget. (For the leanest hamburger meat you can buy, ask the butcher to trim the fat off a round steak and grind it.)

If You'd Trade Your Right Arm for a Hamburger

If nothing but a large, 100 percent regular ground-beef hamburger will satisfy you, save fat calories for your splurge by keeping your fat intake extra low for a few days. But remember, saving for a splurge is a better policy than paying for it later. When you splurge without prepayment too often, you're off your diet. (See Splurging in Chapter 8.)

Dieter's Plate: Guaranteed to Put On Weight

Now that you know about the fat in beef, you will scorn the diet plate offered in thousands of American restaurants. The "Diet Special" features a hamburger (without the bun), whole milk cottage cheese, and a canned peach half. The star of the dieter's special contains 58 fat calories per ounce or about 348 fat calories per 6-ounce patty. (Compare this to the 18 calories of fat spared you by eliminating the bun.)

Veal: Expensive and Fattening

Veal may be pale in color like chicken and turkey breast, but that is where the similarity ends. Veal is not a diet food. Braised veal breast contains 54 fat calories per ounce or 216 fat calories for 4 ounces. Veal cutlet (before it becomes breaded and fried veal cutlet or even sautéed veal cutlet) has 27 calories per ounce or 108 calories per 4 ounces. Try turkey cutlets instead. Pound them thin, and your guests will think they are eating veal scaloppine.

	FAT CALORIES	
	PER OZ	PER 4 OZ
Veal breast, braised	54	216
Veal cutlet, braised	27	108
Turkey cutlet, braised	8	32

Lamb: Not Just the Wool Keeps It Warm

Lamb is also a poor choice for a dieter. It should come as no surprise that a 4-ounce rib lamb chop has 300 calories of fat. You can see it. Ground lamb is no substitute for ground beef. Four ounces of ground lamb has 200 fat calories. The best lamb choice is roasted leg of lamb trimmed of fat (20 fat calories per ounce or 80 fat calories for a 4-ounce serving) or a broiled loin lamb chop trimmed of fat (19 fat calories per ounce or 76 fat calories for a 4-ounce chop).

But remember, if a lamb chop would make you incredibly happy, just make room for it in your budget.

	FAT CALORIES	
	PER OZ	PER 4 OZ
Rib lamb chop	75	300
Ground lamb, broiled	50	200
Leg of lamb (trimmed)	20	80
Loin lamb chop (trimmed)	19	76

Pork: You Are What You Eat

Except for roasted lean pork tenderloin at a mere 12 fat calories per ounce (48 fat calories per 4 ounces), all pork products are high in fat. With a high of 94 fat calories per ounce (376 per 4 ounces) for blade loin, fat calories for pork products hover around 65 fat calories per ounce (260 per 4 ounces). Your favorite roasted ham with the fat is 53 fat calories per ounce (212 per 4 ounces). It is not surprising that one

	FAT CALORIES	
	PER OZ	PER 4 OZ
Blade loin	94	376
Other pork products (average)	65	260
Ham	53	212
Pork tenderloin (lean, roasted)	12	48
	PER STRIP	4 STRIPS
Bacon	28	112

skinny (ha!) strip of bacon has 28 fat calories. But would you kill for a BLT sandwich? Make it with one strip of bacon. You'll get the taste without all the fat.

Fitting It In

Although beef, veal, lamb, and pork are all high-fat foods, you can make room for them in your budget. If you want to eat an occasional steak or chop, reduce the fat calories by trimming off the visible fat before you broil or grill it. Marinate less fatty cuts of meat to make them tender. Instead of choosing a thick steak or roast as the centerpiece of your meal, choose dishes in which small amounts of meat are added to vegetables, rice, or pasta.

Be sure to check the **Meats** (Beef, Lamb, Pork, Veal, and Game), **Fast Foods, Frozen and Microwave Foods,** and **Sausages and Luncheon Meats** sections of the food tables to familiarize yourself with the fat content of meat products not mentioned in this chapter.

POULTRY

Chicken: Basically Great

White meat chicken, properly prepared, beats beef, veal, pork, and lamb in the low-fat marathon. Half a roasted chicken breast without skin has only 28 fat calories. Chicken has the potential to be part of an infinite number of low-fat, delicious recipes. Try Cajun Chicken (page 154), Lemon Chicken (page 155), Chicken with Rice, Tomatoes, and Artichokes (page 158), or *Grilled Apricot-Ginger Chicken** for delectable proof.

Dark meat is fattier than light meat. A roasted drumstick without skin has only 22 fat calories. But then, one drumstick isn't much of a meal. A thigh without skin has 51 fat calories. A roasted thigh isn't all that much to eat, either. However, if you moderate the amount, dark meat chicken can fit into your fat budget.

. . . But Easily Ruined

White meat chicken cooked without skin is a low-fat food. Chicken *with* the skin has a fat content approaching or even surpassing that of many cuts of beef. Half a roasted chicken breast without skin has 28 fat

---

*All italicized recipes can be found in *Eater's Choice: A Food Lover's Guide to Lower Cholesterol,* by Dr. Ron Goor and Nancy Goor. Revised edition 1989, Houghton Mifflin.

calories. Half a roasted chicken breast with skin has 69 fat calories. Take that breast, dip it in flour and fry it, and the fat calories rise to 78. Batter-dip and fry it and the calories climb to 166. Eat it extra crispy or spicy at a Kentucky Fried Chicken fast-food restaurant and the breast becomes, at 216 fat calories, almost eight times as fattening as the original skinless breast.

CHICKEN PART	PREPARATION	FAT CALORIES
Drumstick	Roasted without skin	22
Thigh	Roasted without skin	51
Breast (half)	Roasted without skin	28
Breast (half)	Roasted *with* skin	69
Breast (half)	Fried *with* skin, flour-coated	78
Breast (half)	Fried *with* skin, batter-dipped	166
Breast (half)	Kentucky Fried Chicken	216

Choose to Lose tip: Always remove the skin from chicken *before* cooking, or the fat from the skin will be absorbed by the meat. To reduce the fat even more, steam chicken breasts in a vegetable steamer rather than sautéing them in oil. Cooking on a cast iron griddle or barbecue grill also helps to reduce added fat.

Turkey: Dieter's Pick

One ounce of completely natural turkey breast without skin has a mere 2 fat calories. Ten ounces is only 20 fat calories. That means you can eat a lot of white meat turkey without remorse. The white meat of deep basted Butterball turkeys is not quite as fat-free. Each ounce contains 10 fat calories. This is not a lot of fat but it can accumulate — particularly with added gravy or mayonnaise. Be sure to keep track of the fat-containing sauces and gravies you add to your turkey.

Dark meat without skin is higher in fat than white meat turkey, even with skin. Totally natural turkey dark meat contains 10 fat calories per ounce. That's 50 fat calories for 5 ounces. A whole leg roasted without skin is 76 fat calories. If you moderate your use of gravy, dark meat turkey doesn't have to overload your fat budget. Read labels. Dark meat from deep-basted Butterball turkeys contains 26 fat calories per ounce. Even without dressings and gravies, this can add up quickly to a lot of fat calories.

	FAT CALORIES	
	1 OUNCE	4 OUNCES
White meat turkey without skin	2	8
White meat turkey (Butterball) without skin	10	40
Dark meat turkey without skin	10	40
Dark meat turkey (Butterball) without skin	26	104
Ground turkey (93% fat free)	18	72

Ground Turkey: Deceptive Advertising

Ground turkey seems to be the answer to a weight-watching hamburger lover's dreams. Because turkey is so low in fat, we assume that ground turkey is also low. Not necessarily true. The ground turkey you buy is often loaded with turkey skin and fat. And because most commercially-ground turkey products have no labeling, you have no idea how much fat you are eating. Even those commercially ground turkeys with labels that claim they are 93 percent fat free contain 18 fat calories per ounce. To ensure that your ground turkey is low in fat, grind your own raw turkey breast or cutlets in a food processor or meat grinder.

Duck: Super Splurge

Have you ever seen a duck frolicking in icy water in fifteen-degree weather? The duck is padded with fat to keep it warm and afloat. Eating duck is a sure way to increase your padding and sink your fat budget. Half a duck with skin contains 975 fat calories — without a sauce. Has duck à l'orange lost some of its appeal? Duck without skin has 29 fat calories per ounce. Perhaps your fat budget can handle a pancake or two of Peking Duck (without the skin).

Be sure to check the **Poultry, Fast Foods, Frozen and Microwave Foods,** and **Sausages and Luncheon Meats** sections of the food tables to familiarize yourself with the fat in poultry and poultry products not mentioned in this chapter.

FISH

Just plain, unadulterated fish is an excellent choice for a dieter. Two calories of fat per ounce for raw cod, dolphin fish, haddock, lobster, pollock, scallops, and sunfish; 3 for flounder, grouper, pike, snapper, and sole; and 4 for monkfish, ocean perch, rockfish, and shrimp, leave plenty of room in your fat budget for more choices later.

A few fish are high in fat and warrant caution: Watch these fat calories per ounce: sablefish 39, Pacific herring 35; Atlantic mackerel 35; Chinook salmon 27; Atlantic herring 23; sockeye salmon 22; butterfish 20; Pacific mackerel 20; orange roughy 18. Check the food tables for the values of the fish you wish to eat.

Orange roughy! Salmon! You don't have to eliminate any of these wonderful fish from your diet — just keep track of their fat calories and fit them in.

	FAT CALORIES	
	1 OUNCE	4 OUNCES
Cod, dolphin fish, haddock, lobster, pollock, scallops, sunfish	2	8
Flounder, grouper, pike, snapper, sole	3	12
Monkfish, ocean perch, rockfish, shrimp	4	16
Orange roughy	18	72
Butterfish, Pacific mackerel	20	80
Sockeye salmon	22	88
Atlantic herring	23	92
Chinook salmon	27	108
Atlantic mackerel, Pacific herring	35	140
Sablefish	39	156

Of course, no matter how lean a fish is, when you bread and deep-fry it, or drown it in a cream sauce or butter, it is no longer a good diet choice. Bake, broil, poach, or grill fish with little or no fat or cover with sauces low in fat to create dishes that are easy to eat with gusto and no guilt.

Choose to Lose tip: Choose canned tuna packed in water. A whole can of undrained tuna packed in water has 30 calories of fat or 4.5 fat calories per ounce. A whole can of undrained tuna packed in (soy) oil has

238 calories of fat or 36 fat calories per ounce. Oil-packed tuna has eight times as much fat as water-packed.

You will find the fat calories for fish listed in the **Fish and Shellfish, Fast Foods,** and **Frozen and Microwave Foods** sections of the food tables.

SAUSAGES AND LUNCHEON MEATS

A Poor Choice

Beware of sausages and luncheon meats. They are loaded with fat (in addition to being filled with dangerous additives and an excessive amount of salt). A 3-ounce link of bratwurst has 198 calories of fat; a 2.4-ounce smoked link sausage has 194. A 2-ounce all-beef frankfurter contains 151 fat calories. Even a 1.6-ounce chicken frank contains 79 fat calories. The five little pepperoni slices atop your piece of pizza take a 110-fat-calorie bite out of your fat budget.

The Cold Facts about Cold Cuts

A thin slice of packaged bologna has 59 calories of fat. Slide two slices of bologna (118 fat calories) between two slices of bread (18 fat calories) slathered with a tablespoon of mayonnaise (99 fat calories) and you have created a sandwich worth about 235 fat calories. Doesn't sound like diet food.

	AMOUNT	FAT CALORIES
Bratwurst	1 link (3 oz)	198
Smoked link pork sausage	1 link (2.4 oz)	194
Frankfurter, beef	1 frank (2 oz)	151
Frankfurter, chicken	1 frank (1.6 oz)	79
Bologna	1 slice (.8 oz)	59
Salami	1 slice (.8 oz)	42
Pork bologna	1 slice (.8 oz)	41
Turkey bologna	1 slice (.8 oz)	39
Ham	1 slice (.8 oz)	27
Turkey, chopped, pressed	1 slice (1 oz)	27
Beef, chopped, pressed	1 slice (1 oz)	18
Peppered loaf	1 slice (.8 oz)	16

Here are some more figures. A slice of peppered loaf has 16 fat calories, ham has 27. Slightly higher is a slice of turkey bologna at 39 fat calories, a slice of pork bologna at 41, or a slice of salami at 42. Don't get carried away. *Remember that these numbers are for only one slice.*

If you use the cold cuts that have less fat and make your sandwiches less thick, you can easily fit cold cuts into your budget. However, you might want to eat cold cuts less often. The cancer-causing nitrites and blood pressure–raising sodium won't make you fat, but they may shorten your life.

Sliced Turkey Breast: A Deli Delight

The only luncheon meat you can eat with abandon is fresh roasted turkey breast (2 fat calories per ounce), which you can find at many grocery store deli counters. However, if you are buying packaged turkey breast, read the label. Some turkey cold cuts have so much added fat, they approach or even exceed some beef or pork cold cuts. For example, one thin slice of chopped, pressed, and cooked turkey has 3 grams* of fat or 27 fat calories, but its beef counterpart has 2 grams of fat or 18 fat calories per slice.

Fat Free?

97% fat free! 93% fat free! 87% fat free! Sausage and luncheon meat packagers have jumped onto the deceptive advertising bandwagon. The problem lies not with the accuracy of the percentages printed so large and colorfully on the package. The problem is that these percentages are deceptive and don't tell you what you need to know. If a package says 87% fat free, it means that 13 percent of the *weight* of the meat is fat. However, what you need to know is how many calories of fat you will be consuming when you eat the slice of turkey bologna or ham.

Behind the Hype

The turkey bologna package that raves it is 83% fat free! has 5 grams of fat or 5 × 9 fat calories per gram = 45 calories of fat per slice. That's what you need to know to fit it into your fat budget. The label states that the bologna has 60 total calories per slice, which means that 75

---

*To convert grams of fat into calories, multiply the number of grams of fat by 9 because each gram of fat contains 9 calories.

percent of its total calories come from fat (45 ÷ 60 = 75%). The package should read 75% fat. Of course, that doesn't sound very good. How about 25% fat free? That doesn't sound so good either. If the bologna manufacturer were forced to advertise the percentage of total calories that comes from fat instead of the percentage of total weight that comes from fat, he wouldn't advertise.

For more illuminating cold cut fat values, take a glance at the **Sausages and Luncheon Meats** section of the food tables.

FROZEN DINNERS

Gain Time and Weight

There has been an explosion in the food industry, which is capitalizing on our changing society. Fast-food restaurants, microwave dinners, and a seemingly endless proliferation of convenience foods have been developed for people who don't take time for food preparation. However, what you gain in convenience you often sacrifice in taste, health, and your weight.

Be Label-Wise: A Survival Skill

Learning how to read a label is mandatory if you want to eat convenience foods. The food label tells it all. The package may advertise a low-fat entrée such as fish, turkey, or chicken, but you need to know more. The package may scream "Lite" or "Lean," but you need to know more.

You need to know exactly how many grams of fat the food processors have added to that dinner to make it palatable — and it is often a lot.

Be sure to check out Reading Food Labels: A Consumer's Most Important Survival Skill, in Chapter 8, Coping in a World You Did Not Make, for more information on deciphering food labels.

Ruining a Good Thing

Most fish are naturally very low in fat. Here's what happens when food companies process fish into a frozen dinner. Mrs. Paul turns two 4-ounce haddock fillets (16 fat calories) into Crunchy Batter Haddock Fillets (153 fat calories); Gorton transforms one 5-ounce flounder fillet (20 fat calories) into Light Recipe Stuffed Flounder (126 fat calories);

and Weight Watchers processes one 4-ounce cod fillet (8 fat calories) into Oven Fried Fish (108 calories of fat). That's some kind of magic.

FISH	FAT CALORIES	
	UNADULTERATED	FROZEN DINNER
Haddock (8 oz)	16	153
Flounder (5 oz)	20	126
Cod (4 oz)	8	108

Abracadabra! Watch the food processors turn a low-fat chicken breast into a high-fat food: one chicken breast half (28 fat calories) gets transformed into Armour Dinner Classics Chicken with Wine and Mushroom Sauce (144 calories of fat) or Le Menu Chicken Parmigiana (180 fat calories) or Swanson Original Chicken Pot Pie (7 oz) at 216 fat calories.

CHICKEN	FAT CALORIES
Chicken breast, roasted without skin	28
Armour Chicken with Wine and Mushroom Sauce	144
Le Menu Chicken Parmigiana	180
Swanson Chicken Pot Pie (7 oz)	216

You'd never recognize three low-fat slices of turkey (6 fat calories) when they become Lean Cuisine Turkey Dijon at 90 fat calories, Tyson Gourmet Breast of Turkey with Dressing at 99 fat calories, or Swanson Turkey Pot Pie (7 oz) at 198 fat calories.

TURKEY	FAT CALORIES
Turkey breast without skin (3 slices)	6
Lean Cuisine Turkey Dijon	90
Tyson Gourmet Breast of Turkey	99
Swanson Turkey Pot Pie (7 oz)	198

Take a look at the **Frozen and Microwave Foods** section of the food tables for a true shock.

EATER BEWARE: The food industry is adding a tremendous amount of gratuitous fat to its frozen dinners — and to you, if you eat them.

Diet (?) Frozen Dinners

Don't assume that "diet" frozen dinners are low in fat. Many Lite! Lean! Low Calorie! Slim! frozen dinners have fewer than 300 total calories but are high in fat calories. For example, Lean Cuisine Vegetable and Pasta Mornay with Ham may contain only 280 total calories, but 117 of those calories come from fat. Of the 290 total calories of The Budget Gourmet Slim Selects Sirloin of Beef in Herb Sauce, 108 are fat calories. Weight Watchers Southern Fried Chicken Patty contains 144 fat calories out of 270 total calories. Don't be fooled by the propaganda. Be sure to calculate the **number of fat calories per serving** before you buy.

FROZEN DIET DINNER	TOTAL CALORIES	FAT CALORIES
Lean Cuisine Vegetable and Pasta Mornay with Ham	280	117
Budget Gourmet Sirloin of Beef in Herb Sauce	290	108
Weight Watchers Southern Fried Chicken Patty	270	144

How would these diet dinners fit into your fat budget?

Select with Care

If you shop and read labels carefully, you can find frozen dinners that are low in fat. For example, Armour has three Classic Lite dinners that contain only 18 fat calories — Chicken Burgundy, Seafood with Natural Herbs, and Sweet and Sour Chicken. Lean Cuisine Oriental

Scallops has a mere 27 fat calories and Breast of Chicken Marsala has 45 fat calories. Weight Watchers Imperial Chicken has 45 fat calories. Of course, you can eat high-fat frozen dinners, too, if you make room for them in your fat budget.

A Box Does Not a Dinner Make

If you decide to buy commercial dinners, be sure to enhance them with fresh vegetables and salad. Steam broccoli, carrots, cauliflower, or zucchini in a vegetable steamer. Bake a potato. Boil a pot of rice. Don't cheat yourself out of the vitamins, minerals, and fiber that you need to maintain your good health. Remember, this is an eating diet. You need lots of complex carbohydrates to make those fat calories vaporize.

FAST FOODS

Fast Foods = Fat Foods

A person who wants to stay thin should avoid fast-food restaurants like the plague. Fast-food restaurants are a plague. Hundreds of thousands of Americans will die from fat-related diseases (heart disease and breast and colon cancer) because of the quantities of fat they consume. Here are some figures that may surprise you:

FAST FOOD	FAT CALORIES
Hardee's Big Country Breakfast Sausage	630
Wendy's Triple Cheeseburger	612
Burger King Double Beef Whopper with Cheese	576
Burger King Beef Whopper	513
Kentucky Fried Chicken Extra Crispy drumstick and thigh	483
Dairy Queen Triple Hamburger with Cheese	450
McDonald's McD.L.T.	396
Jack-in-the-Box Supreme Nachos	360
Roy Rogers Bacon Cheeseburger	351
Dairy Queen Super Hot Dog with Cheese	306

And these figures may come as a bigger surprise:

FAST FOOD	FAT CALORIES
Long John Silver **Fish** Dinner, fried (3 pieces)	630
Long John Silver **Seafood** Platter or Clam Dinner	522
Dairy Queen **Chicken** Sandwich	369
Roy Rogers Egg and **Biscuit** Platter with Sausage	369
McDonald's **Biscuit** with Sausage and Egg	360
Burger King Specialty **Chicken** Sandwich	360
Arby's **Baked Potato,** superstuffed, deluxe	342
Arby's **Chicken** Salad Croissant	324
Wendy's **Baked Potato** with cheese	306
McDonald's Filet-o-**Fish**	234
Jack-in-the-Box **Onion** Rings	207
Jack-in-the-Box **Pasta Seafood** Salad	198
Wendy's **Coleslaw** (½ cup)	72

Baked potato, chicken, pasta salad, fish — what happens to all those good, low-fat foods when a fast-food chef gets hold of them?

Slim Pickin's

There are no "no-no"s in *Choose to Lose*. You can eat even the highest-fat fast foods if you can fit them into your budget. But is a Wendy's Triple Cheeseburger (612 fat calories) or a Kentucky Fried Chicken Extra Crispy drumstick and thigh (483 fat calories) worth all those fat calories? Fast-food restaurants offer you such poor choices, you will do yourself a favor by staying away.

However, if you have been knocked on the head, tied up, and dragged to a fast-food restaurant, here are a few choices that won't totally decimate your fat budget.

FAST FOODS	FAT CALORIES
Arby's Junior Roast Beef	72
Long John Silver Ocean Chef Salad (no dressing)	72
Arby's Chicken Breast, roasted	63
Roy Rogers Chicken Leg	63
Wendy's Baked Potato with Chicken à la King	54
Arthur Treacher's Chowder	45
Long John Silver Clam Chowder	45
McDonald's English Muffin with Butter	45
Dairy Queen Chocolate Sundae, small (3.5 fl oz)	36
Kentucky Fried Chicken Corn on the Cob	27
Wendy's Baked Potato	18
Roy Rogers Baked Potato, plain	trace

You might try the salad bar, but beware of its major pitfalls — salad dressings and toppings. (See the discussion of Salad Dressings later in this chapter.)

MILK AND MILK PRODUCTS
Milk: A High-Fat Food

It seems un-American to regard whole milk as anything but wholesome and pure. However, whole milk should be viewed as a high-fat and thus a fattening food. One glass of whole milk (8 fl oz) contains 73 calories of fat. If your fat budget is 280, a glass of whole milk at each meal and one at bedtime would shoot your entire day's allotment. That is not to say that all milk products are high in fat. We are fortunate to live in an age in which we can buy low-fat and nonfat milk products that are truly delicious.

Shift to Skim Milk

If you currently drink whole milk and find the thought of drinking skim milk disgusting, first switch to 2% milk. You probably think 2% milk is truly low-fat. Two percent is barely above zero. But a glass of 2% milk contains 42 calories of fat. How can a drink that is 2% fat contain so many fat calories? Remember the 93% fat-free cold cuts? The 2 percent refers to the percentage of the weight of the milk that is fat, not the percentage of the total calories that are fat. If the milk producers called this milk 35% fat milk (42 fat calories ÷ 121 total calories = 35%), would you rush to buy it?

At 42 fat calories a glass, 2% milk is a better choice than whole milk at 73 fat calories a glass, but it's still pretty high. After you get used to 2% milk, try 1% milk for a while. You'll find it tastes pretty similar, and you'll be down to 23 calories of fat per glass. **Skim milk has only 4 fat calories and more calcium than whole milk** — so go for it!

MILK	AMOUNT	FAT CALORIES
Whole milk	8 fl oz (1 glass)	73
2% milk	8 fl oz	42
1% milk	8 fl oz	23
Nonfat skim milk	8 fl oz	4

Butter: A Spread That Increases Your Spread

Butter is 100 percent fat. A pat contains 36 calories of fat, a tablespoon 100. Each time you spread a knifeful of butter over a roll or piece of toast you are preparing to make a large dent in your fat budget. Keep track. Measure a half teaspoon (17 fat calories) or a teaspoon (33 fat calories) and then spread. Try eating the bread plain.

Butter adds fat calories while you're not even looking — when you eat baked goods, cream sauces, casseroles, and vegetables. Avoid foods containing unknown amounts of butter. Whatever the amount, it's certainly more than you need to stay thin.

You may have heard that margarine is a better choice than butter because margarine has so much less saturated fat (18 calories of saturated fat per tablespoon) than butter (at 65 per tablespoon). Saturated fat contributes to raising your blood cholesterol and thus your risk for heart disease. However, **both margarine and butter are 100 percent fat** and both have about 100 calories of fat per tablespoon. So, although margarine may be more heart-healthy, it is just as fattening as butter and should be limited.

Cream

It hardly seems necessary to advise dieters that cream is full of fat. But do you know exactly how bad it really is? It is necessary to keep a watchful eye on cream, for it sneaks into meals and wreaks havoc on diet goals. Cream in coffee can devastate your fat budget. One tablespoon of light table cream has 26 calories of fat. If you drink four cups of coffee a day, that adds up to 104 fat calories, and you haven't eaten anything of substance. Half-and-half is better, but not great. One tablespoon of half-and-half has 15 fat calories. Enough half-and-half for your four cups of coffee quickly adds up to 60 fat calories.

However, if you want to use cream or half-and-half, why not drink less coffee? Or better still, use whole milk at 5 fat calories per tablespoon, 2% at 3, or skim milk at zero. Best yet, drink your coffee black.

WARNING: Coffee whiteners may be as fattening as cream. One tablespoon of powdered creamers such as Cremora has 27 fat calories; Coffee-mate has about 25. Frozen creamers such as Coffee Rich and Poly Rich have 18 fat calories per tablespoon. Are they worth it?

Cream in Soups and Sauces: Riches to Avoid. Cream in soups can ruin your whole day. A bowl of cream of mushroom soup has about 155 calories of fat, New England clam chowder about 145, vichyssoise 210. These may be low estimates. When eating out, be sure to ask whether a soup contains cream, and if it does, then choose another appetizer or figure out how to budget it in.

And cream sauces! The half cup of curry cream sauce the chef ladles over your chicken costs you 250 fat calories, the cheesy cream sauce 170. If you want cream sauces to be part of your fat budget, insist that they be served on the side. Then you can determine how many spoonfuls (at about 30 fat calories each) you want. But remember. Don't fool yourself. Spoonfuls quickly become cups.

Whipped Cream: For Your Eyes Only. Whipped cream looks and tastes so light and airy, it is hard to believe its fat content is so high. But it is. The 2-tablespoon dollop that perks up your pumpkin pie has 52 fat calories. The little cloud that nestles atop your ice cream sundae may have more than 350 calories of fat. Whipped cream is not a diet food. Whipped cream splurges should be saved for very, very special occasions.

Cheese: Be Aware and BEWARE

If you have been a cheese nibbler, your nibbling days are numbered. Snacking on cheese is a fattening habit. Most whole milk cheeses derive 70 to 80 percent of their calories from fat. One ounce of Cheddar has 85 calories of fat; 1 ounce of Gruyère has 83. One ounce of Camembert cheese has 62; 1 ounce of Gouda has 70. Those chunks of Roquefort cheese in your salad dressing add 78 calories of fat to your greens (and to your thighs). If cheese is not one of your great loves, for the sake of your body, leave cheese off of your shopping list. And if it is, buy a small amount and fit it into your fat budget with great care. You will appreciate every bite.

"Lo" and "Lite": Read the Labels. Low-calorie cheeses abound. Most Lite-line brand cheeses have 18 fat calories per ounce. Eighteen calories isn't too bad if you watch the amount you eat. But be careful. Cheeses labeled "lite" or "lo-cal" are not necessarily low in fat. Light may refer to lower salt content or even a lighter color or texture. Some "light" cheeses, such as Dorman's Light Swiss at 72 fat calories per ounce, are as high in fat as whole milk cheeses. If you really love cheese, you might want to skip the filled cheese imitations and budget in a small piece of the real stuff very occasionally.

Mozzarella Loses Its Reputation. Mozzarella and Parmesan cheese have gained the reputation of being low in fat. However, 1 ounce of whole milk mozzarella has 55 fat calories and 1 ounce of part skim milk mozzarella has 41. One ounce (⅓ cup) of Parmesan cheese has 77 fat calories. When you bite into that slice of pizza oozing with mozzarella and Parmesan cheese, think about all those fat calories being deducted from your budget and added to your hulk. For delicious, low-fat pizzas, try Focaccia (page 167), a delicious cross between pizza and bread, or other pizza and calzone variations to be found in *Eater's Choice.*

Cottage Cheese: Not Always a Great Diet Food. We think of cottage cheese as diet food. And low-fat cottage cheese really is. However, not all cottage cheeses will help you lose weight. That half-cup scoop of whole milk cottage cheese on the "diet plate" has 43 fat calories. Two percent cottage cheese is a better choice at 20 fat calories per half cup. One percent is even better at a mere 10 fat calories per half cup. Mix cut-up fruit with your 1 percent–fat cottage cheese, or scoop cottage cheese on half a cantaloupe for two super, low-fat lunches.

Yogurt: The Good and the Bad

Before you gorge yourself on any brand of yogurt, read the label. Some yogurts contain cream and whole milk. Whitney's 6-ounce (it looks smaller because it *is* smaller) 100% Natural vanilla, lemon, or tropical fruit yogurts contain 54 fat calories; Colombo's 8-ounce whole milk French Vanilla yogurt contains 72 fat calories. These yogurts are

---

Dieters: Don't Give Up Dairy Products

You are embarking on a new way of eating that will keep you slim and healthy for the rest of your life. Your goal is to lose weight, but not by giving up nutritious foods. For you to succeed, your diet must be well-balanced. And that means eating dairy products — nonfat and low-fat dairy products.

Dairy products supply your body with calcium (skim milk has slightly more calcium than whole milk) to keep your bones and teeth strong. Women and girls especially need calcium to prevent osteoporosis. Children need calcium for strong bones and teeth and to grow. Fill your diet with nonfat and low-fat dairy products — nonfat yogurt, low-fat cottage cheese, skim milk, buttermilk.* Cook with nonfat yogurt, buttermilk, and skim milk. Save high-fat dairy products for splurges.

---

*Check the nutrition label on your buttermilk carton. Fat calories of buttermilk range from 0 to 36 (0–4 grams of fat) per cup. One gram (9 fat calories) is common. If you can't find a carton with fat information where you usually shop, buy your buttermilk at a different store.

hardly worth the fat calories, especially since the new nonfat flavored yogurts taste so creamy and good. Nonfat flavored and unflavored yogurt has fewer than 9 fat calories per serving.

Cooking with "Cream." It is possible to make delicious dishes by substituting nonfat yogurt, buttermilk, or skim milk in recipes that call for cream, sour cream, or whole milk. The divinely delicious *Deep-Dish Pear Pie* made with nonfat yogurt has 433 fewer fat calories than deep-dish pear pie made with a cup of sour cream. *Cantaloupe Soup* (page 146) is equally as scrumptious made with buttermilk (0–36 fat calories) as with cream (333 fat calories). Potato Salad (page 174) made with nonfat yogurt instead of sour cream saves 184 fat calories.

For a more detailed discussion of cooking with low-fat ingredients, see Silent Substitutions in Chapter 8.

Eggs: A Fat Surprise

Before you fix yourself a four-egg omelet for a light "diet" dinner, be aware that each egg yolk contains 50 calories of fat. A four-egg omelet contains 200 fat calories. Make your omelet with three egg whites (0 fat calories) and one egg for a similar-tasting but less-fat-filled dish.

FATS

Cut Down on Fat to Cut Down Your Fat

Most recipes contain more fat than they need to taste good. Experiment with reducing the fat in your recipes. Instead of using a quarter cup of margarine in the watercress soup, try 3 tablespoons. If the dish tastes just as good, try reducing the fat further. Use 2 tablespoons of margarine. See if eliminating the dabs of butter on top of the peach pie reduces its appeal. Use more vinegar and less oil in your salad dressings. You will find that your taste will gradually change and you will prefer less fat in your food. Now you may say, "Ha! I only wish!" but wait and see. We wager that soon eating a bowl of heavily creamed soup will turn your stomach.

Don't slather the butter on your bread or load it into your potato. Think! Measure! One tablespoon of butter has 100 fat calories. Ask, "Do I really need all that butter?" Two teaspoons of butter has 67 fat calories. Ask again, "Do I really need all that butter?" Try eating foods without adding fat. Sweet corn is heavenly without butter or margarine. Good bread and baked potatoes are delicious plain. When order-

Fat Facts

Total fat is the sum of three types of fat: saturated, monounsaturated, and polyunsaturated. While all three types of fat are fattening, each has a different effect on your heart-health.

Saturated fat raises your blood cholesterol and your risk of heart disease. It is found predominantly in animal fats (beet fat, veal fat, lamb fat, lard or pork fat, chicken fat, turkey fat, and butterfat) and the following vegetable fats: coconut oil, palm kernel oil, palm oil, cocoa butter, and hydrogenated vegetable oil. If you think these vegetable fats are rare, check out the labels on convenience and snack foods. Saturated fat is easily recognizable because it is solid at room temperature.

Monounsaturated fat and polyunsaturated fat, both of which are liquid at room temperature, lower your blood cholesterol and your risk of heart disease. The major source of monounsaturated fat is olive oil. The major sources of polyunsaturated fat are safflower, sunflower, corn, and soybean oils.

Olive oil is considered the healthiest of all the oils because it lowers the bad type of cholesterol without lowering the good type of cholesterol. (See *Eater's Choice* for a fuller discussion of diet, cholesterol, and heart disease.) Consumption of olive oil also seems to be associated with lower incidences of fat-related cancers such as breast and colon cancer.

Most fats and oils contain about 100–120 calories of fat per tablespoon. For both dieters and the health conscious, fats and oils should be limited in the diet.

CAUTION: All fats are 100 percent fat and thus are fattening.

ing out, ask for vegetables without any fat; ask for fish or potatoes with the butter on the side. You be the boss. It's your body, not the chef's.

Mayonnaise

One hundred percent of the calories of mayonnaise come from fat. One tablespoon of regular mayonnaise has 99 fat calories. Reduced-calorie mayonnaises are better: 1 tablespoon of reduced-calorie mayonnaise has 45 calories of fat. But a mere tablespoon is still a good percentage of your fat budget.

Mayonnaise Salad Sandwiches. Although tuna, shrimp, and chicken are basically low-fat meats, when they are mixed with mayonnaise and made into salads, they lose their low-fat label. If you can't avoid ordering a meat salad sandwich, insist that no additional mayonnaise be spread on the bread. Turkey breast meat is a better choice — with mustard. If you must have mayonnaise, ask the sandwich maker to use no more than a teaspoonful — just enough to wet the bread. For added taste, sprinkle on hot peppers.

Salad Dressings

Many salad dressings are loaded with fat calories: 1 tablespoon of Russian or blue cheese dressing has about 70 fat calories, 1 tablespoon of Italian 64. The salad dressings you get in a restaurant are almost always high in fat. Ask to have your dressing served on the side so you can regulate the amount you use. Unless otherwise labeled, salad bar dressings are high-fat. A small ladle holds 1 ounce, which is 2 tablespoons of salad dressing (140 fat calories of Russian dressing, 128 fat calories of Italian dressing). A large ladle holds 2 ounces, which is 4 tablespoons (280 fat calories of Russian dressing, 256 fat calories of Italian). Look for the number of ounces on the ladle handle or ask.

Keep track of how much dressing you put on your salad. Measure by tablespoonfuls (or soup spoons in a restaurant) so that you don't use up your day's fat budget before you get to the main course.

Low-Fat Dressings: A Boon to Dieters. Good news! Many low-calorie dressings are truly low in fat calories. Read the label. Some Russian low-calorie dressings have 6 fat calories per tablespoon; some French low calorie dressings have 8. Salad dressings with zero fat calories do exist. Or make your own. Try substituting nonfat yogurt in salad dressing recipes that call for sour cream.

DESSERTS

No dieter has to be told that desserts can cause a fat budget blowout. But what's the fun of living, after all, if you can never have a dessert? The beauty of *Choose to Lose* is that it allows you to eat any dessert as long as you can fit it into your fat budget. Just eat under your budget for several days to save up enough fat calories for a big splurge. (See Splurging in Chapter 8.) But beware. Desserts are not going to make you thin.

Cakes: Sweet Temptation

Think very carefully before that piece of cheesecake (at least 160 fat calories), carrot cake with cream cheese frosting (190 fat calories), or a 2-ounce Rachel's Double Chocolate Brownie with Walnuts (153 fat calories) passes between your lips. Check the food tables for the fat calories of your favorites. Try eating a sliver of cake. Eat it very slowly. Savor every bite.

For *very special* occasions you might also try baking other scrumptious desserts — Key Lime Pie at 36 fat calories per slice (page 185) or Tante Nancy's Apple Crumb Cake at 66 fat calories per slice (page 184) or, from *Eater's Choice,* such delights as *Divine Buttermilk Pound Cake* (66 fat calories per slice) or *Strawberry Tart* (57 fat calories per slice). While not especially low in fat, many have fewer than half the fat calories of their commercial counterparts. But before you bake a different *Eater's Choice* dessert for each day of the week, remember: "reduced" fat does not mean "little" fat, and eating these desserts too often may frustrate your effort to lose weight.

Cookies: Who's Counting?

Now that you are so fat-savvy, would you be surprised to learn that one small Pepperidge Farm Lido cookie has 50 fat calories, one Mint Milano cookie has 39 fat calories, an Almond Supreme or Southport has 45? Would you be shocked to find that one FFV TC Round has 36 fat calories, one Sunshine Vienna Finger has 27? That one Keebler Soft Batch Walnut Chocolate Chip cookie or one Stella D'oro Dietetic Peach Apricot Pastry cookie has 36 fat calories? Even one thin Nabisco Nilla Wafer has 5 fat calories.

Generally small, cookies don't look fat-packed. But commercially baked cookies range from a low of 3 fat calories for one Nabisco Animal Cracker to a high of 50 for one Pepperidge Farm Lido cookie. (Pepperidge Farm has added oversized cookies filled with chocolate chips and nuts to its cookie line. As with most cookies, these gustatory gems sport no nutrition labeling. A guesstimate should begin at 100 fat calories per cookie.)

Read the food tables to find the fat calories of your favorites. The problem with cookies is that they are addictive and additive. One tastes so good, why not have two? Or three? Or ten? If you know you can limit yourself to one cookie, or however many you can accommodate in your fat budget, do. That's why *Choose to Lose* is a workable plan. However, if you know that you are truly a cookie monster, leave temptation in the store and keep your home and office cookie jars filled with fruit.

Frozen Desserts: Fat on a Stick

The moment you bite into a Dove Bar or let a spoonful of Häagen-Dazs settle in your mouth, you know. Rich ice cream is full of fat. A Dove Bar is so high in fat that no nutrition information is printed on the label. A Häagen-Dazs Vanilla Milk Chocolate bar has 225 fat calories. A cup of Häagen-Dazs Vanilla Swiss Almond ice cream has 396 calories of fat. All ice cream is not that high-fat, but it is definitely not diet food. A cup of ordinary vanilla ice cream has about 129 fat calories. Read the label. Some ice creams have 90 fat calories a cup. Of course, you can have half a cup or a quarter of a cup or a tablespoon or two. But don't bring a gallon of ice cream into the house "for the kids" if you know that you are the kid the ice cream is for.

The Best Fat Buy: Nonfat Frozen Yogurt

If you are an ice cream purist, no other frozen confection may satisfy you. However, frozen desserts that have less fat do exist. An average ice milk* has about 25 calories of fat per half cup. A half cup of sherbet has 17 fat calories. And then there is frozen yogurt. Frozen yogurt parlors have sprouted up all over the United States. Many frozen yogurts are quite low in fat. The server may know the number of fat grams per serving (or ounce). A typical small serving (4 fl oz or ½ cup) of Colombo low-fat frozen yogurt has 18 fat calories. ICBIY and TCBY low-fat yogurts are not quite as low. A typical small serving of TCBY (4 fl oz) has 36 fat calories. The greatest treat is nonfat frozen yogurts (Colombo, ICBIY, and TCBY), which have zero calories of fat and are truly delicious. Check your local frozen yogurt parlors for their nonfat frozen yogurt choices.

Cold News Hot Off the Presses

Just in — some new "light" ice creams and ice milks that will not deeply depress your fat budget when eaten with thought. Be careful to read the labels to find the flavor with the lowest number of fat grams (to convert grams to calories, multiply the number of fat grams by 9).

---

*Some ice milks have as many as 54 fat calories per half cup. Read the label.

Safeway has introduced a line of Lucerne Light Supreme Ice Milk that includes strawberries and cream at 18 fat calories a half cup and vanilla at 27 fat calories per half cup. Breyers Light Natural, while not dipping quite as low as the ice milks, offers Vanilla and Chocolate Fudge Twirl at 36 fat calories per half cup. Be aware that although lower than most ice creams, these "light" varieties still have enough fat calories to demand extra vigilance.

Don't Let Fake Ice Cream Fake You Out

Nondairy Tofutti may be low in saturated fat and cholesterol-free, but it is brimming with fat. One cup of Chocolate Supreme Tofutti has 234 calories of fat. A cup of Tofutti Wildberry Supreme has 216. That is more than twice as high as many ice creams. How can that be? Read

FROZEN DESSERT	AMOUNT	FAT CALORIES
Häagen-Dazs Vanilla Milk Chocolate	1 bar	225
Häagen-Dazs Vanilla Swiss Almond ice cream	½ cup (4 fl oz)	198
Tofutti Chocolate Supreme	½ cup (4 fl oz)	117
Tofutti Wildberry Supreme	½ cup (4 fl oz)	108
Breyers Vanilla ice cream	½ cup (4 fl oz)	72
Hood Light Chocolate Macadamia Crunch ice milk	½ cup (4 fl oz)	54
TCBY low-fat frozen yogurt	½ cup (4 fl oz)	36
Breyers Light Vanilla and Chocolate Fudge Twirl	½ cup (4 fl oz)	36
Lucerne Light Vanilla ice milk	½ cup (4 fl oz)	27
Hood Light Vanilla ice milk	½ cup (4 fl oz)	27
Colombo low-fat frozen yogurt	½ cup (4 fl oz)	18
Lucerne Light Strawberries and Cream ice milk	½ cup (4 fl oz)	18
Sherbet	½ cup (4 fl oz)	17
Nonfat frozen yogurt (Colombo, ICBIY, TCBY)	½ cup (4 fl oz)	0

the ingredient list: water, high fructose, corn sweeteners, **corn oil,** and **tofu.***

Candy Packs a Fat Wallop

A candy bar may be small in size but it's gigantic in fat-calorie count. A 1.85-ounce Mr. Goodbar has 180 fat calories. A 1.625-ounce Kit Kat has 117 fat calories. One little caramel has 27 calories of fat. When the taste is gone, much too quickly, all you have left is fat deposits on your frame and a few extra cavities in your mouth. However, if never eating candy would cause you deep remorse, budget candy into your diet — *carefully.*

Although candy has no redeeming nutritional value, some candy has little or no fat. Gumdrops, hard candies, jelly beans, and marshmallows have no fat, but they are also devoid of any vitamins, minerals, or fiber. So think before you eat.

SNACKS

The problem with snacks is not just their high fat content. The problem with snacks is that they are addictive. You can't eat just one — one peanut or one cracker or one potato chip. Or even two. Or even three. Try fifty.

Sitting in front of the television set or among a group of friends, the snacker reaches into a bowl of nuts, crackers, chips, over and over and over: bowl to mouth, bowl to mouth. He barely tastes what he is eating, much less thinks about it. Dieters must be thinkers. Here are some truths about snacks.

Popcorn

Homemade Air-Popped Popcorn: The Best Buy. We start with popcorn because it has the potential to be one of the greatest snacks of all time. Popcorn that you pop in an air popper has no fat. It is chock-full of fiber — half insoluble (important for effective bowel function and reducing risk of colon cancer) and half soluble (helps to lower blood cholesterol and risk of heart disease). It is a perfect snack. It fills you up and satisfies that hand-to-mouth craving at no punishment to your budget. Air-popped popcorn may taste a bit like bumpy cardboard at

---

*Tofu is actually a high-fat food. A 2½ × 2¾ × 1–inch piece contains 50 fat calories.

first, but in a short time you'll develop a yen for it. And because it contains no fat, you can eat as much as you want.

Homemade Popcorn Popped in Oil: Not Such a Great Buy. The dietary benefits of popcorn diminish when other popping methods are used, because it takes a lot of fat to pop popcorn. Each cup of popcorn prepared in a saucepan with sunflower or corn oil contains about 25 fat calories. That's 1 cup. Who eats one cup of popcorn? (To help put one cup into perspective, note that the smallest container of popcorn you can buy at a movie theater holds 5 cups, and the largest bucket holds 22 cups.) And then, if you flavor it with melted butter or margarine, add 100 fat calories per tablespoon. And who uses just 1 tablespoon of butter or margarine?

Commercial Air-Popped Popcorn: The Pits. It's a cruel world out there. The food industry has perfected deception to its highest level. And we are the victims, unless we fight back by reading labels. The newest treachery in the food industry's bag of tricks is commercially packaged air-popped popcorn. Wow, how healthy. Ha! Read the label. Bachman's All Natural (another catchword for healthy) Air-popped Popcorn has 11 grams of fat or 99 fat calories for 1 ounce — 5 cups. The first fat ingredient is coconut oil. Bachman took a perfect dieter's food and made it highly fattening by covering it with the most saturated, heart-risky fat available. How sad.

Microwave Popcorn: No Buy. Microwave popcorns do not save you money, time, or fat calories. Microwave popcorn costs about $2.00 a pound (versus 40 cents a pound for plain popcorn kernels), takes three

POPCORN	COST PER POUND	FAT CALORIES PER OUNCE
Microwave	$2.00	99–214
Popcorn popped in oil	$0.40	138
Bachman's "Air-popped"	$4.36	99
Homemade air-popped popcorn	$0.40	0

to five minutes to make (versus four to five for air-popped), and ranges from 18 to 36 fat calories per cup (versus zero fat calories for plain air-popped popcorn).

Movie Popcorn: Bring Your Own. Beware of movie popcorn. It is almost always prepared in coconut oil, the most saturated (heart-risky) oil there is. Don't even consider buying buttered popcorn unless you want to bankrupt your fat budget. Bring your own air-popped popcorn. For a splurge, mix in some melted margarine (100 fat calories per tablespoon) . . . *carefully.*

Nuts to Nuts

Nuts make a delicious snack, add zest to entrées and desserts, possess delectable taste and crunch, and (sigh) are loaded with fat. They range from 70 to 86 percent fat, which turns out to be a lot of fat calories. And they are habit-forming. You might want to save nuts for cooking and then, when a recipe calls for half a cup of peanuts (323 fat calories), use only a quarter cup (161 fat calories) or 3 tablespoons (121 fat calories). If having nuts around for any reason demands more self-control than you are able to muster, leave them on the shelf in the store.

Nuts to Coconut

When the soda jerk asks you if you want your dish of nonfat frozen yogurt covered with shredded coconut, you might offer him a lecture on nutrition. There are two reasons to avoid coconut: first, it is a high-fat food, and almost 100 percent of the fat is saturated. (Saturated fat raises blood cholesterol, which raises your risk for heart disease.) Coconut is what scientists feed rats (who are quite resistant to heart disease) to give them heart disease. Second, and of most importance to the new thin you, coconut is incredibly high in fat calories. One cup of shredded coconut has 241 fat calories. One half cup of coconut cream has 375 fat calories. One half cup of coconut milk has 258 fat calories. A little dab will undo you.

Nuts to Seeds

Seeds represent another sneaky fat carrier. They are so small and seem so healthy, but just a few handfuls can deplete your whole fat budget. Whole pumpkin seeds contain 50 fat calories per ounce. One tablespoon of sesame seeds contains 39 fat calories. Shelled sunflower seeds contain 127 fat calories per ounce, 36 fat calories per tablespoon. The little package (1⅛ oz) of shelled sunflower seeds you pick up at the grocery store checkout line has 152 fat calories. And they are filled with salt, so you want to eat more and more. If you love to nibble on sunflower seeds, apportion yourself 1 tablespoon and consider that a hefty treat.

For a real education, check the **Nuts and Seeds** section of the food tables.

Trail Mix

Trail Mix (mixed nuts, seeds, and dried fruit) conjures up the aura of outdoor vitality and good health. Out on the trail, hiking up a mountain, forging a stream (or, perhaps, sitting in your den watching TV) you gobble up handfuls of this tasty mix. *Stop.* Consider the contents — almonds (132 fat calories per ounce), cashews (118 fat calories per ounce), peanuts (126 fat calories per ounce), sunflower seeds (127 fat calories per ounce), flaked coconut (82 fat calories per ounce), dried fruit (0–13 fat calories per ounce). This "healthy" snack food could contain anywhere from about 85 to 120 fat calories per ounce.

Just Say No to Chips

If you are like most normal human beings, you will find it impossible to keep from eating potato chips if they are in your house. Since one cup of potato chips has 75 fat calories, you might want to avoid bringing temptation home from the store. If you have an uncontrollable urge to eat potato chips, buy a small snack bag (113 fat calories). It may be worth that big chunk out of your fat budget every once in a while.

Any chips — Fritos, Chee-tos, nachos, etc., etc. — should be eaten with considerable thought. Chips are basically fat stiffened with a bit of vegetable. In fact, the first ingredient of Durkee's French Fried Onions is partially hydrogenated vegetable oil (soy, palm).* And the fat calories show it. Both 1 ounce of Bugles and 1 ounce of Fritos corn chips contain 72 fat calories. An ounce of Cornuts has 36 fat calories. Snack chips are truly addictive and can be consumed by the hundreds and thousands. The last one always invites another. Our strong recommendation is to leave temptation out of the house by not bringing chips in. No one needs them.

---

*Ingredients on a food label are listed in descending order by weight.

Crackers

Your suspicions should be aroused when you note that almost no cracker package sports a food label. What are they hiding? *Fat.* Crackers are a high-fat food and like potato chips and peanuts, crackers are consumed in great numbers with nary a thought. They are little but they add up. One cracker may have only 9 calories of fat, but ten have 90, and it is very easy to eat ten crackers. Dieters must pay attention. The best policy is to avoid the cracker section of your grocery store. But if you must have crackers, be sure to fit them into your fat budget. Perhaps as a treat have two crackers a day. You know yourself. Will the box of crackers be so tempting that you will eventually weaken and gobble them all up? If so, leave the crackers in the store.

The Rare Exceptions. Devonsheer's Melba Toast and Melba Rounds and Wasa's Crispbreads have zero calories of fat and lots of crunch. Eat them plain or with jelly. Nonfat crackers covered with cheese, cream cheese, or some other high-fat spread are no longer diet food.

THE GOOD NEWS

Dry your tears. You can still fit any of these fat-laden foods into your fat budget. But now that you know how to choose carefully and wisely, you might ask yourself some questions. Why eat a can of solid white tuna packed in oil at 238 fat calories when a can of solid white tuna packed in water has only 30 fat calories? Do I really want that greasy cheese smokie at 112 calories of fat? Will a bite of that apple pie (about 16 fat calories) instead of a whole slice (160 fat calories) satisfy me? Refer to this chapter and to the food tables in the back of the book to make educated choices that will produce a streamlined and glorious you.

Coming next . . . sniffing out the fat in the foods *you* eat.

Remember:
1. Red meats such as beef, veal, lamb, and most pork products are high in fat. The higher the grade of meat, the more fat it contains.
2. Turkey and chicken with the skin removed (always remove the skin before cooking chicken) and many fish are low in fat. But these low-fat foods are easily made high-fat foods by the way they are prepared.

3. Most sausage and luncheon meats are extremely high in fat (in addition to containing cancer-risky nitrites and blood pressure–raising sodium).

4. Many frozen dinners and convenience foods are riddled with hidden fat. Read the labels to see how you can fit these foods into your fat budget.

5. Most fast foods are loaded with fat (and sodium). Do your diet a favor and approach fast-food restaurants with caution.

6. Dairy products are excellent sources of calcium, but many are high in fat. A glass of whole milk contains 73 fat calories. An ounce of Cheddar cheese contains 85 fat calories. Choose low-fat dairy products such as low-fat or nonfat yogurt, low-fat cottage cheese, and skim milk. Fit cheeses into your budget sparingly and you will really enjoy them.

4. Self-Discovery

NOW THAT you know *generally* where fat lurks in foods, you will want to discover *exactly* where the fat lurks in the foods *you* eat. Before you evaluate your own food diary, let's look at Ellen's.

BREAKFAST: DON'T MISS IT

	Ellen's breakfast			
TIME	FOOD	AMOUNT	TOTAL CALORIES	FAT CALORIES
8:15 A.M.	blueberry muffin	1 large	290	**99**
	coffee	1 cup	0	**0**
	half-and-half	1 tbsp	20	**15**
		Total Fat Calories:		**114**
		Ellen's Daily Fat Budget:		**280**

Ellen was wise to eat breakfast. Eating three meals a day (low-fat, high-carbohydrate meals, natch) is *extremely* important for weight loss. You want to start burning calories as soon as you get up. In addition, when you miss breakfast, you are apt to satisfy your midmorning cravings with a high-fat snack. However, the blueberry muffin was a poor choice. It tastes a lot like pound cake because it is made with all the same high-fat ingredients — butter, lard, or vegetable oil, whole milk, sometimes cream. Next time Ellen will have to decide if the blueberry muffin is worth more than one-third of her fat budget.

Ellen uses half-and-half in her coffee. At 15 for each tablespoon, the fat calories add up. How about 2% milk? 1% milk? Nonfat milk? Why not drink it black?

For better breakfast choices, see Chapter 6, Putting *Choose to Lose* to Work for You.

MIDMORNING SNACK

Ellen knows that her snack will get her into trouble.

	Ellen's morning snack			
TIME	FOOD	AMOUNT	TOTAL CALORIES	FAT CALORIES
10:30 A.M.	glazed doughnut	1 large	235	117
	coffee	1 cup	0	0
	half-and-half	1 tbsp	20	15
		Total Fat Calories:		132
		Ellen's Daily Fat Budget:		280

Ellen has eaten 246 fat calories so far today.

Instead of the doughnut, how about eating a carton of nonfat flavored yogurt at zero fat calories or a few slices of Onion Flat Bread (page 179) at 7 fat calories a piece?

LUNCH: SIT DOWN, CHOOSE WELL, AND ENJOY

Don't skip lunch to save calories or because you have to finish a job. You'll only end up bingeing when you get home or overeating at dinner. Take advantage of lunchtime to unwind and enjoy a good meal — a good low-fat, high-carbohydrate meal. Eating at least three meals a day is important for weight loss because your body needs the fuel to maintain your basal metabolic rate.

Ellen had second thoughts about going to a fast-food restaurant for lunch. Next time she will have first thoughts. But, it won't be easy. Friends or coworkers often choose restaurants that offer no food options for weight-conscious diners. Peer pressure is a poor excuse. Ellen has to stand up for her rights. The companionship of people who don't

		Ellen's lunch		
TIME	FOOD	AMOUNT	TOTAL CALORIES	FAT CALORIES
Noon	mixed salad			
	lettuce	2 cups	20	0
	tomato	½	12	0
	cucumber	¼	10	0
	carrot	¼	8	0
	Russian dressing	4 tbsp*	308	280
	sunflower seeds	1 tbsp	46	36
	biscuit	1	231	108
	butter	1 pat (tsp)	36	36
		Total Fat Calories:		460
		Ellen's Daily Fat Budget:		280
	Ellen has eaten 706 fat calories so far today.			

*Two ladlefuls = 2 ounces = 4 tablespoons

respect your diet wishes is not worth a lethal gash in your fat budget. Ellen might even convince her friends that they can enjoy a restaurant with low-fat options.

Ellen's notion that the salad bar is a good diet choice is not completely accurate. Many of the salad bar options are items made with high-fat ingredients — mayonnaise salad with a macaroni or two, cold cut salad drowning in oil, apple salad with walnuts and sour cream. Eating at a salad bar takes much care. Ellen's choice of salad vegetables — carrots, lettuce, tomatoes, and cucumbers — was diet-wise. Salad vegetables are complex carbohydrates that are high in fiber, vitamins, and minerals and almost completely fat-free. However, very few people enjoy salad without salad dressing.

Salad Dressing

Ellen poured 2 ladles or 4 tablespoons of Russian dressing (70 fat calories per tablespoon or 280 fat calories for four) on her salad. A low- or reduced-calorie dressing would have been a better choice, although creamy-type reduced-calorie dressings at fast-food restaurants are still high in fat calories. (At Wendy's the reduced-calorie creamy cucumber dressing has 45 fat calories per tablespoon, the reduced-calorie Italian dressing 18.) Using 2 tablespoons of dressing instead of 4 cuts the fat calories in half, and 1 tablespoon cuts them even more.

BEWARE: The small dressing ladle at the salad bar holds 2 tablespoons of salad dressing. Two dunks and you have a quarter cup of dressing.

Sunflower Seeds

Ellen sprinkled a tablespoonful of sunflower seeds over her salad. That casual gesture cost her 36 fat calories. Seeds and nuts are high-fat foods.

Biscuits

Biscuits don't *look* fattening. A biscuit made in your kitchen may have from 10 to 30 fat calories, depending on how much butter or shortening you add. A fast-food biscuit ranges in fat calories from 108 (Roy Rogers) to 162 (McDonald's). Add a little pat of butter and your "innocent" biscuit creates a 144- to 198-calorie dent in your fat budget.

Ellen was surprised to find that her "diet" lunch contained 460 fat calories.

Dieters should steer clear of fast-food restaurants. The temptation to splurge with a Big Mac (315 fat calories), Roy Rogers hamburger (255 fat calories), or a Wendy's baked potato with cheese (306 fat calories) is hard to resist. As you can see from Ellen's food record, even the salad bar can be a disaster. Choose a sandwich shop, a real restaurant, or bring your lunch from home. For more on eating out, see Chapter 6, Putting *Choose to Lose* to Work for You.

DINNER

Ellen is like millions of working people. They labor all day and when they get home, they don't feel like cooking. They feel pressured for time and want food that takes no effort to prepare and seconds to cook. This mind-set has created a multibillion-dollar frozen food industry. In an ideal world, one could shove a box into a microwave oven and produce delicious, healthy meals. This is the real world. Meals in a box do not taste great and they are often shot up with fat and sodium as well as artificial colors and flavors.

If you are dieting or just interested in good health and sensory plea-

Ellen's dinner

TIME	FOOD	AMOUNT	TOTAL CALORIES	FAT CALORIES
6:15 P.M.	Chicken Enchiladas Suiza			
	(Weight Watchers)	1 dinner	350	**153**
	cucumber	½	20	**0**
	coffee	1 cup	0	**0**
	half-and-half	1 tbsp	20	**15**
	yogurt (Whitney's 100%			
	Natural) vanilla	6 oz	200	**54**

Total Fat Calories: 222
Ellen's Daily Fat Budget: 280

Ellen has eaten 928 fat calories so far today.

sure, you need to cook your own food, using real ingredients. Ellen has all evening to make dinner. She is cheating herself by eating plastic food. Read the section on frozen dinners in Chapter 3, Where's the Fat? and check out the fat calories of frozen dinners in the food tables.

Frozen Dinners: Packaged Fat

The Weight Watchers Chicken Enchiladas Suiza has 153 fat calories. Is it called Weight Watchers because you watch your weight increase? Ellen would do better to make Apricot Chicken Divine (page 153), which has 39 fat calories, or Broiled Ginger Fish (page 160) at 50 fat calories. Both take little time to prepare and taste superb.

The Missing Vegetable

Ellen's diet is vegetable-bare. Vegetables can be steamed in minutes, add color and texture to your meal, contain fiber, vitamins, and minerals, and taste wonderful. They fill you up, improve your bowel function, and help reduce your risk of breast and colon cancer. What's more, vegetables can be eaten with abandon because they contain little or no fat.

All Yogurts Are Not Equal

Ellen's choice of yogurt for dessert could have been weight-wise — except she chose a high-fat yogurt (54 fat calories in 6 ounces). She could have selected any number of nonfat flavored yogurts that have 0 to 9 calories of fat in 8 ounces. Even a low-fat flavored yogurt, at 27 fat calories in 8 ounces, would have been a better choice.

SNACKS: DIETER'S DOWNFALL

Ellen's snack

TIME	FOOD	AMOUNT	TOTAL CALORIES	FAT CALORIES
7–11 P.M.	oil-roasted salted peanuts	½ cup	420	**321**

Total Fat Calories: **321**
Ellen's Daily Fat Budget: **280**

Ellen has eaten 1249 fat calories so far today.

Snack foods are the downfall of weight watchers. Snacks are almost always filled with fat, and they are addictive. It is impossible to eat one peanut. One peanut leads to another and another, until finally the whole bowl of peanuts has disappeared. The snacker eats without thought. When the bottom of the bowl appears he wonders where all the potato chips went. A tip for snackers: put out no more than you plan to eat.

As you can see from Ellen's food diary, she consumed a half cup of peanuts — 321 calories of fat. A better choice would have been 8 cups of air-popped popcorn with zero fat calories, loads of soluble and insoluble fiber, and lots of crunch.

Ellen adds up her total calories and fat calories for the day:

	TOTAL CALORIES	TOTAL FAT CALORIES
Breakfast	310	**114**
Morning snack	255	**132**
Lunch	671	**460**
Dinner	590	**222**
Evening snack	420	**321**
Total:	2246	**1249**

Ellen ate 928 fat calories from breakfast through dinner. By the time she finished her evening snack and went to bed she had eaten 1249 calories of fat. Is it any wonder she is fat? Remember, Ellen's fat budget is 280. She's *only* 969 fat calories over her budget. You may think that her fat calorie intake is unusually high, but if you look back at Ellen's food record you will see nothing out of the ordinary. In fact, you may have noticed that she ate no fattening desserts. Fat calories have a sneaky habit of adding up.

Reducing Fat Intake Brings Total Calories into Line

It is interesting to note that Ellen's total caloric intake is 2246 calories — 842 calories over her recommended total daily caloric intake of 1404 calories. Since we know she ate 969 fat calories over her budget, it is clear that all the 842 total calories she over-ate were fat calories. Ellen did not become fat overeating carbohydrates. Like most people who are overweight, when Ellen reduces her intake of fat to her budgeted amount, she will automatically bring her daily caloric intake close to her recommended level.

BEFORE YOU KNOW IT

Think of your $1000 monthly credit card bill. "What?" you cry in despair. "I didn't buy anything big." You take out your calculator: a pair of $42 shoes, a gasoline charge of $9, a TV repair bill for $59, and on and on. Nothing over $60. And, of course, it all adds up to a whopping $1000. Fat calories work the same way. A 42–fat calorie glass of 2% milk, a 9–fat calorie cracker, a 59–fat calorie slice of bologna. They all add up until you've bankrupted your budget.

A FOOD RECORD = AN EDUCATION

Reviewing her three-day food diary has been invaluable for Ellen, and quite a surprise. She no longer wonders why she is overweight. She has discovered the sources of fat in her diet. She won't regard biscuits with such a friendly eye. She'll think before dumping 4 tablespoons of dressing on her salad. Ellen now knows where to cut out fat. She knows which foods she still wants to eat and how much it will cost her — fat-wise.

LOOKING AT YOUR OWN FOOD RECORD

Now it is your turn for self-discovery. What about the fat content of the foods you eat? Will you be as shocked as Ellen was? With your fat budget in mind, use the food tables at the back of the book to calculate the total and fat calories of the foods you ate and recorded in your three-day food diary. If you did not keep a food diary, you might want to do it now. Reread Chapter 2 and Appendix A for helpful details. If you decide not to keep a food diary, read on, because you will need to know the following information for choosing foods and evaluating your food records in the future.

Using the Food Tables

The food tables are an invaluable source of information — and surprises. They give you insight into why you did not wear a bikini last summer. Would you have thought that fifteen potato chips have 95 fat calories? Four ounces of lean flank steak have 140 fat calories? Nine little cashews have 60 fat calories?

The food tables are organized alphabetically according to the following categories: Beverages, Dairy Products and Eggs, Fast Foods, Fats and Oils, Fish and Seafood, Frozen and Microwave Foods, Fruits and Fruit Juices, Grain Products, Meats (Beef, Lamb, Pork, Veal and Game), Nuts and Seeds, Poultry, Sauces and Gravies, Sausages and Luncheon Meats, Soups, Sweets, Vegetables and Vegetable Products, and Miscellaneous.

If you have difficulty locating specific foods in the food tables, check the Food Tables Index following the food tables. In this index, foods are listed alphabetically rather than by category.

How Much Did You Actually Eat?

The amount that you ate and the portion size listed in the food tables may differ. You can easily calculate the number of calories you consumed by multiplying the portion size that is listed by the amount you ate. For example, if one cup of Tofutti Chocolate Supreme contains 234 calories of fat, and you ate half a cup, you consumed 234 × ½ or 117 fat calories. On the other hand, if you ate two cups, you consumed 234 × 2 or 468 fat calories.

Comparison Value

Data for many foods is given in 1-ounce amounts to help you compare their fat content so you can make informed choices. However, keep in mind that although 1-ounce portions are listed for a food, 1 ounce may be much less than you eat and you must adjust your figures accordingly.

For instance, at first glance, the meats (beef, veal, lamb, pork, poultry, fish) all look like low-fat foods because the fat values are given for 1 ounce portions. But as you rarely eat a single ounce of meat, you must multiply the 1-ounce portion by the number of ounces you actually ate. If you ate 4 ounces of lean ground beef, multiply the fat content of lean ground beef (47 fat calories) by 4 to determine the number of fat calories you actually ate: 4 × 47 = 188 fat calories.

You may find the Table of Equivalent Measures on page 296 helpful.

Guesstimate

You may not be able to find *exactly* what you ate listed in the food tables. Perhaps you had French fries at Jack-in-the-Box, but can find no French fries listing under Fast Foods, Jack-in-the-Box. Look at the other fast-food restaurant entries and make a guess. Roy Rogers regular French fries contain 126 calories of fat; Kentucky Fried Chicken fries have 117; Hardee's fries have 112. Your French fry estimate might be 117 calories of fat.

Guesstimate When Eating Out

If you ate out and butter was added to your vegetables, add 36 fat calories per serving. If your meat was fried, add 20 fat calories per ounce of meat. If your meat was breaded and fried, add 40 calories of fat per ounce of meat.

If you were served a dish or dessert that isn't in the food tables, look for the recipe in a cookbook (not a low-fat cookbook) to estimate the fat calories. To estimate the fat calories you consumed, add up the fat calories for the fat-containing ingredients and divide by the number of servings given for the recipe.

Say you ate lasagna. According to your cookbook, the fat-containing ingredients are the following:

INGREDIENT	FAT CALORIES
⅓ cup olive oil	640
2 lb (32 oz) ground beef	2176 (68 fat calories per ounce × 32)
¾ lb (1½ cups) ricotta cheese	435 (145 fat calories per half cup × 3)
⅓ lb (5.3 oz) mozzarella cheese	292 (55 fat calories per ounce × 5.3)
½ lb (8 oz) grated Parmesan cheese	616 (77 fat calories per ounce × 8)

Total fat calories: 4159

The recipe makes sixteen servings, so to get the figure for one serving, divide the total fat calories by 16 (4159 ÷ 16 = 260). Your serving of lasagna contained about 260 fat calories. To estimate the total calories for your serving, add up the total calories of all the ingredients and divide by the number of servings.

REMEMBER: Be honest with yourself. When in doubt, over-estimate.

Convert Grams to Calories

If you ate any commercial products, read the food label to learn how much fat you ate. (If you did not save the label or write down the nutrition information from the package, take a pencil and paper to the grocery store and copy the information from a similar package.) To convert grams of fat into calories of fat, multiply the grams of fat by 9. For example, if your fish stick contains 7 grams of fat, to find out how many fat calories it has, multiply 7 grams of fat by 9 calories per gram (7 × 9 = 63 fat calories).

Be sure to adjust the serving size to the amount you actually ate. If one serving of cookies contains 10 grams of fat, then to find the calories of fat per serving, multiply 10 grams by 9 calories per gram (10 × 9 = 90 calories of fat per serving). One serving of cookies contains four cookies, so four cookies contain 90 calories of fat.

If you ate twelve cookies, you actually ate three servings (12 cookies

÷ 4 cookies per serving = 3 servings). To find the fat calories for three servings, multiply the fat calories per serving by the number of servings (90 × 3) to get 270 calories of fat.

FILLING IN THE FAT CALORIES

Okay, do it! First, fill in the headings of the last two columns with Fat Calories and Total Calories so it looks like this:

TIME	FOOD	AMOUNT	TOTAL CALORIES	FAT CALORIES

Starting with day one of your food diary, determine the fat calories and total calories for each entry and write them down. Be sure that you figure out the calories for the actual amounts you ate.

If you find that you did not write down enough information to calculate the fat calories of the food you ate, start all over and record everything you eat for three more days. This time, keep better records. The food diary is for you. It must be detailed if it is going to help you discover the sources of fat in your diet.

Adding It All Up

When you have completed your fat-calorie evaluation, add up the fat calories for each day and then add up the total calories.

Gaining Insight

Look at your results and answer these questions:

• How does your daily fat calorie intake compare with your fat budget?
• How does your daily total calorie intake compare with your recommended daily total caloric intake?
• How much greater is your fat intake than your fat budget? (If your fat intake and fat budget are similar, take three more days to record your food intake and *be honest*. You're fat for some reason and it isn't because you are eating lots of spinach.)

- Can you target the foods that are making you fat?
- Are there many different foods that are full of fat or just a few?
- Do you eat them at certain meals? Snacks? Throughout the day?
- What have you learned about the foods you are eating?

With the answers to these questions in mind, read the next chapter to find out about foods you *can* eat, great foods you may have been avoiding that you can now gobble up, great low-fat foods to replace high-fat offenders.

Remember:
1. Your food record is the key to discovering the sources of fat in your diet.
2. Use the food tables to determine the fat calories of the foods you ate.
   a. Adjust the serving size to the actual amount you consumed.
   b. Don't forget that meat is listed in 1-ounce portions.
3. Analyze your food record for high-fat foods.

5. Eat without Fear

THINK BACK to the science you learned in Chapter 1. The earthshaking truth is that you *must* eat to lose weight. Of course, you must eat foods that are low in fat, but you should eat *lots* of low-fat foods.

It is crucial that you eat enough calories. You figured out your ideal caloric intake in Chapter 2. Make sure that you keep track of your total calories for a few days to ensure that you are eating enough food. When you reduce fat in your diet, there is a real danger that your total caloric intake will fall too low. You must replace some of the fat you eliminate with foods rich in complex carbohydrates — grains, fruit, vegetables. Keep saying to yourself over and over, "I must eat to lose."

CARBOHYDRATES GALORE

And which foods these are may surprise you.

Here's the great news. You may eat bread. You may eat potatoes. You may eat rice. You may eat spaghetti. You may put jelly on your toast. Remember, carbohydrates help you to *lose* weight. This is probably still difficult for you to believe and may be even more difficult for you to implement, but the more bread, potatoes, rice, and pasta you eat and the less fat you eat (within reason), the faster you will lose.

Adding Carbohydrates to the Fire

Let's review the reasons why this miraculous statement is true. Carbohydrates have a thermogenic effect, causing your body to burn calories at a faster rate. Did you ever notice that you become warm when you eat? That's the thermogenic effect in action. Eating carbohydrates is like adding wood to a fire — the fire burns hotter and faster until the wood (carbohydrate) is burned up.

Putting Fat into Cold Storage

Fat does not have this thermogenic effect. The fat you eat on a mixed diet doesn't get burned up, doesn't add fuel to the fire, but gets stored almost entirely as fat in your fat cells. So while occasionally you can even eat up to 2000 calories of carbohydrates in excess of your normal mixed diet and not gain weight, any fat you eat above your fat budget turns into fat on your bod.

Misguidance

Carbohydrates used to be (and remain to a great extent) the Number One Forbidden Food Group in every diet. You are advised to eat the 2 ounces of Cheddar cheese and toss the 2 slices of bread, eat the 5-ounce sirloin steak and chuck the baked potato. Let's see what that means in fat calories. Keep the cheese — 170 calories of fat — and toss the bread — 18 calories of fat. Keep the steak — 230 fat calories — and chuck the potato — trace fat calories. Huh? They must be kidding.

Not The *Choose to Lose* Diet. Here are some good things to eat.

Bread: A Yes-Yes

Hey! You can eat *bread!* Consider bread diet food. A slice of commercially baked bread has 1 gram of fat (9 fat calories). Check the labels — some have more. You can eat it for a snack. Shun open-face sandwiches. Give your sandwich a top and a bottom. You need those calories of carbohydrate. Besides, you will feel more full eating both slices of bread.

BEWARE: Even the fat calories of low-fat foods can add up if eaten in excess. Keep track of your bread consumption. Nine fat calories times 10 slices of bread equals 90 fat calories.

Homemade Breads: Mmmm Good! Try baking your own bread. Bread dough is quickly and easily made in a food processor (it takes less than five minutes). Even baking the bread doesn't take much time. You have to be around an hour after you make the dough to roll it out and put it in loaf pans. Then you have to return an hour later to bake it. Start the bread when you finish dinner if you're staying home for the evening and you'll have it warm for a late-night snack. Make two loaves and freeze one. A slice of Onion Flat Bread (page 179) or Anadama (page 177) or any of the breads in *Eater's Choice* will enhance your diet and your life.

These homemade breads are not without fat calories — on the average a slice has 15 fat calories (some have as many as 25), but homemade bread tastes so good and is so filling it is worth a small bite into your fat budget. Have a slice for breakfast, toasted and piled high with banana slices and 1% cottage cheese. Have a slice with your fruit salad and nonfat yogurt for lunch. Even a slice or two may find a place in your budget to satisfy afternoon or evening pangs of hunger.

An aside: choose whole-grain breads. They are healthier than white. They are rich in fiber, protein, thiamine, riboflavin, niacin, folic acid, vitamin E, iron, phosphorus, magnesium, zinc, and other trace minerals. Check labels. Some breads labeled "wheat bread" may contain no whole wheat. Some bread manufacturers use caramel coloring to create the darker appearance of whole-wheat flour.

Eat Potatoes to Avoid Looking Like One

Can you believe it? Eating potatoes will help you lose weight. Bake them, boil them, broil them. Fill them with nonfat yogurt or eat them plain. Bake Potato Skins (page 165), but use only 1 teaspoon of olive oil. At 5 fat calories a serving, you can eat them with gusto. Bake an extra potato for dinner and eat it cold as a snack.

Your mouth drops open in disbelief. How can potatoes be diet food? Potatoes are almost completely free of fat. And, they are a good source of vitamin C, thiamine, niacin, and iron. Sweet potatoes are also loaded with vitamin A. Screw up your courage and eat a potato or two every day. See if you don't look less and less like a potato.

Low-Fat Potato + Fat = High-Fat Potato. Of course, if you stuff your potato with a fat (butter, margarine, sour cream) or slice and fry it into French fries or slice it even thinner and fry it into potato chips, you can no longer consider potatoes diet food. French fries and potato chips are among the worst offenders on the Most Unwanted Fat list.

Pastas and Rice

Here are two more complex carbohydrates to add to your diet list — pasta and rice. Don't be shy. Pile a heap of rice on your plate and top it with a low-fat chicken or vegetable dish. Fill a large bowl with spaghetti and cover it with a low-fat tomato sauce. Eat more of the pasta or rice and less of the topping.

Are you having difficulty imagining piles of rice or spaghetti on your plate? And actually eating them? Those who have always considered a quarter cup of rice or spaghetti extravagant must make an effort to regard them in a positive light. Repeat over and over: "Pasta and rice are *not* fattening. Eating pasta and rice will help me *lose* weight." You'll see.

Pasta + Cream Sauce = Weight Gain. Of course, pasta and rice are not always reducing foods. Mix in butter or margarine or cover them with high-fat sauces or cheese and you destroy their beneficial weight loss properties.

Veggies

No one needs to tell you that vegetables are an important part of a diet. You have probably followed diets in which the fear of turning into a rabbit was justified. But don't disparage vegetables. Not only are they low in fat, high in vitamins, minerals, and fiber, they are also just plain delicious. Eat them raw. Cut them into match-size strips. They taste better that way. Steam them until just tender and press garlic or grind pepper over them or sprinkle them with herbs. Create a vegetable dip by mixing Dijon mustard into nonfat yogurt. Try vegetables you have never tried before. Have you ever baked spaghetti squash? When you scrape out the cooked interior, it separates into strands, exactly like spaghetti but more nutritious and delicious. Top with tomato sauce.

Fruit: Food of the Gods

Fruit makes a great snack, a great lunch, and a great dessert. In fact, we should emulate the Europeans and top off our meals with fruit instead of rich desserts. In season, cantaloupe, honeydew melon, watermelon, strawberries, raspberries, peaches, nectarines, pears, and plums taste divine. Packed with vitamins, minerals, fiber, fruit is nutritious and puts no strain on your fat budget.

Fattening Fruit. Of course, even fruit can be ruined. Vanilla ice cream covered with strawberries, raspberries in cream, or blackberries in sour cream may taste delicious, but they won't keep buttons from popping off your shirts. Substitute nonfat yogurt or nonfat frozen yogurt for a similar but nonfattening effect.

SUGAR GUILT

Sugar guilt is intense in dieters. Intense, but misguided, because sugar by itself will not make you gain weight. It is the fat that accompanies the sugar that makes you fat. Think of all those wonderfully rich desserts you have been avoiding. They contain sugar *and* butter, chocolate, whipped cream, cream, or sour cream. The big *and* makes the dessert fattening.

"So big deal," you say. "Even if sugar doesn't make you fat, I still can't pig out on cheesecake or ice cream." True, but you can occasionally fit high-fat desserts into your fat budget. You can put jelly or jam on your English muffin without a twinge of conscience. (In fact, you should use jelly and forget about the margarine or butter.) You can suck an occasional peppermint or butterscotch hard candy without guilt.

Sweet Treat

No, you should not binge on sugar, either. Not only does it cause tooth decay, sugar is just a lot of empty calories containing no vitamins, minerals, or fiber. If you are diabetic or have high triglycerides you should avoid sugar. But treating yourself to an occasional hard candy may give you a lift. (Be sure to check labels for ingredients; some hard candy is made with heart-risky, fattening coconut oil.) If you ordinarily skimp on maple syrup on French toast, pouring a little more of the maple syrup and eating a lot less of the French toast will do both your psyche and diet a lot of good. Vanilla nonfat yogurt may have 120 calories of sugar, but since it has zero calories of fat, eat away.

SNACKS

Popcorn

Air-popped popcorn — that is, *true* air-popped popcorn that you pop yourself as opposed to commercial packaged brands, which add 99 calories of fat per ounce — has no fat. If you ate the same amount of air-popped popcorn with no added fat that fills the large container of coconut-oil-popped movie theater popcorn — twenty-two cups — you would not gain weight. (However, your jaws might never open again.)

Pretzels

Pretzels can make a good diet snack. Some are very low in fat. Ten two-inch pretzel sticks may have only trace amounts of fat. One large twisted pretzel may have only 9 fat calories. However, before you invest in a warehouse of pretzel tins, note that most brands are heavily encrusted with salt (sodium raises blood pressure and causes fluid retention), and as your aim is to control your appetite and not continue to be an eating machine, you don't want to go hog-wild on even the lowest-sodium pretzels. Be sure to read the labels. Some pretzels are made with significant amounts of fat.

Self-Control

You are following *Choose to Lose* because you want to lose weight and eat healthfully. Keep this in mind at all times. Eating a million pretzels or hard sucking candies because they have little or no fat is pushing the system.

CHOICE MEATS

Chicken: Infinite Variety

Chicken can be prepared in umpteen million delicious ways without harming your diet. The chicken part lowest in fat is the breast. Always remove the skin *before* you cook it. Steam, bake, broil, or stew to minimize added fat. Use spices for interest. Substitute nonfat yogurt, skim milk, or buttermilk for cream, sour cream, or whole milk to create tasty, low-fat dishes.

Turkey without Skin: Low-Fat Treat

White turkey meat has only 2 calories of fat per ounce. You can't do much better than that. Fill your sub roll to overflowing with turkey breast meat and dress it with mustard, tomato, lettuce, and hot peppers for a low-fat treat. Throw cooked turkey into low-fat sauces. Roast a big Tom and you'll have turkey leftovers to freeze and use for weeks.

Fish: Lean Cuisine

Many fish are irresistibly lean and delicious: 2 calories of fat per ounce for raw cod, dolphin, haddock, lobster, pike, pollack, scallops, and sunfish; 3 for flounder, grouper, snapper, and sole; and 4 for monkfish, perch, rockfish, and shrimp. Just bake it, grill it, poach it, or broil it. Skewer it with vegetables. Cover it with low-fat sauces. Eat away.

WARNING: Chicken, turkey, and fish can be exceedingly fattening if prepared incorrectly. Read the Chicken, Turkey, and Fish sections in Chapter 3, Where's the Fat? to learn how easily these low-fat meats can be pumped up with fat.

YOGURT: TOO GOOD TO BE TRUE

Nonfat flavored yogurts (0–9 fat calories per 8-ounce container) are truly a treat. Choose coffee, lemon, vanilla, and a variety of fruit flavors. Even if you don't think you like yogurt, check these out. They make good snacks and desserts. Try the Roland Lippoldt special for a nonfat dessert delicacy: mix applesauce and nonfat plain yogurt and top with a sprinkle of pumpkin pie spice; add a cut-up apple for extra crunch.

Low-fat yogurts can easily be fitted into your fat budget, but not eaten with abandon. Coffee, lemon, and vanilla low-fat yogurts have 36 fat calories per 8 ounces, and low-fat fruit yogurts have 27 fat calories per 8 ounces.

Alcohol — Not a Fat-Free Panacea

Although alcohol has no fat, its consumption should be limited for other reasons. Not only are alcohol calories empty — they provide no nutritional benefits — drinking too much alcohol can wreak havoc on your health. Limit alcoholic beverages to a maximum of one to two drinks a day.

DIET FOOD CAN BE DELICIOUS

How does Chili Non Carne (page 169) sound? Barley-Vegetable Soup (page 145)? Sweet Potatoes with Oranges, Apples, and Sweet Wine (page 165)? All real food. Most will easily find room in your fat budget. *Really!* Read Cooking Low-Fat in Chapter 8 to learn how to reduce the fat in your favorite recipes. When you start changing your eating habits and eat wonderful low-fat foods, you will find life worth living. Not only will your fat melt away, your whole life will be richer. You'll see.

DON'T FORGET: THIS IS A DIET . . .

. . . Not a License to Overdo

Now that you're feeling free as a bird, here is a warning. You need not count complex carbohydrates, but you must use sense. Don't gobble up a whole loaf of bread. One slice of bread has only 9 calories of fat. But try multiplying 9 calories of fat by 17 slices — 153 fat calories is no longer inconsequential. Be sure that what you are eating is pure complex carbohydrate. A croissant, for example, is made of flour (complex carbohydrate) and lots of butter (fat), about 110 calories of fat. Croissants are not exactly in the complex carbohydrates category.

Watch Simple Sugars

Choose to Lose allows you to eat jelly on your bagel or pop a Life Saver into your mouth. But don't abuse the system by consuming handfuls of hard candy (110 total calories per ounce) and mixing half a cup of honey (520 total calories) into your tea. Eating too much simple sugar will do nothing for your health and could cause a massive overrun of your recommended daily caloric intake. Don't deprive yourself; just use sense.

Coming Next . . .

Read the next chapter to get the scoop on making *Choose to Lose* work for you.

Remember:

1. You must eat foods rich in carbohydrates to lose weight.
2. Carbohydrates are burned and not stored as fat.
3. Some low-fat foods you will want to eat in abundance are potatoes, bread, rice, pasta, fruit, vegetables, and low-fat and nonfat dairy products. Be sure to keep track of any fat you add to them.

6. Putting *Choose to Lose* to Work for You

ARMED with your own fat budget and three-day food record, insight into the sources of fat in your diet, and a desire to be light as a feather, you are ready to . . . begin making changes!

Take Your Time

But whoa! Don't expect to revamp your entire eating repertoire today and lose 25 pounds tomorrow. (Ah, were it so easy.) You have been eating the way you have been eating for a long time. Changes made too quickly are rarely permanent, and you want to be permanently slim. Take a few weeks to work into your new eating plan. You'll even lose during this time because you will be making changes — enduring changes.

Cut to the Bone

For those of you who want to cut your fat intake to budget level immediately and know that you can stick to these big changes, disregard the last paragraph. Each to his or her own style.

Paring Down by Stages

One approach to making gradual changes is to focus your attention on the worst culprits. Can you eat these less often, in smaller amounts, or eliminate them entirely? Go for the worst first. Make changes in stages. Don't go from whole milk to skim. Go from whole milk to 2% milk (the taste is very similar), then from 2% milk to 1% milk (the taste is close), then from 1% milk to nonfat skim milk. You made it.

Choices and Changes

First you want to target your high-fat food choices. Make four lists:

1. high-fat foods you can eat in smaller amounts
2. high-fat foods you can eat less often
3. high-fat foods you can eliminate entirely
4. low-fat foods you can substitute for high-fat favorites

Study these lists and use them to plan your meals.

Choose Smaller Amounts. Perhaps you find that nuts, potato chips, cheeseburgers, and waffles made with whole milk are your high-fat downfall. (If you can pinpoint just a few offenders, you are lucky. For most people, no one item is making them fat — fat is riddled throughout their diet.) You decide that peanuts are a high-fat food that you are willing to eat in smaller amounts. Check the food tables. Thirty-five peanuts (126 fat calories) would find no space in your fat budget, but ten peanuts (41 fat calories) or five peanuts (21 fat calories) could fit in just fine.

Choose Less Often. Your food records show that you have eaten three cheeseburgers in a three-day period. Realizing that you are not that crazy about cheeseburgers, you choose to eat them less often. According to the food tables (and your food diary) cheeseburgers have 286 fat calories (4 ounces of lean hamburger = 188 fat calories, 1 ounce of American cheese = 80, 1 hamburger roll = 18). You decide to fit that 286–fat calorie cheeseburger into your budget no more than once every two weeks.

Choose Not at All. How do you want to treat your third high-fat booby trap, potato chips? You look at the food tables under Vegetables and Vegetable Products, Potatoes. Eliminating potato chips at 64 fat calories for a mere 10 chips (and who eats only 10 potato chips?) is a change you can make with no pain.

Choose Low-Fat Alternatives. You love making waffles Sunday mornings. Light streaming through the kitchen window, the aroma of coffee filling the air, maple syrup flowing over a pile of light brown, crispy, sour cream waffles — a scene to warm the heart. Why start such a beautiful day with a dent in your fat budget? Why not replace the 2 cups of sour cream (866 fat calories) with 2 cups of buttermilk (18 fat calories)?

A Day to Be Reckoned With

Let's look at a meal plan (pretend it's one day of your food record) and see what changes can be made for the whole day.

FOOD ITEM	CALORIES	
	TOTAL	FAT
Breakfast		
6 oz orange juice	80	0
1 cup whole milk	150	73
1 soft-boiled egg	79	50
1 Danish pastry	235	117
1 cup coffee	0	0
1 tbsp half-and-half	20	15
Lunch		
Roy Rogers roast beef sandwich with cheese	424	171
1 order regular French fries	268	126
12-oz Coke	160	0
Dinner		
Weight Watchers Southern Fried Chicken Patty	270	144
1 cup salad	8	0
2 tbsp French dressing	134	116
1 cup vanilla ice cream	269	129
1 cup coffee	0	0
1 tbsp half-and-half	20	15
Snack		
6 oz Yoplait fruit yogurt	190	36
Total:	2307	992

It's amazing how total calories and fat calories accumulate while you're not paying attention. If your ideal caloric intake were 1500 and your fat budget 300 fat calories (20%), and this is your meal plan, you need to reduce your fat intake by 692 calories; if your fat budget is 225 fat calories (15%), you need to reduce your fat intake by 767 calories.

Look over the meal plan. Which are the biggest fat offenders? The Roy Rogers roast beef sandwich with cheese contributes 171 calories of fat. Hold the cheese and your sandwich is down to 90 fat calories. Better still, how about a turkey sub (with mustard instead of mayo) at a mere 12 fat calories? Even if you eat the plain roast beef sandwich, your total fat intake is reduced by 80 fat calories, down to 912. Eat the turkey hoagie and you reduce it by 159 fat calories, to 833. Eat potato chips (a high-fat item at 64 fat calories) instead of fries (a super-high-fat item at 126 fat calories) and save 62 fat calories, bringing down your total to 771.

Is the chicken patty dinner worth 144 calories of fat? Why not make Lemon Chicken (page 155) at 29? That's a saving of 115, reducing your fat calories to 656. Your fat intake is looking better and better.

Do you need a whole cup of ice cream? How about half a cup at 65 fat calories? How about ice milk at 51? Would you believe an apple? With half a cup of ice cream your fat intake is 592. You're getting closer.

If you use 1 tablespoon of French dressing (58 fat calories) instead of 2 tablespoons (116 fat calories), you're down to 534.

Can you give up the 117–fat calorie Danish pastry and eat an English muffin with jam at 9 fat calories instead? And that glass of whole milk (73 fat calories) — why not try a glass of 2% at 42 fat calories? It tastes almost the same and you save 31 fat calories. That makes 395 before your snack. Just think, you started at 992. Fantastic! Why not have nonfat yogurt (5 fat calories) instead of high-fat yogurt (36 fat calories) for your snack and you'll end the day with a total of 364 fat calories. You're only 59 calories from your 20 percent goal and 134 from your 15 percent goal. You have done a great job, and you can do even better — tomorrow.

See, it didn't hurt a bit. You'll notice that the modified menu is filled with much more food — more interesting tastes, more bulk, a more balanced and healthier menu. And you still were able to eat your ice cream. Amazing. You'll find that you feel pleasantly full after every meal, not bloated and lethargic.

First Cut. In this first round of fat modification, you may not be able to make as many changes as we have. You might keep your roast beef sandwich but eliminate the cheese. If giving up the Danish would make you cry, you might eat it today and substitute an English muffin tomorrow. When you feel ready — perhaps in a few days — try to modify more of your high-fat choices.

Try a Little Harder. Next round, take another look at your food record to see if there are other foods you wouldn't mind eating less often or in smaller amounts or eliminating entirely. Do you need those potato chips? Or half-and-half in your coffee? Why not give 1% milk a

Baseline

FOOD ITEM	CALORIES TOTAL	FAT
Breakfast		
6 oz orange juice	80	0
1 cup whole milk	150	73
1 soft-boiled egg	79	50
1 Danish pastry	235	117
————		
1 cup coffee	0	0
1 tbsp half-and-half	20	15
Breakfast subtotal	564	255
Lunch		
Roy Rogers roast beef sand-		
wich with cheese	424	171
1 regular French fries	268	126
12 oz Coke	160	0
Lunch subtotal	892	297
Dinner		
————		
Weight Watchers		
Southern Fried		
Chicken Patty	270	144
1 cup salad	8	0
2 tbsp French dressing	134	116
————		
————		
————		
1 cup vanilla ice cream	269	129
1 cup coffee	0	0
1 tbsp half-and-half	20	15
Dinner subtotal	701	404
Snack		
6 oz Yoplait fruit		
yogurt	190	36
Total	2307	992

Replacement

FOOD ITEM	CALORIES TOTAL	FAT
Breakfast		
6 oz orange juice	80	0
1 cup 2% milk	121	42
1 soft-boiled egg	79	50
1 English muffin	140	9
2 teaspoons jam	36	0
1 cup coffee	0	0
1 tbsp half-and-half	20	15
Breakfast subtotal	476	116
Lunch		
1 turkey sub:		
6-inch sub roll	200	4
4 oz turkey breast	152	8
1 tsp mustard	5	0
1 oz potato chips	105	64
8 oz apple juice	80	0
Lunch subtotal	542	76
Dinner		
Cucumber Soup	78	0
Lemon Chicken	200	29
1 cup salad	8	0
1 tbsp French dressing	67	58
1 baked potato	104	0
1 tbsp nonfat yogurt	6	0
Steamed Zucchini Match-		
sticks	17	0
½ cup vanilla ice cream	135	65
1 cup coffee	0	0
1 tbsp half-and-half	20	15
Dinner subtotal	685	167
Snack		
8 oz Colombo Lite fruit		
yogurt	190	5
	1843	364

chance? Try replacing the French dressing (58 fat calories per tablespoon) with low-calorie dressing (8 fat calories per tablespoon). Before you know it, you'll be eating at your 20 percent budget level and feeling no pain.

You may find that the 20 percent budget provides more fat than you need. Lower your fat budget to 17 percent or even, eventually, to 15 percent. Then again, maybe 20 percent suits you to a tee.

The *Word*

Always keep in mind that you are trying to lose weight, and the less fat you eat, *without feeling like a martyr,* the faster you will lose. You can easily fit many wonderful foods into your budget. You just have no room for a lot of greasy, ugly high-fat foods.

Educated Choices

Of course, you could have modified the original menu in an infinite number of ways to suit your tastebuds. It is your choice. But now when you make choices, you will think before you choose. The quarter cup of butter you pour over your popcorn will scream **400** FAT CALORIES! You'll pause before you bite into the 77 fat calories of a Reese's peanut butter cup.

Don't worry. You'll still be able to enjoy and love food. You'll just be able to make more informed choices. When you do choose that hot apple turnover with vanilla ice cream after a month of low-fat desserts, you'll love every bite. You'll even taste every bite.

Remember:
1. Gradual changes are more likely to be lasting.
2. Four ways to change your fat intake:
    a. Choose some high-fat foods in smaller amounts.
    b. Choose some high-fat foods less often.
    c. Eliminate some high-fat foods entirely.
    d. Substitute low-fat foods for high-fat foods.
3. Use the food tables to choose lower-fat alternatives.

7. Taking the Show on the Road: Planning Your Meals

Moving Right Along

You are ready to make wise choices for the rest of your life. You have a fat budget, so you know how much fat you should eat each day. You have targeted your high-fat favorites, so you know how often and in what amounts you plan to fit them in. Now for the actual meal planning.

To Plan or Not to Plan?

If planning is impractical or not in your nature, you can keep a running total of what you eat each day as you eat it. When your fat consumption equals your fat budget, just stop eating fat — until the next day.

Or you can plan your meals for the day or week and add up your fat calories in advance. Planning ahead gives you the opportunity to make choices before you eat. "Hmm," you say, "I'll spend ——— calories on ——— and ——— calories on ———. Better still, if I eat ——— instead of ———, I'll have ——— fat calories left for dessert." Advance planning also makes grocery shopping more efficient.

When you plan ahead, you can save up fat calories for splurges (see Chapter 8). If some great food emergency arises (your mother-in-law bakes your very favorite chocolate cheesecake as a special treat *just for you*), you can deduct those added fat calories from your budget and compensate for the splurge by eating less the next day. Of course, your fat budget has just so much room for emergencies. Too much borrowing from tomorrow's fat budget and you're off your diet.

Benefits of Keeping Track

You may think adding up fat calories will take all the fun out of eating. However, you probably eat a limited number of foods and dishes, so sooner than you think you will know their fat values as well as you know the telephone numbers of your family and friends.

You may feel that you can lose weight without keeping a record of the foods you eat. While just knowing your fat budget and the fat calories in foods will help you to make educated choices, if you don't keep track of what you are eating, you may be consuming more fat than you realize. It is very easy to overeat fat calories when you are not counting.

To help you record your fat intake, you may want to use the order form at the end of the book to order the handy portable Passbook (checkbook size), which includes the *Choose to Lose* food tables and a balance book for keeping a two-week record of the total and fat calories you consume.

EATING WELL WITHIN BUDGET

Here are some suggestions for easing into your new eating pattern.

Making Changes: Breakfast

A low-fat breakfast can be nourishing and delicious. Some quick and easy choices are: hot cereal (0–18 fat calories per ounce); cold cereal (generally 0–18 fat calories per ounce; check the label) with skim milk and fruit (0 fat calories); toast (9 per slice) with jelly (0); 1% cottage cheese (10 fat calories per ½ cup); nonfat yogurt (less than 9 fat calories per cup); fruit or juice (0 fat calories). Take a few minutes to eat at home. (That doesn't mean slipping a 54–fat calorie toaster pastry into

---

Skipping Meals: A Dieter's Undoing

Do you nobly skip breakfast and/or lunch to save calories? Don't. Skipping a meal only makes you hungrier for the next meal or snack. So hungry, in fact, you may eat twice the calories you saved by not eating. Missing a meal may even depress your basal metabolic rate so that everything you eat later is burned more slowly. You need carbohydrates to stoke your calorie-burning fires. No breakfast or lunch makes for an empty furnace.

---

your toaster or heating a 288–fat calorie Great Starts breakfast sandwich in your microwave oven.) You narrow your choices (but not your waist) when you pick up breakfast at a snack or coffee shop.

Making Changes: Lunch

Brown-bag it. Leftovers make great (and quick) sandwiches. Fill a small pita or two with last night's Indonesian Chicken with Green Beans (page 155) to create a tasty, low-fat lunch.

Make a scrumptious sandwich by thinly slicing the Bar-B-Que Chicken (page 156) breast you had for dinner onto whole-wheat bread. Use mustard instead of mayonnaise and add tomatoes and lettuce. Mix 1% cottage cheese or nonfat yogurt with cut-up fruit. Pack a nonfat flavored yogurt, fruit, carrot and celery sticks. Add air-popped popcorn for a crunchy, filling "dessert."

If you have to buy lunch, select a sandwich shop where you can order turkey (with mustard or a teaspoon or less of mayonnaise) rather than a fast-food restaurant where your options are few. A fancier restaurant might offer grilled chicken breast for lunch. If the only chicken breast on the menu is breaded and deep-fried, ask that it be grilled (without the skin and with no fat) instead. If the menu offers Cajun steak, have the grilled chicken cooked with Cajun sauce. Ask for a baked potato, plain, instead of French fries. Have a chef's salad, but hold the cheese and ham. Ask for the dressing (preferably low-fat) on the side so that you control the amount you use. Cold shrimp, although expensive, have almost no fat and can be dipped fat-free into cocktail sauce (not tartar sauce, which is made with mayonnaise). If you're forced to have a higher-fat-than-you-want lunch, keep track of the fat so you can balance it with low-fat dinner choices.

Be Salad-Bar-Wise

Salad bars offer a tempting array of greens and sliced vegetables, fresh fruits, and — high-fat salads. Red potatoes in sour cream dressing, bacon pieces lurking in apple salad, mayonnaise salad with a bit of cabbage mixed in, cold cut strips marinated in oil — each one is overflowing with fat calories. A little bit of this and a little bit of that adds up to triple your fat budget for the day. Unless you eat only the fruit or vegetables with little or no dressing, salad bars are not a buy for the diet-conscious.

Making Changes: Dinner

For Starters. Stay home for dinner and give your diet goals a boost. Start dinner with soup. Soup is a wonderful invention for weight watchers. It cheers the soul as it fills you up. With a low-fat soup as a filling first course, you are less tempted to gorge yourself on the higher-fat main course or dessert. If you have regal tastes, try Sour Cherry Soup (page 148), Oriental Noodle Soup (page 148), or *Vegetable Soup Provençal.*

For equally wonderful results, substitute nonfat yogurt, buttermilk, skim milk, or evaporated skim milk in soup recipes that call for sour cream, cream, or whole milk. Try Zucchini Soup (page 152). Make large batches of soup and freeze them in small containers for future use.

Spice Up the Main Course. Delectable food does not have to be made with cream. Beef doesn't have to be eaten in a slab. Rethink your preferences and retrain your palate. Make "cream" sauces with skim milk, nonfat yogurt, or buttermilk. Use spices instead of fat. For fewer fat calories and more texture and flavor, cut meat into small pieces and mix them with a sliced vegetable or two. Pile on the pasta or rice. Modify favorite recipes by reducing the fat. It's easy to eat well on a low-fat diet. Does Turkey Mexique (page 158) or Chicken with Rice, Tomatoes, and Artichokes (page 158) sound like diet food? With 40 or fewer fat calories each, they slip easily into anyone's fat budget.

Fitting In Your Favorites

Don't forget: the reason you have a fat budget is so that you can occasionally splurge on a thick steak or cherry cheesecake. You just have to make enough low-fat choices to balance your high-fat favorites.

A Balanced Diet

It is *your* fat budget, and you can decide how you want to spend it. However, it is extremely important that you do not just cut out fat. You must replace some of the fat you eliminate with complex carbohydrates (fruits, vegetables, and whole grains) and low-fat or nonfat dairy products. Your body needs all the vitamins, minerals, and fibers that these foods provide. You need to eat lots of complex carbohydrates to keep up your basal metabolic rate to burn the fat. (See Chapter 10, Ensuring a Balanced Diet.)

Eat, Eat, My Darling

When you reduce the fat in your diet, you will also reduce the total calories. For many of you, this dual reduction works out perfectly so that you are eating the number of total calories recommended for your desirable weight. However, if you find that your total caloric intake is falling below the recommended caloric intake level, you must make an effort to eat more. (Did you ever think you would be urged to eat more?) Eat more fruits, vegetables, and whole grains, that is. Keep the fires burning. Don't be distressed if you are eating more than ever and still losing weight. Celebrate.

And in the Next Chapter . . . Practical advice to fit *Choose to Lose* into your life.

Remember:

1. Budget fat into your diet by keeping a running total for each day or planning ahead for a day or a week.
2. Keep track of your fat intake so that you know you are truly eating under your fat budget.
3. Be sure your total caloric intake does not fall below the desirable level to ensure that you
   a. maintain your BMR.
   b. consume an adequate supply of vitamins, minerals, and fiber.

8. Coping in a World You Did Not Make

YOUR GOALS are high. You are making all the right changes — and loving it. Soon you will find that your clothes are slipping off your bony body. You'll be so perky and alert your boss will give you a raise, or if you're the boss you'll give yourself a bonus. You are beginning to prefer plain air-popped popcorn to buttered. Your life is shaping up. And so are you.

Hopefully this first paragraph describes you. However, the road to thinness may not be quite so smooth. Temptation abounds. Television ads assault you with rich, sweet chocolate flowing smoothly over a cluster of peanuts, cheese merrily bubbling amidst pepperoni and anchovies. Birthday parties, office parties, dinner parties threaten your resolve. Here are some tips to get you through the hard times.

> Important: *Choose to Lose* is quantitative. You have a fat budget. If you weaken and gorge yourself, just compensate by making low-fat choices for the next few days — and you know exactly how many fat calories that is. *Don't give up and pig out for the rest of the day because you splurged. You can fit it in. You are in control.*

SPLURGING

The beauty of *Choose to Lose* is that you can go to a party and eat what you want. You just have to prepare for the event. Say you are going out to dinner Saturday night and want to eat a 6-ounce steak (276 fat calories), a baked potato with a teaspoon of butter (34 fat calories), and a piece of cheesecake (162 fat calories) for a total of 472 fat calories.

Wow! Even if your budget is 268, you can afford this splurge. Here's how.

If you eat 220 fat calories each day from Sunday to Saturday you will have accumulated 268 − 220 = 48 fat calories per day; 48 fat calories × 6 days = 288 extra fat calories to spend on Saturday. Add these to your budget (288 + 268) and you have 556 fat calories for Saturday. You can enjoy your splurge and have 84 fat calories left for Saturday's breakfast and lunch. Just plan ahead.

Here are some hints for the many occasions that will arise when you haven't saved for a splurge but don't want to decimate your budget.

PARTIES

It's guaranteed — any party you attend will be overloaded with high-fat foods. In fact, at some parties the only low-fat choice will be soda water.

Pre-party

Ask your host or hostess if you can bring something — hors d'oeuvres, bread, salad, vegetable, main course, dessert — and of course, you'll make it low-fat. Most hosts will be delighted, but if one should resist, you insist. Your contribution may be all you get to eat.

Eat a light snack before the party so that blinding hunger won't cause you temporary failure of will power and overeating.

Don't starve all day so that you go wild when you arrive. You'll break your fat bank in a millisecond or two. If you want to save fat calories for the party, just eat extra-low-fat all day or for several days. (See Splurging, above.)

At the Party

The first glance may make your heart sink. How can you resist the sumptuous array of the most delectable foods you have craved your entire life? But look again. Does the breaded shrimp look luscious or just greasy? Does the twelve-layer rum cake taste good or just look beautiful? Granted, some of the food will be delicious, but not all. Pick and choose.

Leave the Scene of the Crime before It Becomes a Crime

When you have finished savoring a few offerings, leave the area. Don't stand around listening to the food cry, "Eat me! Eat me!" Go to a room where there's no food. Out of sight, out of mind; in sight, in mouth.

Regrets to the Hostess

Before you arrive at a dinner party, devise a plan of action. Be ready with an appeasing comment: "You know I adore your desserts, but I'm off sweets until I can button my slacks." Or privately, before dinner: "Please give me small portions. I'm trying so hard to lose weight."

At Your Own Party

This is a perfect opportunity to show your friends how well they can eat without eating high-fat foods. Give a dinner party with Cantaloupe Soup (page 146) to start — 4 fat calories per cup. Then Bar-B-Que Chicken (page 156) for a main course — 13 fat calories per breast or 24 fat calories per thigh; steamed carrot sticks with garlic for a vegetable — 0 fat calories; Cucumber Salad (page 172) — 0 fat calories; and for dessert, Pineapple Pound Cake (page 186) — 47 fat calories. When's the party? We'll be there.

If time limitations force you to weaken and buy a high-fat dessert (better to serve fruit), be sure any leftovers leave with your guests. Stuff them into their pockets and purses if necessary. Don't leave a trace even in your garbage can, because we all know that food in garbage cans can be retrieved.

AT A RESTAURANT

Eating at home makes keeping to your fat budget a breeze. Although you can't always be expected to eat at home, keep eating out to a minimum.

REMEMBER: If you eat out once or more a week, it is no longer a special treat that justifies splurging. Eat as you do at home — with care.

Here are some tips for eating out.

Be Choosy

If possible, *you* pick the restaurant. If others choose, you may have no options. Select a restaurant that you know serves food you can eat. Want to try someplace new? Call early in the day to ask what's on the menu. If nothing suits your fat budget, ask if the chef can prepare something with little fat or with a low-fat sauce.

Beforehand

Don't starve all day in preparation for dinner or you'll frantically gobble up your fat budget before you get through the soup and salad. Eat low-fat all day, but eat. In fact, you might want to munch on a carrot or two or even snack on a nonfat flavored yogurt an hour before you depart for the restaurant.

Ask

Don't be shy. Always ask the waiter what you want to know. It's your body, not his. Ask how the sole amandine or chicken Dijon is prepared. Is it fried? Baked? Broiled? Is it made with butter? Oil? What's in the soup or the sauce? Cream? Milk? Sour cream? Ask enough questions so you can make educated choices.

And Ask Again

Ask the waiter whether the chef will broil, bake, poach, or grill the chicken or fish without fat. Then you add it later in the amounts you choose. Ask if the mustard sauce that spices up the steak dish can be used on a grilled fish. Be creative.

On the Side

Always ask to have butter, salad dressings, and sauces served on the side so that you can regulate how much you use. You'll see how quickly a few tablespoons add up to more than you need to eat.

Dip In or BYO

When you order your salad dressing on the side, keep it in the serving dish instead of pouring it over your salad. Dip your fork into the dressing, then spear your salad greens or vegetables. You will get the salad dressing taste with many fewer fat calories. You might want to order your salad plain and enhance it with packets of nonfat or low-fat salad dressing you bring from home.

Give It Away

If a portion served is more than you should eat, give what you don't want to your dining partner. If you are eating alone, place the extra on a salad plate and ask the waiter to take it away. Send back the butter served with the bread. Ask for the potato plain. You can't eat what's not there.

You may feel compelled to lick your plate clean because you paid for your meal, but resist the urge. The cost to your fat budget is not worth the salve to your conscience.

Share

If you are dying for a taste of that Black Forest cake, share it with a friend, or better yet, several friends. Choose your friends wisely, and you might find one who will give you a bite of everything he eats. Main dishes and appetizers can also be shared without anyone starving. Restaurants often serve single portions that are large enough for two.

Taste

Don't just shovel in the food. Concentrate. Taste. Think when you eat. Don't rush. If you have the patience, place your fork on the table between bites.

AT HOME

Choose to Lose is not a diet — it is an eating plan for life. It is not a two-week exercise in starvation or balancing exchanges. It is an education that will last a lifetime. You are learning about fat in food so you can make choices.

Free to Eat

You will find that this new approach to food will free you from food anxiety. No food is forbidden. You learn to judge food in relation to your fat budget and to other foods. A Mr. Goodbar was much more tempting before you knew that it has 180 fat calories and your budget is 240. A baked potato filled with nonfat yogurt entices you both because it tastes delicious and is jam-packed with vitamins, minerals, and fiber and because it has no fat calories.

Being food-smart will have a profound effect on your eating habits. In addition, you may want to make some changes in your behavior that will make losing weight even easier. First, you might want to ask yourself why you eat.

Boredom

Many people eat because they are bored or lonely. They spend their evenings and weekends watching television. To satisfy their feeling of emptiness, they fill up on food. Of course, the food industry makes thinking about high-fat foods as easy as flicking on the TV. You can't avoid fantasizing about food you shouldn't eat, because it pops out at you every ten minutes.

A solution: How about taking up a hobby? It's never too late. How about photography, oil painting, or ceramics? Take an adult education course at your local high school or Y. What about square dancing or folk dancing? Join a barbershop quartet or a chess club. Work for your local politician or volunteer at your library or neighborhood hospital. Get out, meet people, get involved. You'll feel better about yourself, and you'll have less time to eat.

Psychology

The emphasis in *Choose to Lose* is not on restructuring psyches. The emphasis is on knowledge. Knowing you can eat what you want and becoming food-smart will remove a lot of psychological stumbling blocks. For those who are fat to avoid sex, fat because of self-hate, fat because of an overprotective parent, *Choose to Lose* will not rid you of these problems. You may find, however, that when the pounds start coming off easily and naturally without much thought, you will feel so much better about yourself, you'll be able to get thin — and stay that way.

It's There

When asked, "Why did you climb Mount Everest?" Sir Edmund Hillary answered, "Because it was there." If that is why you overeat high-fat foods, make sure they are not "there." You can't devour a gallon of ice cream if it isn't in your freezer. You can't demolish a bowl of macademia nuts if you never buy them. Keep high-temptation foods out of your house. Splurge elsewhere.

How "Clean" Is Your House?

The amount of high-fat food that still lingers in your home is an indication of how seriously you are trying to change your way of eating to lose weight. What about your hidden fat stores? Do you keep ice cream in the freezer? Do you keep crackers in the cupboards? Do caches of high-fat foods offer irresistible temptation? Why not give them away to neighbors? Feed them to your dog? Take a deep breath and throw them into the garbage.

Plenty

Instead of fixating on the high-fat food you are eliminating, pamper yourself with an abundance of delicious low-fat food. How about starting dinner with cool, creamy, and completely fat-free Cucumber Soup (page 147)? Take time (and it takes very little) to marinate skinless chicken breasts in a mixture of equal amounts of mustard, molasses, and vinegar, and then broil or grill them until cooked through. Place fish fillets in a lightly oiled shallow baking dish, pour in ¼–½ cup of vermouth or white wine, grind pepper over the fish, then cover with 2–4 tablespoons of chopped shallots and bake until the fish flakes easily. Press a garlic over steamed broccoli. Sprinkle vinegar, basil, salt, and pepper over sliced tomatoes. You can create a feast in almost no time. Eat well the low-fat way, and you'll find the pounds melting away.

ALL IN THE FAMILY

There is an excellent chance that if you are overweight, so are your children and your spouse. You probably share the same eating habits. Start your children on the thin road early; good eating habits begin in childhood. Don't let your plump toddlers become your chubby children and your obese adolescents. Fat children are not cute. Fat children often suffer discrimination. Fat children almost always become fat adults. Teach your children to enjoy low-fat food at an early age so they can live long, healthy, slim-bodied lives.

Why not ease your whole family into your new regime? Food preferences are established at an early age. Don't bring high-fat chips, crackers, cookies — junk, into the house. If you hear complaints, re-

Facts about Obesity in Children and Teenagers Today

- Twenty-five to 30 percent of children are obese, about a 54 percent increase in the last fifteen years.
- Twenty to 25 percent of teenagers are obese, about a 40 percent increase in the last fifteen years.
- Fifty to 95 percent of obese adolescents become obese adults. The chance of an obese teen attaining normal weight in adulthood is 1 in 28.
- Obese children and teenagers have an increased prevalence of irregular periods, hypertension, respiratory problems, and hyperinsulinemia. They often suffer from peer and adult discrimination, social isolation, low self-esteem, depression, and a negative body image.

member — you're the boss. Keep plenty of fruit, nonfat yogurt, low-fat crackers, and air-popped popcorn in the house. Plan ahead so that you have lots of good, healthy food to make satisfying meals. Running to a fast-food restaurant or ordering a pizza because your cupboard is bare or you don't feel like cooking is unacceptable if you truly want to lose weight and keep your family thin and healthy.

The Snack Law

Very important!! Make sure that your kids don't snack — even healthy snacks — too close to dinner. A full child will reject all but junk food. A hungry child will be willing to try your luscious, low-fat meals. *Be firm.* If they balk at a new type of soup or chicken dish, ask them to try just a bite. They'll change their tune after a taste.

Smooth and Svelte

If you have overweight teenagers, encourage them to read this book. (Even thin teenagers can learn a lot from reading *Choose to Lose.*) Knowing that fat makes fat and how much fat lurks in the food they eat will have a profound effect on their food choices. By giving your teens control over their diets, *Choose to Lose* can free you from being a food warden and improve your relationship. You may find your roles reversed, with your teens keeping *you* true to *your* fat budget.

Note to Overzealous Parents

In your zeal to keep your children thin, don't eliminate all fat from their diets. For proper growth and development, young children require a diet that is about 30 percent total fat and filled with vitamins, minerals, and fiber found in fruits, vegetables, and whole grains. (Frankly, drastically reducing children's fat intake is a rare problem. The more widespread and serious problem is allowing children to eat 40 to 50 percent of their calories as fat.)

ASK FOR HELP

Tell your family that you don't feel good being fat, that they can help you by keeping fat-filled foods out of the house and by eating your low-fat meals. Eventually they will realize that they are doing themselves a favor as well. They will look and feel better. By eating the low-fat way they will also lower their own risks for heart disease, cancer, and diabetes.

How Often Should You Weigh In?

Try to overcome the urge to weigh yourself daily (or even hourly!). Short-term changes in your weight only reveal changes in your water balance and can be misleading or discouraging. Weigh yourself no more than once a week, or even once every other week, for a more realistic reflection of your fat loss. Make sure the circumstances are approximately the same each time you weigh in. Try to weigh yourself on the same day of the week, at the same time of the day, wearing the same amount of clothing, and using the same scale. Then the only variable will be your weight. See Appendix C for a record to help you keep track of your weight loss.

AT THE SUPERMARKET

Strolling down the aisles of a supermarket can be a dieter's undoing — if the shopper is unprepared. Use the *Choose to Lose* food tables to make a shopping list of low-fat choices *before* you go to the store and stick to the list. (Unless, of course, you see some fruits or vegetables that you can't resist.)

Reading Food Labels: A Consumer's Most Important Survival Skill

Dieters! The health conscious! All consumers! For survival, you must learn to read food labels. Read beyond the bright lettering on the package that screams "NATURAL," "LOWER IN FAT," or "LITE." The truth can be found in the nutrition label.

Before you read on, select a can or package from your kitchen or pantry so that you can examine the label.

List of Ingredients

Most packaged foods have some nutrition labeling, even if it is only a list of ingredients. Although ingredient lists do not give you quantitative information, they may give you enough facts to help you make wise choices. Find the ingredient list on your package. What ingredient is listed first? Ingredients are always listed in descending order by weight.

For example, the Granola Bar label (page 101) lists granola (rolled oats, coconut oil, brown sugar, honey, salt, natural flavor), crisp rice, corn syrup, dextrose, coconut oil, raisins, brown sugar syrup, almond pieces, corn syrup solids, sugar, cinnamon, salt, malt syrup, natural vanilla.

This ingredient list tells you that rolled oats accounts for more weight than any other ingredient. Unfortunately, since the actual weights of the ingredients are not provided, you have no way of knowing if the rolled oats comprise 50 percent of the granola bar or 40 percent or 10 percent. You know that coconut oil is the ingredient second in weight, but how much coconut oil is there? You will notice that coconut oil appears again later in the list. Does this mean that if the manufacturer had combined the two weights of coconut oil, coconut oil would be the first ingredient? We'll never know. But since we know that coconut oil is 100 percent fat, and extremely saturated and heart-risky at that, you would do well to return this granola bar to the shelf.

What does the ingredient list on your label tell you?

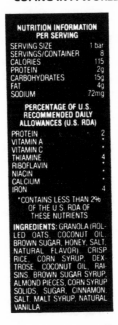

**NUTRITION INFORMATION
PER SERVING**

SERVING SIZE	1 bar
SERVINGS/CONTAINER	8
CALORIES	115
PROTEIN	2g
CARBOHYDRATES	15g
FAT	4g
SODIUM	72mg

**PERCENTAGE OF U.S.
RECOMMENDED DAILY
ALLOWANCES (U.S. RDA)**

PROTEIN	2
VITAMIN A	*
VITAMIN C	*
THIAMINE	4
RIBOFLAVIN	*
NIACIN	*
CALCIUM	*
IRON	4

*CONTAINS LESS THAN 2%
OF THE U.S. RDA OF
THESE NUTRIENTS

INGREDIENTS: GRANOLA (ROL-
LED OATS, COCONUT OIL,
BROWN SUGAR, HONEY, SALT,
NATURAL FLAVOR), CRISP
RICE, CORN SYRUP, DEX-
TROSE, COCONUT OIL, RAI-
SINS, BROWN SUGAR SYRUP,
ALMOND PIECES, CORN SYRUP
SOLIDS, SUGAR, CINNAMON,
SALT, MALT SYRUP, NATURAL
VANILLA

Nutrition Information

You will learn most from labels that provide the nutrient content per serving in addition to the listing of ingredients. Let's look at the Granola Bar nutrition information.

Fat..........4g. Fat is always listed in gram amounts. The fat content looks smaller that way. Four grams of fat sure sounds like a tiny amount of fat. However, we know that each gram of fat has 9 calories. To figure out how many calories of fat the product contains, multiply the number of grams (4) by the number of calories of fat (9). Each granola bar has $4 \times 9 = 36$ calories of fat.

Calories..........115. Total calories are always interesting. As you know, a product relatively low in total calories can be a high-fat item. This is often true in many "lite" and "lean" diet frozen dinners.

Serving Size, 1 bar. It is most important to check the serving size. The manufacturer's idea of a serving size and the amount you actually eat may differ. For example, the label states that one granola bar contains 4 grams or 36 calories of fat. If you eat one serving (1 bar) you are consuming 36 calories of fat. But if you normally eat three bars, you must multiply 3 by the fat calories per serving (36) to find the number of fat calories you are really eating: $3 \times 36 = 108$ fat calories.

More for Your Money Is Not Always a Bargain

You buy a small bag of shelled sunflower seeds that seems perfect for just one serving. A quick glance at the nutrition label shows you that the seeds contain 15 grams of fat (135 fat calories). Look again. The serving size is 1 ounce. However, the bag contains 1⅛ ounces of sunflower seeds. You are actually eating 1⅛ servings or 17 grams of fat, which add up to 153 fat calories.

QUIZ YOURSELF

Here's nutritional information for a 4½-ounce bag of air-popped popcorn. Nonfattening and healthy? Sure. You figure it out.

NUTRITIONAL INFORMATION
PER SERVING

SERVING SIZE	1 oz.
SERVINGS PER CONTAINER	4½
CALORIES	160
PROTEIN	2g
CARBOHYDRATE	13g
FAT	11g
CHOLESTEROL**	0
SODIUM	310mg
POTASSIUM	.95mg

PERCENTAGES OF U.S. RECOMMENDED DAILY ALLOWANCES (U.S. RDA)

PROTEIN	2
VITAMIN A	0
VITAMIN C	*
THIAMIN	*
RIBOFLAVIN	*
NIACIN	*
CALCIUM	*
IRON	4

*CONTAINS LESS THAN 2% OF US RDA OF THESE NUTRIENTS.

**INFORMATION ON CHOLESTEROL CONTENT IS PROVIDED FOR INDIVIDUALS WHO ON ADVICE OF A PHYSICIAN, ARE MODIFYING INTAKE OF CHOLESTEROL.

INGREDIENTS: POPCORN, VEGETABLE OIL (COCONUT AND/OR CORN AND/OR SUNFLOWER AND/OR PARTIALLY HYDROGENATED SOYBEAN AND/OR PARTIALLY HYDROGENATED COTTONSEED), SALT AND ANNATTO COLORING.

Answer these questions about the popcorn label.

1. Which ingredient provides the most weight?
2. Does this ingredient normally contain fat?
3. When this ingredient is air-popped, does it normally contain fat?
4. The popcorn has_____grams of fat per ounce. This equals_____fat calories per ounce.
5. Where does all this fat come from?
6. Do you know what the serving size represents in terms of cups?
7. How many ounces are you likely to eat?
8. How many calories of fat are you likely to eat?

Answers:

1. Popcorn is the first ingredient, so it provides the most weight.
2. Popcorn is a fat-free food.
3. Normally, air-popped popcorn contains no added fat.
4. The popcorn has 11 grams of fat per ounce; each gram of fat has 9 calories. To convert 11 grams of fat into calories of fat, multiply 11 by 9 = 99 fat calories per ounce.
5. How did fat-free popcorn accumulate 99 calories of fat? Look at the second ingredient on the label: vegetable oil (coconut and/or corn and/or sunflower and/or partially hydrogenated soybean and/or partially hydrogenated cottonseed). That's pure fat. The manufacturers took fat-free popcorn, air-popped it (so they could claim AIR-POPPED!!!), and then added 99 calories of fat.
6. To figure out what 1 ounce means in terms of how much you eat, first measure the popcorn in the bag. This bag contains 22 cups of popcorn and weighs 4½ ounces. To determine how many cups make up an ounce, divide 22 cups by 4½ ounces: 1 ounce = about 5 cups of popcorn.
7. The smallest movie theater popcorn container holds 5 cups of popcorn. A household air-popped popcorn maker produces about 12 cups. If you are unsure of how much you eat, measure it next time.
8. If you normally eat about 12 cups of popcorn, to find out how many ounces you eat, divide 5 cups (1 ounce) into 12 cups. Five cups goes into 12 cups about two and a half times. You eat about 2½ ounces. Since the popcorn has 99 fat calories per ounce, you would be eating more than 2 ounces or 248 fat calories.

CONSUMER BEWARE!

The food industry has you pegged. They know that you and millions like you want to buy products that are limited in total calories. They count on your not being wise enough to read and understand food labels.

Watch out for these advertising claims:

1. CLAIM: Lite, light, slim, lower-fat, or lean

    TRUTH: Claims for "lite" may refer to color, amount of sodium (salt), fat content, or serving size. Dorman's Lite Swiss Cheese, for example, has 7 grams (63 calories) of fat. Dorman's regular Swiss also has 7 grams (63 calories) of fat. Obviously the "lite" does not refer to the fat content. "Lite" refers to the sodium content.

        Klondike regular ice cream bars are 5 fluid ounces and contain 207 fat calories. Klondike Lite ice cream bars are 2.5 fluid ounces and contain 90 calories of fat. The "Lite" bar, so labeled because it is half as big, is hardly less fat-packed. To call an ice cream bar with 90 calories of fat "lite" is laughable.

    TRUTH: A "light" or "slim" product may have fewer fat calories than the regular version, but may still be high in fat. Regular cream cheese has 10 grams (90 calories) of fat per ounce. "Light" cream cheese has 5 grams (45 calories) of fat per ounce. While half as fat as regular cream cheese, light cream cheese still has a lot of fat.

        One ounce of Dorman's Slim Jack has 63 calories of fat; 1 ounce of regular Monterey Jack has 77. While Slim Jack has less fat than regular Jack, it is still a high-fat food.

2. CLAIM: Only 4% fat

    TRUTH: 4% fat. Sounds good. But what does it really mean? Whole milk is 4% fat; that is, 4% of the total weight of the milk is fat. Milk is mostly water, so the percentage contributed by fat to the total weight is small. Of much more importance, whole milk derives 50 percent of its calories from fat (73 fat calories divided by 150 total calories per cup). The whole milk ads should say, "50% fat."

3. CLAIM: 91% Fat-free

    TRUTH: Chopped turkey ham is 91% fat free or 9% fat — by weight.

Again, the 9% fat refers to the fat content as a percentage of the weight. If we were concerned with percentages we would want to know what percentage of the total calories, not the weight, come from fat. In this example, the turkey ham contains 3 grams of fat ($3 \times 9 = 27$) or 27 fat calories per slice out of its total of 45 calories. Thus, the fat calories are 60 percent of the total calories ($27 \div 45 = 60\%$). The label should read 60% fat or 40% fat-free. What is more important to weight watchers is that the slice of turkey ham contains 27 fat calories. How do 27 fat calories per slice fit into your fat budget?

4. CLAIM: Less than 300 calories

   TRUTH: This claim is true but irrelevant. We know that total calories don't make you fat. Many of the diet frozen dinners, while relatively low in total calories, are extremely high in fat calories. The Weight Watchers Cheese Enchiladas Ranchero contains only 360 total calories, but 189 of those calories come from fat. That's a pretty big bite out of anyone's budget. Read the label.

COOKING LOW-FAT

You can't help but notice how many times we have mentioned the *fantastic!* recipes in *Eater's Choice*. We are not trying to strong-arm you into buying another book, but as you can see from our hearty endorsement, we believe you would greatly enjoy the 180 additional recipes in *Eater's Choice*. They are generally quite low in fat, delectable, and helpful for losing weight. In fact, one of the reasons we wrote *Choose to Lose* was that so many people told us they lost weight using *Eater's Choice* recipes. (See Appendix B for the total fat calories of the recipes from *Eater's Choice*, revised edition, third and subsequent printings.) You probably also have favorite recipes that are too high in fat to keep your fat budget in the black. By making a few substitutions and modifications you may be able to fit these favorites into your new eating plan.

Silent Substitutions

In most cases, the following low-fat or nonfat substitutions will greatly reduce the fat content of your recipes without diminishing the taste or texture.

WHEN THE RECIPE CALLS FOR	SUBSTITUTE
Cream	Nonfat yogurt, buttermilk, skim milk, evaporated skim milk
Whole milk	Skim milk
Sour cream	Nonfat yogurt, buttermilk
Veal cutlets	Turkey cutlets
Pork	Chicken, white meat
3 egg yolks*	1 egg yolk
2 whole eggs	1 whole egg + 1 egg white
Ground beef	Ground turkey (without skin and fat) that you grind yourself

Reduce the Fat

Recipes often recommend more fat than is necessary. If the recipe calls for ¼ cup olive oil or margarine, try 3 tablespoons. If this works, try 2 tablespoons. If you are to sauté garlic in 2 tablespoons of oil, try 1 tablespoon or ½ tablespoon. Try *not* dotting the top of your fish or pie with margarine or butter. You may find the dish doesn't need the extra fat.

Modifying a Recipe

The following high-fat recipe for Curry Soup was easily modified into a tasty low-fat treat. This is how we did it:

- Four tablespoons of butter was more fat than necessary to sauté the onions. We reduced the fat to 1½ tablespoons of olive oil and saved 220 fat calories. (We chose olive oil because it is a heart-healthy oil, but being heart-healthy does not make it any less fattening.)
- Instead of dark and light chicken meat, we used only white breast meat and saved 17 fat calories.
- Straining the chicken fat from the broth saved 179 fat calories.
- Replacing the cream with nonfat yogurt saved 417 fat calories.

The resulting soup tastes fine and at 20 fat calories per cup easily fits into anybody's fat budget.

---

*The egg yolk contains all the fat (50 calories) as well as all the cholesterol in an egg; the egg white has neither fat nor cholesterol.

The Recipe Modified

HIGH-FAT CURRY SOUP		LOW-FAT CURRY SOUP	
INGREDIENTS	FAT CALORIES	INGREDIENTS	FAT CALORIES
4 tbsp butter	400	1½ tbsp olive oil	180
2 medium onions	—	2 medium onions	—
3 stalks celery	—	3 stalks celery	—
2 tbsp flour	—	2 tbsp flour	—
1 tbsp curry powder	—	1 tbsp curry powder	—
2 apples	—	2 apples	—
1 cup diced chicken (light and dark meat)	31	1 cup diced chicken (white meat)	14
2 qt chicken broth	184	2 qt strained chicken broth	5
1 cup light cream	417	1 cup nonfat yogurt	0
Total fat calories	1032	Total fat calories	199
Makes 10 cups		Makes 10 cups	
Per cup of soup	103	Per cup of soup	20

Cooking Tips

The following cooking tips will help you stay within your fat budget:

- Steam vegetables. Purchase an inexpensive metal steamer and place in a saucepan filled with about an inch of water. Spread out the steamer and place cut-up fresh vegetables on top. Cover the saucepan and steam the vegetables until they are tender. Steamed vegetables need no fat. For added flavor, mix in some pressed garlic or herbs (thyme, basil, etc.).
- Steam skinless and boneless chicken breasts whole or in bite-size pieces in a vegetable steamer or on the steamer tray in a wok.
- Always remove skin *before* cooking chicken to keep the chicken from absorbing the fat from the skin. Eating the skin more than triples the fat calories in a chicken breast.
- *Never* deep-fry fish or chicken. *Never, ever* flour or bread and fry fish or chicken. Breading absorbs fat like a sponge.
- Bake, broil, grill, or poach chicken and fish. Limit the amount of fat you use. Use low-fat sauces for added taste.
- If you cook beef, lamb, pork, or veal, trim off all visible fat. Broil or

bake on a rack to drain the fat. Wrap cooked meat in paper towels to remove more fat. Avoid pan-frying.

Fat-Reducing Cooking Equipment

• Cast iron makes a great nontoxic, nonstick cooking surface. Small cast iron grills are available that fit over one stove burner and grill chicken with little or no added fat in about five minutes. Large cast iron griddles fit over two stove burners and effectively cook French toast and pancakes with little or no added fat.
• Steamer: see Cooking Tips, above.
• Clay cooker: keeps chicken moist and tender without adding fat.

Is Low-Fat Cooking and Eating Expensive?

No way. Replacing foods high in fat with vegetables, fruits, and whole grains will keep you thin and your wallet fat. Convenience foods and snacks are high in fat and expensive. Beef costs more than chicken or turkey. Sour cream, sweet cream, and cheese make a large dent in both your monetary budget and your fat budget. In contrast, a variety of vegetables, rice, or pasta with small amounts of chicken or beef keep both budget and body trim. Even if eating low-fat were more expensive — which it definitely is not — the saving in health costs and the psychological benefits of being slim would balance the expense.

Remember:
1. Splurging: *Choose to Lose* allows you to splurge without guilt. By eating fewer fat calories than allowed on your fat budget, you can save up for special occasions.
2. Party survival
   a. Eat a light snack before the party.
   b. Station yourself *away* from the food.
   c. Make low-fat choices.
   d. Serve low-fat dishes at your own parties.
3. Restaurant survival
   a. Choose a restaurant with low-fat options.
   b. Ask questions about preparation and ingredients.
   c. Have sauces, dressings, gravies, toppings, and butter served on the side so you can regulate the amount you use.
   d. Eat with care. When you dine out once a week or more, it is no longer a special occasion justifying high-fat gluttony.

4. Home survival
   a. Keep tempting high-fat foods out of your home.
   b. Stock up on delicious low-fat/high-carbohydrate foods.
   c. Cook your own food from scratch to reduce the fat content and increase your satisfaction.
   d. Let everyone in the family enjoy and benefit from low-fat eating.
5. Supermarket survival
   a. Use the food tables to plan low-fat choices.
   b. Read food labels to make wise selections.
   c. Beware of misleading advertising claims such as lite! lean! xx% fat free!
6. Low-fat cooking
   a. Reduce the fat content of recipes.
      (1) Use less fat than called for.
      (2) Substitute low-fat or nonfat ingredients for high-fat counterparts.
   b. Prepare food with little or no fat.
      (1) Steam, broil, grill, bake, poach, or boil rather than fry.
      (2) Use cast iron cookware, vegetable steamers, or clay cookers for low-fat cooking.

9. Exercise:
Is It Necessary?

EATING RIGHT + EXERCISE = PERFECTION

You're almost there. You now know how to modify your fat intake to lose weight. Soon you will be watching your clothes get baggier and baggier as you become slimmer and slimmer. To keep *you* from getting baggier and baggier as you change your eating habits, you will need to indulge in an activity you may have tried to avoid — *exercise.*

Relax. We are not proposing marathon running, Olympic swimming, 2000 pushups six times a day. We are suggesting that you walk 20 to 30 minutes three to five times a week. Is that so bad?

LET'S HEAR IT FOR EXERCISE

Exercise will help you lose weight as well as benefit your health and make you feel good.

As we discussed in Chapter 1, exercise helps you lose weight because you burn up more calories when you are exercising than when you are sedentary. If you do not increase the amount you eat, your body must use stored energy to supply the increased energy demands. But remember, the body prefers to burn protein from the muscle rather than fat from the adipose tissue. So, when you exercise you protect your muscle from being broken down and burned for energy. By exercising you force your body to burn fat from the fat stores rather than protein from the muscle tissue.

110

Exercise Raises Your Metabolic Rate

Exercise increases your metabolic rate, the rate at which you burn calories. Not only does your metabolic rate increase *while* you are exercising, there is evidence, though it is somewhat controversial, that your metabolic rate *remains elevated* for a number of hours *after* you finish exercising. If this is true, then you continue to burn off calories at an accelerated rate even after you stop exercising.

Exercise Builds Lean Body Mass, A.K.A. Muscle

If you exercise as you diet you will lose body fat and preserve or even develop new muscle tissue. You want to maximize your muscle mass because muscle is metabolically active and burns off calories. Fat just sits there. Increasing your lean body mass — muscle — by exercising will help you attain and maintain your ideal weight. In other words, muscle helps you burn up what you eat.

Fat but Not Overweight

If you do not exercise when you diet, you will lose muscle tissue. You can end up weighing less but being fatter, that is, a higher percentage of your weight is fat. "So what," you say. "As long as I weigh less, who cares what percentage is what?" You *should* care. Being fatter and having less lean body mass means that you are in greater danger of regaining weight because you don't have as much metabolically active muscle tissue to burn off the fat you eat.

Losing Pounds Doesn't Always Make You Thin

To make this concept clearer, let's look at George and Henry. Initially, George and Henry both weighed 180 pounds and both were 30 percent fat (54 pounds of body fat). They both lost 20 pounds, but because George exercised, he lost 25 pounds of fat and gained 5 pounds of muscle. Sedentary Henry lost 4 pounds of fat and 16 pounds of muscle. If you subtract George's fat loss from his original body fat (54 lb − 25 lb = 29 lb of fat) you will find that George is now 18 percent fat (29 lb body fat ÷ 160 lb weight = 18% body fat) and considered lean. Although Henry also lost 20 pounds, his fat loss (54 lb − 4 lb = 50 lb) is much less than George's, making his percentage of body fat considerable (50 lb ÷ 160 lb weight = 31% body fat). Henry is fatter than when he started, even though he weighs less than he did.

BEFORE WEIGHT LOSS	GEORGE (EXERCISE)	HENRY (SEDENTARY)
Total weight	180 lb	180 lb
Body fat	54 lb	54 lb
Percent body fat	30%	30%
AFTER WEIGHT LOSS		
Total weight	160 lb	160 lb
Body fat lost	25 lb	4 lb
Body fat remaining	29 lb	50 lb
Percent body fat	18%	31%

George and Henry may weigh the same, but George has much more metabolically active muscle and much less metabolically inactive fat. George will have an easier time maintaining his new weight.

Give a Cheer for Exercise

In addition to helping you become lean, exercise provides the following important benefits:

- Cardiovascular fitness — helps protect you against fatal heart attacks
- Helps protect you against osteoporosis
- Lowers blood pressure
- Helps you cope with anxiety, stress, and tension
- Relieves insomnia
- Enhances mood — makes you feel good
- Strengthens, tones, and shapes muscles
- Increases stamina

What Is This Thing Called Exercise?

By exercise we mean aerobic exercise. Aerobic exercise is repetitive and rhythmic and includes walking, jogging, continuous aerobic dancing, biking, and swimming. It does not include lifting weights, bowling, golf, tennis, or most other competitive sports.

Aerobic exercise need not be strenuous nor does it require any athletic ability. But in order to realize the weight loss benefits, you must do at least twenty to thirty minutes of aerobic exercise continuously three to five times a week. For that small expenditure of time and energy, you can raise your metabolic rate, improve your cardiovascular fitness, lower high blood pressure, build muscle tissue, reduce anxiety and tension, and just generally feel great.

Consult your physician before you begin an exercise program if you are over forty, have heart trouble, experience pain during or after exercise, or suffer from arthritis, dizzy spells, or any condition that would lead you to believe you should consult your physician.

Why Aerobic Exercise?

Back to the science. When you eat carbohydrates your body breaks them down into glucose, a simple sugar. Some of that glucose is burned immediately, some is stored as glycogen. When you exercise in spurts and bursts, as when you play tennis, your body burns mainly glucose for quick energy. Burning glucose has no effect on removing fat from your fat stores. When you do aerobic exercise your body supplies the fuel largely by burning fat from the fat stores.

THE NUMBER ONE BEST EXERCISE, BAR NONE

The best, easiest, and safest exercise is plain old walking, which almost anyone can do almost anywhere. This is the least expensive and least punishing exercise. You need no special facility or special equipment, except good walking shoes. The risk of injury is negligible. So go to it. Work up to thirty minutes a day, five days a week. Walk briskly if you can or work up to walking briskly. For the greatest aerobic effect, bend your elbows at a 90-degree angle and move them straight back and forth, slightly brushing your sides as you walk.

If you are overweight, you may find that walking literally takes your breath away. Don't give up. Walk slowly at first. Stop for a few moments when you get out of breath. But keep walking. And continue to walk — a little faster and a little longer each day. As you get thinner, you will find that walking will become easier.

A Sample Walking Program

Exercise at least three to five times each week. Walk slowly during warm-up and cool-down.

| | MINUTES | | | |
WEEK	WARM-UP +	BRISK WALK +	COOL-DOWN =	TOTAL TIME
1	5	5	5	15
2	5	7	5	17
3	5	9	5	19
4	5	11	5	21
5	5	13	5	23
6	5	15	5	25
7	5	18	5	28
8	5	20	5	30
9	5	23	5	33
10	5	26	5	36
11	5	28	5	38
12	5	30	5	40

Adapted from *Exercise and Your Heart,* U.S. Department of Health and Human Services, Public Health Service, National Institutes of Health, Pub. No. 81-1677, 1981.

AEROBIC ACTION

Many local YMCAs, hospitals, adult education programs, and spas offer aerobic dancing classes. Aerobic dancing is fun and, for some, paying for a class that meets on a schedule is a strong incentive to exercise. These classes are offered at both low-impact and high-impact levels. Even if you are not Jane Fonda, there is a class you can handle. Be sure, however, that you keep moving even when the music stops. Dancing in starts and stops will cause your body to burn carbohydrates for quick energy and have little effect on protecting your muscle mass.

Be careful. It is easy to injure yourself doing aerobic dancing.

Video Exercise

If you prefer exercising in the privacy of your home, an extensive array of exercise and aerobic workout tapes are available at your local video store and through catalogues. They range from low-impact to strenuous and are adjusted to different ages and exercise goals. Try to schedule your video exercise at the same time four or five times a week. Make it part of your routine.

Bicycling

Riding a bicycle outdoors in fair weather is a visual and emotional treat as well as excellent exercise. If your area has accessible bike paths or streets that are safe for riding, and you enjoy biking, budget half an hour of bicycling into your daily routine.

However, if the weather or terrain of your area does not encourage biking out of doors, a stationary bicycle is an excellent substitute. You can do it at any time and in any weather. For those with bad feet, biking has the advantage of supporting your weight as you exercise. The drawback to riding a stationary bike is that it is incredibly boring and a lot of work. Some exercisers overcome this problem by watching TV or reading while they bike.

Swimming

Swimming is a particularly effective exercise for those who find walking difficult. Swimmers use muscles in both the upper and lower body, but their weight is supported by the water. The disadvantage of swimming is that, as most of us do not own our own pools, we must fight kiddies for swimming lanes in the summer and endure overchlorinated indoor pools in the winter. As with any exercise, start slowly and work up to swimming twenty minutes of laps five times a week.

Jogging

We do not recommend jogging for most people. Jogging incurs a high risk of injury to backs, knees, calves, and ankles. Walking is much safer and just as effective in terms of permanent weight loss.

Heavy Equipment

We have just described the safest and easiest forms of aerobic exercise that require the least equipment and expense and can be easily incorporated into anyone's routine and budget. Of course, you can buy expensive exercise equipment such as treadmills, stationary rowing machines, and cross-country skiing machines. All these machines provide perfectly acceptable aerobic exercise if used properly and regularly.

Combination Exercise

You may choose to swim in the summer and walk or bike in the winter or do aerobic dancing in the morning and walk in the evening.

Whatever exercise or combination of exercises you choose, be sure you do some aerobic exercise at least three to five times a week. Soon, exercise will become a part of your routine, like taking a shower or bath, and you will miss it sorely when circumstances force you to forgo it.

BUT NOT FOR ME

"Of course I know how important exercise is and I'd love to do it but . . ."

Choose one of the following excuses:

☐ I'm too busy to exercise.
☐ Exercise takes time from my family.
☐ I get all sweaty.
☐ I look funny in leotards.
☐ I get out of breath.
☐ It's too dark, too light, too cold, too wet, to exercise.
☐ I (fill in the blank)_____

Have you found your favorite excuse(s) for not exercising? Here's why your excuse is no excuse:

☐ **I'm Too Busy to Exercise.** No one is too busy to exercise. You can always fit it in. Get up a few minutes early and ride a stationary bike or take a walk before you leave for work. Walk during your lunch hour. Take a walk before you go to bed. What do you do that is more important than exercising? Watch TV? Work overtime? Exercise is essential to your well-being, both physical and mental.

☐ **Exercise Takes Time from My Family.** Include your family when you exercise. Take a walk after dinner with your daughter, son, husband, wife. Leave the car at home and walk your spouse to and from the subway or train. Take a bike ride with your family on the weekend. Exercise won't hurt them a bit.

☐ **I Get All Sweaty.** Walking should not make you sweaty. If your chosen activity causes excessive perspiration, exercise at a time and place where you can arrange to shower.

☐ **I Look Funny in Leotards.** Almost everyone looks funny in leotards. They exaggerate what you want to flatten and flatten what you want to exaggerate. Don't wear leotards. Wear comfortable shorts. If you look funny in shorts, who cares? The exercise is for you. And if you eat right and exercise, you will soon look great in shorts.

☐ **I Get Out of Breath.** Take it easy. After all, if you haven't exercised in a long time you are probably out of shape. If you are overweight you are carrying a lot of extra pounds. Start slowly, a few minutes a day, and work up to thirty minutes of vigorous walking. However, you should check with your physician before you begin any exercise program.

☐ **It's Too Dark, Too Light, Too Cold, Too Wet, to Exercise.** Come on! You can find a solution to any problem if you try. If the weather is poor, take a walk in a covered mall, exercise at home on a stationary bike or a treadmill, or pop an exercise tape in your VCR and move with the beat.

TIPS TO KEEP YOU ON THE STRAIGHT AND NARROW

It is so easy to put off exercise. The following tips will help you incorporate exercise into your life and keep it there.

1. Schedule Exercise.

Schedule exercise at a specific time so you will really do it. Reserve twenty minutes every weekday morning for a ride on your stationary bicycle. Walk for thirty minutes every day after dinner. Work out to a videotape every morning at 9:30. Make exercise a habit. Do it even if you're not in the mood. Force yourself. You'll be glad you did.

Walking Fits Right In Everywhere. Incorporating walking into your schedule is probably the easiest and most practical exercise program. Make it an integral part of your lifestyle rather than an activity grafted onto an already busy schedule. For example, walk to work or part way by getting off the bus early or parking your car twenty to thirty minutes away.

Walk on Your Lunch Break. Walk for thirty minutes at lunchtime. It's good to get out of the office and into the fresh air. You can combine the walk with errands. But, remember, the exercise *must be continuous.* Walking five minutes to the bank and standing in line for fifteen minutes doesn't count as exercise.

2. Do Exercise You Enjoy.

Choose an exercise you enjoy or make the exercise you do more enjoyable. If you find a stationary bike too strenuous, walk. If you find walking boring, plug in earphones, turn on your Walkman, and listen to your favorite music or talk show. Slide in language tapes and teach yourself Italian. Watch television as you stride along your treadmill or ride your bike.

3. Exercise with a Buddy.

Exercising with another person (spouse, child, neighbor, friend) can be more fun than exercising alone. Instead of spending an hour every evening gathered around the kitchen table nibbling and chatting, spend the time taking a walk and chatting. Let it become a ritual. Exercising with a friend can also give you the added nudge you need. How can you say no when Barbara phones to ask if you need a ride to your nine o'clock aerobics class?

However, if you exercise with a partner, do not use his or her absence (due to illness or other commitments) as an excuse to stop. Either find another partner or go it alone. If you know you do not have the commitment to continue to exercise on your own, join a spa or exercise group. But do whatever it takes.

4. Wear the Best Equipment — Good Shoes.

Be sure to wear comfortable shoes with good support. You need not buy $99 superwalker sneakers with double soles filled with bubbles of air and foam-layered heels especially constructed for walking on pavement in temperate climates. In fact, you might find tie-up leather shoes more comfortable for walking because they don't get as hot as sneakers. Whatever type of shoes you prefer, make sure they fit and offer support.

THE MESSAGE

Exercise will both help you lose weight and keep it off. It will enhance your life. Start now. Schedule it in. You'll be glad you did — and your body and psyche will be ecstatic.

Recommended Reading. To learn more about exercise, check the reference list for Chapter 9. In particular, the exercise books by Kenneth Cooper, M.D., are an excellent resource.

Remember:

1. Regular aerobic exercise is a necessary part of The *Choose to Lose* Diet Plan because it
   a. protects your muscle from being burned for energy.
   b. maximizes the burning of stored fat.
   c. increases your metabolism.
   d. increases your energy expenditure.
   e. helps you maintain your desirable body weight.
   f. improves cardiovascular fitness, reduces risk of osteoporosis and other diseases, and enhances your sense of well-being.
2. Walking is the preferred aerobic exercise. Alternatives include bicycling and swimming.
3. Make exercise a regular part of your daily schedule.

10. Ensuring a Balanced Diet

IN YOUR fervor to reduce your intake of fat, don't forget to balance your diet with foods that give you adequate amounts of vitamins, minerals, protein, and fiber.* Eating a well-balanced diet should be no problem if you replace your excess fat calories with fruits, vegetables, and whole grains.

More specifically, to maintain your health it is essential that you eat foods from each of the following food groups each day. At the end of the chapter you will find a table that summarizes the recommended servings and serving sizes of foods from each group.

VEGETABLES

Vegetables contribute vital fiber, vitamins, and minerals to your diet. They should be varied and eaten daily.

Dark green vegetables should be included several times a week. They are an excellent source of vitamins A and C, riboflavin, folic acid, iron, and magnesium. Choose from:

---

*You may find a computer nutrient-analysis program useful in analyzing your food intake to ensure that your diet is well balanced. With a database of over 5600 food items, the user-friendly DINE Windows system analyzes the fat content in the food you eat and compares your intake of 26 food components with established guidelines. Also available is a comprehensive nutrition book, *The DINE System: How to Improve Your Nutrition and Health.* Included in the price of the book is a free dietary cholesterol and fat analysis of your food choices for one day. For more information, write to DINE Systems, Inc., 5 Bluebird Lane, West Amherst, New York 14228.

beet greens	endive	spinach
broccoli*	escarole	turnip greens
chard	kale	watercress
chicory	romaine lettuce	

Deep yellow vegetables are an excellent source of vitamin A. Choose from:

| carrots | sweet potatoes |
| pumpkin | winter squash |

Other vegetables also contribute varying amounts of vitamins and minerals. Choose from:

artichokes	chinese cabbage	okra
asparagus	cucumbers	onions
beets	eggplant	radishes
brussels sprouts*	green beans	summer squash
cabbage*	green peppers	tomatoes
cauliflower*	lettuce	turnips*
celery	mushrooms	zucchini

Starchy vegetables are rich in starch, fiber, vitamin B_6, folic acid, iron, magnesium, potassium, and phosphorus. Choose from:

corn	potatoes (white)
green peas	rutabaga*
lima beans	sweet potatoes (rich in vitamin A)

Dried beans and peas are excellent sources of protein, soluble fiber (known to reduce blood cholesterol levels), calcium, magnesium, phosphorus, potassium, iron, and zinc.

Choose from these dried beans and peas, which should be included as a starchy vegetable several times a week:

black beans	lentils	split peas
black-eyed peas	lima beans	other types of dried
chickpeas	navy beans	beans and peas
kidney beans	pinto beans	

*These cruciferous vegetables may reduce your risk of colon cancer.

FRUITS

Fruits contain fiber, vitamins, and minerals. They should be varied and eaten daily.

Citrus, melon, and berries are rich sources of vitamin C, other vitamins, folic acid, and minerals. Choose from:

blueberries	lemon	tangerine
cantaloupe	orange	watermelon
grapefruit	orange juice	other citrus fruits,
grapefruit juice	raspberries	melons, and
honeydew melon	strawberries	berries

Other fruits have smaller amounts of the same nutrients. Choose from:

apples	nectarines	prunes
apricots	peaches	raisins
bananas	pears	other fruit
cherries	pineapples	fruit juices
grapes	plums	

WHOLE GRAINS, BREADS, AND CEREALS

Whole grains, breads, and cereals are rich in protein, starch, fiber, vitamins, and minerals and should be consumed daily.

The following whole-grain products are rich in starch, fiber, protein, thiamine, riboflavin, niacin, folic acid, vitamin E, iron, phosphorus, magnesium, zinc, and other trace minerals. Choose from:

brown rice	oatmeal	whole-wheat bread
buckwheat groats	pumpernickel	and rolls
bulgur	bread	whole-wheat pasta

The following enriched-grain products contain starch and protein, but thiamine, riboflavin, niacin, and iron have been added. Be careful that fat has not also been added. *Read the labels carefully!*

Eat these foods in moderation. Whole-grain products are far more nutritious.

bagels   French bread   pasta
cereal (ready-to-eat) noodles   rice

MILK PRODUCTS

Milk products are rich in protein, calcium, riboflavin, vitamin B_{12}, magnesium, vitamin A, thiamine, and, if fortified, vitamin D. Milk products need not be high in fat to contain high amounts of calcium. In fact, low-fat milk products contain slightly more calcium than their high-fat counterparts. Choose from these milk products daily:

buttermilk   low-fat and nonfat yogurt
low-fat cottage cheese (1%)   skim milk

Calcium is also found in dark green vegetables.

Women need more calcium than men in order to avoid developing the bone-thinning disease osteoporosis.

MEATS, POULTRY, FISH, AND EGGS

Meats, poultry, fish, and eggs are good sources of protein, phosphorus, niacin, iron, zinc, and vitamins B_6 and B_{12}.

Choose often from the following:

white meat chicken with no skin
white meat turkey with no skin
fish
shellfish

Choose less often from the following:

beef   lamb   veal
ham   pork   eggs

Eat organ meats such as liver, pancreas, and brain rarely. They are loaded with cholesterol, and pancreas and brain are also high in fat.

Cooked dried beans or peas, as well as nuts and seeds, may be substituted for meat, poultry, fish, and eggs. However, as these plant foods lack vitamin B_{12}, this vitamin must be supplied by other foods. Nuts and seeds are high in fat and should be eaten in moderation.

Minimum Basic Nutritional Requirements

FOOD GROUP	DAILY RECOMMENDED SERVINGS	SERVING SIZES
VEGETABLES	at least 3 to 5	½ to 1 cup
FRUITS	at least 2 to 4	½ to 1 cup, 1 medium piece of fruit
WHOLE GRAINS, BREADS, AND CEREALS	at least 6	1 slice bread, 1 oz cereal, ½ cup pasta, ½ cup rice
DAIRY PRODUCTS	2	1 cup skim milk
LEAN MEAT, POULTRY, FISH, EGGS	2	2 to 3 oz lean, trimmed

Epilogue: *Choose to Lose for Life*

CHOOSE to Lose is more than a diet. It is an education, a way of life. Not only will you learn how to make the right food choices to keep you lean forever, a whole new world of eating will open up to you as you replace fat with complex carbohydrates. Your life will become richer and your palate will expand as you explore new foods and recipes that fit into your fat budget.

You will be amazed at how you will change, not only in size and shape, but in attitude. At first you may find yourself hungrily eyeing a croissant. But, instead of gobbling it down, you will see a number pop

---

What Next?

After you achieve your desired weight you may want to determine a new fat budget that is slightly higher. Perhaps you were on a 15 percent fat budget (237 fat calories), and now that you weigh 135, you want to follow a 17 percent fat budget (268 fat calories). Keeping a food record for a few days will give you an idea of how much more you can eat on the new budget. You will need to experiment to find the fat budget with the best fit.

Having lived on a budget and generally knowing the fat calories of the foods you like, you will probably be able to maintain your new weight forever. If, however, you find that you are beginning to gain back the weight you lost, have no fear. Just reread *Choose to Lose*, determine a budget, and *pay attention*. Write down what you eat, find the sources of fat in your diet, and make the right choices and changes. Within a short time you will be lean once more.

---

out at you: *croissant = 108 calories of fat,* and then you'll ask yourself, "Is that soggy croissant worth almost half my fat budget? Wouldn't French bread taste just as good and leave not a trace of fat in my fat stores?" You'll begin to prefer low-fat choices. You may find it hard to believe, but you may eventually lose your craving for high-fat food.

KEEP THOSE MUSCLES MOVING

As part of your new start on life you have made aerobic exercise a regular part of your daily life. Be sure to keep exercising even after you achieve your weight goal. Not only will exercising help you maintain your new weight, but it is beneficial for the many reasons discussed in Chapter 9. See Appendix C for a chart to record the amount of time you exercise.

IT'S UP TO YOU

You've got the tools. It's your move. Go to it and have fun! Expect to see a lean, gorgeous *you* in the mirror pretty soon.

POSTSCRIPT: HOW *CHOOSE TO LOSE* DIFFERS FROM *EATER'S CHOICE*

In 1987, the first edition of *Eater's Choice: A Food Lover's Guide to Lower Cholesterol* was published. It was one of the first books to deal with the problem of high cholesterol. It was (and still is) the only book of its kind. It focuses on food. It is specific and quantitative so that you know you have made enough changes in your diet to lower your blood cholesterol.

The approach is simple and effective. You first determine your personal sat-fat budget because the main culprit in the diet that raises blood cholesterol level is saturated fat. Thus, by limiting saturated-fat intake, you lower your blood cholesterol. Knowing your sat-fat budget and the sat-fat calories of the foods you want to eat, you can eat any combination of foods as long as you stay within your budget and still lower your blood cholesterol level.

Since *Eater's Choice* was published, thousands of people have lowered their cholesterol levels and thus their risk for heart disease. Many have lost weight as a side effect. Limiting saturated fat will cause you to lose weight because foods that are high in saturated fat are even higher in total fat. When you limit total fat, you lose weight.

As we mentioned in the Introduction, we wrote *Choose to Lose* because so many people following *Eater's Choice* lost weight. However, we realized that just lowering saturated fat does not cause weight loss in every individual. Some foods, such as margarine, most vegetable oils (olive, corn, sunflower, and safflower), and peanut butter are low in saturated fat and would fit easily into a cholesterol-lowering diet. But because they are so high in total fat, consuming them without keeping track could make you gain weight.

Choose to Lose uses the same simple approach as *Eater's Choice,* but instead of a sat-fat budget, you determine a fat budget. Knowing your fat budget and the fat calories of the foods you choose to eat, you can eat any combination of foods as long as you stay within your budget and still lose weight. With either plan you need never feel deprived, because you can always eat your favorite foods, you learn to appreciate new, healthy foods, you feel better than you ever did, and you look great. As a side effect of *Choose to Lose* you may even lower your cholesterol because when you reduce total fat, in many instances you also reduce your intake of saturated fat.

Meal Plans

WE CREATED the following meal plans to show you how easy it is to fit delicious food into your fat budget and how to save calories for a splurge. These are only *sample* meal plans, not menus designed to be repeated twenty-six times each year until you are ninety-nine years old. It is your body and your tastebuds, and you will have to devise meal plans that suit you and your fat budget. Don't worry. It will be fun.

The first week of meal plans illustrates a 20 percent fat budget based on three different daily caloric intake levels: 1200, 1500, and 2000. The second week of meal plans illustrates how to save up calories for a splurge following a sample budget of 225 fat calories (a 15 percent fat budget based on a daily caloric intake of 1500).

The recipes for dishes printed in italics are adapted from *Eater's Choice* and are included in this volume.

Key to Abbreviations

amt	amount	pkg	package
br	breast	sl	slice(s)
c	cup(s)	sm	small
cal	calorie(s)	sv	serving(s)
lg	large	T	tablespoon(s)
med	medium	tot	total
oz	ounce(s)	tr	trace
pc	piece(s)	t	teaspoon(s)
(PF)	Pepperidge Farm		

Meal Plans — Week 1
20% Fat Budget

Sunday — Week 1	1200 CAL/DAY			1500 CAL/DAY			2000 CAL/DAY		
		CALORIES			CALORIES			CALORIES	
	AMT	TOT	FAT	AMT	TOT	FAT	AMT	TOT	FAT
Breakfast									
Buttermilk Waffle	1	173	47	2	346	94	2	346	94
Maple syrup	2 t	33	0	1 T	50	0	1 T	50	0
Honeydew melon	1/10	46	tr	1/10	46	tr	1/10	46	tr
Skim milk	1 c	86	4	1 c	86	4	1 c	86	4
Coffee or tea	1 c	tr	0	1 c	tr	0	1 c	tr	0
Lunch									
Tomato-Rice Soup	1 c	93	0	1 c	93	0	1½ c	140	0
Roast turkey breast	3 oz	114	6	3 oz	114	6	4 oz	152	8
Baked potato	1 sm	75	tr	1 med	112	tr	1 med	112	tr
Steamed broccoli	½ c	20	tr	½ c	20	tr	1 c	40	tr
with margarine	½ t	17	17	½ t	17	17	1 t	33	33
Sliced fresh peaches	½ c	37	tr	½ c	37	tr	½ c	37	tr
Coffee or tea	1 c	tr	0	1 c	tr	0	1 c	tr	0
Dinner									
Grapefruit	½	38	tr	½	38	tr	½	38	tr
Chili Non Carne	1 c	142	30	1½ c	213	45	2 c	284	60
Tossed salad	1 c	10	tr	1 c	10	tr	1 c	10	tr
Italian dressing	1 T	69	64	1 T	69	64	1½ T	104	96
Steamed Zucchini									
Matchsticks	½ c	17	0	½ c	17	0	½ c	17	0
Margarine	½ t	17	17	½ t	17	17	½ t	17	17
Onion Flat Bread	1 sl	83	7	1 sl	83	7	2 sl	166	14
Coffee or tea	1 c	tr	0	1 c	tr	0	1 c	tr	0
Mandelbrot	2 pc	92	36	2 pc	92	36	3 pc	138	54
Snack									
Skim milk	½ c	43	2	½ c	43	2	½ c	43	2
Bran Chex	⅔ c	90	0	⅔ c	90	0	⅔ c	90	0
Totals		**1295**	**230**		**1593**	**292**		**1949**	**382**

Meal Plans — Week 1
20% Fat Budget

**Monday —
Week 1**

	1200 CAL/DAY			1500 CAL/DAY			2000 CAL/DAY		
		CALORIES			CALORIES			CALORIES	
	AMT	TOT	FAT	AMT	TOT	FAT	AMT	TOT	FAT
Breakfast									
Apricot Oat Muffin	1	135	32	2	270	64	2	270	64
Skim milk	1 c	86	4	1 c	86	4	1 c	86	4
Strawberries, fresh	1 c	45	tr	1 c	45	tr	1 c	45	tr
Coffee or tea	1 c	tr	0	1 c	tr	0	1 c	tr	0
Lunch									
Chickpea Sandwich									
on pita bread	1	195	39	1	195	39	2	390	78
Tangerine	1	35	tr	1	35	tr	1	35	tr
Oatmeal Cookies	1	75	25	2	150	50	3	225	75
Coffee or tea	1 c	tr	0	1 c	tr	0	1 c	tr	0
Nonfat fruit yogurt	—	—	—	—	—	—	½ c	95	3
Dinner									
Tortilla Soup	1 c	155	36	1½ c	233	54	1½ c	233	54
Indonesian Chicken									
with Green Beans	1 sv	185	54	1 sv	185	54	1½ sv	278	81
Rice, white	½ c	112	tr	½ c	112	tr	½ c	112	tr
Margarine	½ t	17	17	½ t	17	17	½ t	17	17
Acorn squash	½ sm	70	tr	½ sm	70	tr	½ sm	70	tr
Coffee or tea	1 c	tr	0	1 c	tr	0	1 c	tr	0
Snack									
Nonfat yogurt	½ c	55	0	½ c	55	0	½ c	55	0
Blueberries, fresh	½ c	40	tr	½ c	40	tr	½ c	40	tr
Sesame Crackers									
(PF)	3	60	18	3	60	18	3	60	18
Totals		**1265**	**225**		**1553**	**299**		**2011**	**394**

Meal Plans — Week 1
20% Fat Budget

Tuesday — Week 1

	1200 CAL/DAY			1500 CAL/DAY			2000 CAL/DAY		
		CALORIES			CALORIES			CALORIES	
	AMT	TOT	FAT	AMT	TOT	FAT	AMT	TOT	FAT
Breakfast									
Whole-wheat toast	2 sl	140	18	2 sl	140	18	3 sl	210	27
Jelly	1 t	17	0	2 t	34	0	2 t	34	0
Cantaloupe	½	94	7	½	94	7	½	94	7
1% cottage cheese	½ c	82	10	½ c	82	10	½ c	82	10
Skim milk	1 c	86	4	1 c	86	4	1 c	86	4
Coffee or tea	1 c	tr	0	1 c	tr	0	1 c	tr	0
Lunch									
Tuna sandwich:									
Tuna, water-packed	2 oz	60	9	2 oz	60	9	6 oz	180	27
Low-fat mayonnaise	2 t	30	30	2 t	30	30	1 T	45	45
Rye bread	2 sl	130	18	2 sl	130	18	4 sl	260	36
Orange	1	60	tr	1	60	tr	1	60	tr
Coffee or tea	1 c	tr	0	1 c	tr	0	1 c	tr	0
Dinner									
Tarragon Squash Soup	1 c	122	4	1½ c	183	6	1½ c	183	6
Turkey Mexique	1 sv	170	40	1 sv	170	40	1 sv	170	40
Rice, white	½ c	112	tr	¾ c	168	tr	¾ c	168	tr
Tossed salad	1 c	10	tr	1 c	10	tr	1 c	10	tr
1000 Island dressing	1 T	59	50	1½ T	89	75	1½ T	89	75
Cooked spinach	½ c	20	tr	½ c	20	tr	½ c	20	tr
Margarine	—	—	—	½ t	17	17	½ t	17	17
Sesame Bread Sticks	—	—	—	2	52	15	3	78	23
Coffee or tea	1 c	tr	0	1 c	tr	0	1 c	tr	0
Snack									
Vanilla ice cream (light)	½ c	120	36	½ c	120	36	1 c	240	72
Totals		1312	226		1545	285		2026	389

Meal Plans — Week 1
20% Fat Budget

**Wednesday —
Week 1**

	1200 CAL/DAY			1500 CAL/DAY			2000 CAL/DAY		
		CALORIES			CALORIES			CALORIES	
	AMT	TOT	FAT	AMT	TOT	FAT	AMT	TOT	FAT
Breakfast									
Raisin bran cereal	¾ c	120	9	¾ c	120	9	1½ c	240	18
Skim milk	½ c	43	2	½ c	43	2	1 c	86	4
Banana	½	52	2	½	52	2	1	105	5
Coffee or tea	1 c	tr	0	1 c	tr	0	1 c	tr	0
Lunch									
Turkey sandwich:									
Turkey breast	2 oz	76	4	3 oz	114	6	4 oz	152	8
Lettuce, tomato		10	tr		10	tr		10	tr
Low-fat mayon-									
naise	2 t	30	30	2 t	30	30	4 t	60	60
Whole-wheat									
bread	2 sl	140	18	2 sl	140	18	4 sl	280	36
Apple	1	81	tr	1	81	tr	1	81	tr
Honey Graham									
Crackers	1	58	12	2	116	24	4	232	48
Coffee or tea	1 c	tr	0	1 c	tr	0	1 c	tr	0
Dinner									
Carrot Soup	1 c	85	17	1½ c	128	26	1½ c	128	26
Shrimp Curry	1 sv	197	46	1 sv	197	46	1 sv	197	46
Rice, white	½ c	112	tr	½ c	112	tr	¾ c	168	tr
Tossed salad	1 c	10	tr	1 c	10	tr	1 c	10	tr
Russian dressing	1 T	76	70	1½ T	114	105	1½ T	114	105
Zucchini, steamed	½ c	18	tr	½ c	18	tr	½ c	18	tr
Margarine	½ t	17	17	½ t	17	17	½ t	17	17
Pear halves	½ c	37	tr	½ c	37	tr	½ c	37	tr
Coffee or tea	1 c	tr	0	1 c	tr	0	1 c	tr	0
Snack									
Frozen nonfat									
yogurt	½ c	80	0	1 c	160	0	1 c	160	0
Fresh strawberries	½ c	22	tr	½ c	22	tr	½ c	22	tr
Totals		**1264**	**227**		**1521**	**285**		**2117**	**373**

Meal Plans — Week 1
20% Fat Budget

Thursday — Week 1	1200 CAL/DAY			1500 CAL/DAY			2000 CAL/DAY		
		CALORIES			CALORIES			CALORIES	
	AMT	TOT	FAT	AMT	TOT	FAT	AMT	TOT	FAT
Breakfast									
Apple Oat Muffin	—	—	—	1	125	32	2	250	64
Skim milk	1 c	86	4	1 c	86	4	1 c	86	4
Grapefruit	½	38	tr	½	38	tr	½	38	tr
Wheatena	1 sv	100	9	1 sv	100	9	1 sv	100	9
Margarine	½ t	17	17	½ t	17	17	½ t	17	17
Coffee or tea	1 c	tr	0	1 c	tr	0	1 c	tr	0
Lunch									
Roast beef sandwich:									
Roast beef	2 oz	108	32	3 oz	162	48	4 oz	216	64
Lettuce, tomato,									
mustard		10	tr		10	tr		10	tr
Rye bread	2 sl	130	18	2 sl	130	18	4 sl	260	36
Peach	1	37	tr	1	37	tr	1	37	tr
Coffee or tea	1 c	tr	0	1 c	tr	0	1 c	tr	0
Dinner									
Cucumber Soup	1 c	78	0	1 c	78	0	1 c	78	0
Spaghetti, cooked	½ c	78	4	1 c	155	9	1½ c	232	13
Tomato sauce with	½ c	37	tr	½ c	37	tr	1 c	74	tr
ground round	3 oz	162	48	3 oz	162	48	4 oz	216	64
Parmesan cheese	1 T	23	14	1 T	23	14	1 T	23	14
Tossed salad	1 c	10	tr	1 c	10	tr	1 c	10	tr
Italian dressing	1 T	69	64	1 T	69	64	1 T	69	64
Italian bread	2 sl	170	tr	2 sl	170	tr	2 sl	170	tr
Margarine with									
garlic	¾ t	25	25	1 t	33	33	1 t	33	33
Coffee or tea	1 c	tr	0	1 c	tr	0	1 c	tr	0
Snack									
Popcorn, air-popped	5½ c	165	tr	5½ c	165	tr	5½ c	165	tr
Totals		**1343**	**235**		**1607**	**296**		**2084**	**382**

Meal Plans — Week 1
20% Fat Budget

**Friday —
Week 1**

	1200 CAL/DAY			1500 CAL/DAY			2000 CAL/DAY		
		CALORIES			CALORIES			CALORIES	
	AMT	TOT	FAT	AMT	TOT	FAT	AMT	TOT	FAT
Breakfast									
Nonfat yogurt with	½ c	55	0	½ c	55	0	½ c	55	0
cut-up fresh fruit	¾ c	60	tr	¾ c	60	tr	¾ c	60	tr
Apricot Oat Muffin	—	—	—	1	135	32	2	270	64
Whole-wheat toast	1 sl	70	9	—	—	—	—	—	—
Margarine	1 t	33	33	1 t	33	33	1 t	33	33
Skim milk	—	—	—	1 c	86	4	1 c	86	4
Coffee or tea	1 c	tr	0	1 c	tr	0	1 c	tr	0
Lunch									
Asparagus Pasta	1 sv	250	38	1 sv	250	38	1 sv	250	38
Blueberries	½ c	40	tr	½ c	40	tr	½ c	40	tr
Cardamom Bread	1 sl	95	15	2 sl	190	30	2 sl	190	30
Coffee or tea	1 c	tr	0	1 c	tr	0	1 c	tr	0
Dinner									
Cantaloupe Soup	1 c	80	4	1 c	80	4	1½ c	120	6
Fish Baked in Olive,									
etc.	1 sv	163	34	1 sv	163	34	1½ sv	245	51
Potato Skins	1 sv	79	20	1 sv	79	20	2 sv	158	40
Steamed carrots	½ c	35	tr	½ c	35	tr	½ c	35	tr
Margarine	½ t	17	17	½ t	17	17	1 t	33	33
Cucumber Salad	½ c	20	0	½ c	20	0	½ c	20	0
Coffee or tea	1 c	tr	0	1 c	tr	0	1 c	tr	0
Snack									
Skim milk	1 c	86	4	1 c	86	4	1 c	86	4
Oatmeal Cookies	2	150	50	3	225	75	4	300	100
Totals		**1233**	**224**		**1524**	**291**		**1981**	**403**

Meal Plans — Week 1
20% Fat Budget

**Saturday —
Week 1**

	1200 CAL/DAY			1500 CAL/DAY			2000 CAL/DAY		
		CALORIES			CALORIES			CALORIES	
	AMT	TOT	FAT	AMT	TOT	FAT	AMT	TOT	FAT
Breakfast									
Cinnamon French									
Toast	2 sl	212	58	2 sl	212	58	3 sl	318	87
Cinnamon sugar	1 t	15	0	1 t	15	0	2 t	30	0
Skim milk	1 c	86	4	1 c	86	4	1 c	86	4
Pineapple slice,									
¾" thick	1	42	tr	1	42	tr	1	42	tr
Coffee or tea	1 c	tr	0	1 c	tr	0	1 c	tr	0
Lunch									
Dijon Chicken-Rice									
Salad	1 sv	265	51	1 sv	265	51	2 sv	530	102
Fresh strawberries	½ c	22	tr	½ c	22	tr	½ c	22	tr
Coffee or tea	1 c	tr	0	1 c	tr	0	1 c	tr	0
Anadama Bread	1 sl	110	15	1 sl	110	15	2 sl	220	30
Dinner									
Mixed citrus fruits	½ c	40	tr	½ c	40	tr	½ c	40	tr
Lemon Chicken	1 sv	200	29	1 sv	200	29	1½ sv	300	44
Rice, white	½ c	112	tr	½ c	112	tr	¾ c	168	tr
Sweet potato, med	1	59	tr	1	59	tr	1	59	tr
Margarine	1 t	33	33	1 t	33	33	1 t	33	33
Tossed salad	1 c	10	tr	1 c	10	tr	1 c	10	tr
Russian low-calorie									
dressing	1 T	23	6	1 T	23	6	1 T	23	6
Coffee or tea	1 c	tr	0	1 c	tr	0	1 c	tr	0
Cinnamon Sweet									
Cakes	—	—	—	1	148	61	1	148	61
Snack									
Sliced peaches	½ c	37	tr	½ c	37	tr	½ c	37	tr
Popcorn, air-popped	—	—	—	4 c	120	tr	—	—	—
Totals		**1266**	**196**		**1534**	**257**		**2066**	**367**

Meal Plans — Week 2
15% Fat Budget with Splurge
(1500 Total Calories)

Sunday — Week 2

	AMOUNT	CALORIES TOTAL	CALORIES FAT

Breakfast

	AMOUNT	TOTAL	FAT
Egg, poached	1	79	50
Canadian bacon	1 sl	43	18
English muffin	1	140	9
Apricots	3	50	tr
Skim milk	1 c	86	4
Coffee or tea	1 c	tr	0

Lunch

Apricot Chicken Divine	1 sv	243	39
Rice	½ c	112	tr
Sliced tomatoes	½ c	20	tr
Coffee or tea	1 c	tr	0
Sliced banana	1	105	5

Dinner

Barley-Vegetable Soup	1 c	100	tr
Focaccia	2 sl	240	48
Italian bread	1 sl	85	0
Tossed salad	1 c	10	tr
Low-calorie Italian dressing	1 T	16	14
Coffee or tea	1 c	tr	0

Snack

Nonfat yogurt	1 c	110	0
Sliced peaches	½ c	37	tr

Totals		1476	187
Budget			225
Saved			38

Monday — Week 2

	AMOUNT	CALORIES TOTAL	FAT

Breakfast

	AMOUNT	TOTAL	FAT
1% cottage cheese	½ c	82	10
Sliced strawberries	½ c	45	tr
Whole-wheat toast	2 sl	140	18
Grapefruit	½	38	tr
Coffee or tea	1 c	tr	0

Lunch

	AMOUNT	TOTAL	FAT
Turkey sandwich:			
Turkey breast	3 oz	114	6
Lettuce, tomato		10	tr
Low-fat mayonnaise	½ T	22	22
Whole-wheat bread	2 sl	140	18
Apple	1	81	tr
Skim milk	1 c	86	4
Coffee or tea	1 c	tr	0

Dinner

	AMOUNT	TOTAL	FAT
Vegetable Soup with Spinach,			
Potatoes, Rice, and Corn	1 c	145	29
Scallop Creole	1 sv	199	35
Rice, white	¾ c	168	tr
Steamed Zucchini Matchsticks	½ c	17	0
Margarine	½ t	17	17
Tossed salad	1 c	10	tr
Low-calorie French dressing	1 T	22	8
Coffee or tea	1 c	tr	0

Snack

	AMOUNT	TOTAL	FAT
Frozen nonfat yogurt	1 c	160	0
Blueberries	¼ c	20	tr

	Totals	1516	167
	Budget		225
	Saved		58
	Carry-over		38
	New Carry-over		96

Tuesday — Week 2

	AMOUNT	CALORIES	
		TOTAL	FAT
Breakfast			
Bagel	1	200	18
Preserves	1 T	50	0
Nonfat yogurt	1 c	110	0
Melon chunks	1 c	57	tr
Coffee or tea	1 c	tr	0
Lunch			
Curried Tuna Salad with Pears	1 sv	220	49
Pita bread	1	165	9
Orange	1	60	tr
Coffee or tea	1 c	tr	0
Dinner			
Oriental Noodle Soup	1 c	64	8
Bar-B-Que Chicken	1 br	165	13
Mashed potatoes (skim milk)	1 c	160	tr
Indian Vegetables	1 sv	96	20
Tossed salad	1 c	10	tr
Low-calorie French dressing	1 T	22	8
Coffee or tea	1 c	tr	0
Snack			
Skim milk	1 c	86	4
Honey Graham Crackers	1	58	12
	Totals	1523	141
	Budget		225
	Saved		84
	Carry-over		96
	New Carry-over		180

Wednesday — Week 2

	AMOUNT	CALORIES TOTAL	FAT
Breakfast			
Oatmeal	1 c	165	27
Raisins	1 T	31	tr
Margarine	½ t	17	17
Skim milk	1 c	86	4
Banana	1	105	5
Coffee or tea	1 c	tr	0
Lunch			
Baked chicken breast sandwich:			
Chicken breast (no skin)	3 oz	142	28
Lettuce, tomato, mustard		10	tr
Rye bread	2 sl	130	18
Peach	1	37	tr
Popcorn, air-popped	4½ c	135	tr
Coffee or tea	1 c	tr	0
Dinner			
Zucchini Soup	1 c	80	2
Cajun Chicken	1 sv	244	58
Baked potato	1 lg	145	tr
Steamed broccoli	1 c	46	tr
Margarine	½ t	17	17
Coffee or tea	1 c	tr	0
Snack			
Nonfat fruit yogurt	1 c	190	5
	Totals	1580	181
	Budget		225
	Saved		44
	Carry-over		180
	New Carry-over		224

Thursday — Week 2

	AMOUNT	CALORIES TOTAL	FAT
Breakfast			
English muffin	1	140	9
Jelly	1 T	50	0
Grapefruit	½	38	tr
Cocoa:			
Cocoa powder	1 t	5	tr
Sugar	2 t	30	0
Skim milk	1 c	86	4
Lunch			
Chili Non Carne	1 c	142	30
Chopped lettuce, tomatoes, onions	¼ c	10	0
French bread	1 sl	100	0
Orange	1	60	tr
Coffee or tea	1 c	tr	0
Dinner			
Sour Cherry Soup	1 c	165	0
Broiled Ginger Fish	1 sv	209	50
Hot and Garlicky Eggplant	1 sv	35	15
Baked potato	1 med	112	tr
Tossed salad	1 c	10	tr
Low-calorie French dressing	1 T	22	8
Grapefruit sections	½ c	37	tr
Coffee or tea	1 c	tr	0
Mandelbrot	1	46	18
Snack			
Frozen nonfat yogurt	1 c	160	tr
Strawberries	½ c	22	tr
	Totals	1479	134
	Budget		225
	Saved		91
	Carry-over		224
	New Carry-over		315

Friday — Week 2

	AMOUNT	CALORIES TOTAL	FAT

Breakfast

Wheatena	1 c	200	18
Margarine	½ tsp	17	17
Skim milk	1 c	86	4
Orange sections	½ c	40	tr
Coffee or tea	1 c	tr	0

Lunch

Fruit Salad with Cottage Cheese:		280	10
1% cottage cheese	½ c		
Blueberries	½ c		
Peach	1		
Cantaloupe	¼		
Honeydew melon	⅙		
Bran Muffin	2	232	46
Coffee or tea	1 c	tr	0

Dinner

Ginger-Carrot Soup	1 c	70	18
Chicken Marrakesh	1 sv	145	13
Indian Rice	¾ c	146	15
Sweet Potatoes with Oranges,			
Apples, and Sweet Wine	1 sv	123	0
Margarine	½ tsp	17	17
Coffee or tea	1 c	tr	0
Fig Newton cookie (Nabisco)	1	50	9

Snack

Bran Chex cereal	⅔ c	90	0
Skim milk	½ c	43	4

	Totals	1539	171
	Budget		225
	Saved		54
	Carry-over		315
	New Carry-over		369

Saturday — Week 2
Splurge Day

	AMOUNT	CALORIES TOTAL	FAT

Breakfast

	AMOUNT	TOTAL	FAT
Pumpernickel toast	1 sl	80	9
Orange juice	½ c	55	tr
Skim milk	1 c	86	4
Coffee or tea	1 c	tr	0
Nonfat flavored yogurt	1 c	160	0

Lunch

	AMOUNT	TOTAL	FAT
Easy Spaghetti Sauce			
à la Sicilia	1 sv	285	24
Nectarine slices	½ c	67	tr
Coffee or tea	1 c	tr	0

Dinner

	AMOUNT	TOTAL	FAT
Sirloin steak	6 oz	354	132
Baked potato	1 lg	145	tr
Sour cream	2 T	52	46
Tossed salad	1½ c	15	tr
Blue cheese dressing	2 T	154	144
Cheesecake	1 sl	280	162
Coffee or tea	1 c	tr	0

Snack

	AMOUNT	TOTAL	FAT
Pepto Bismol	2 T	tr	tr

		TOTAL	FAT
	Totals	1743	521
	Budget		225
	Saved		−296
	Carry-over		369
	New Carry-over		73

RECIPES

Soups

BARLEY-VEGETABLE SOUP

½ cup pearl barley, washed
2 quarts homemade chicken
   stock, or 3 cans (10¾ oz
   each) chicken broth,
   strained, + 3 cans water
1 small onion, cut into fourths
1 carrot, cut into thirds
1 stalk celery, cut into 1 inch
   slices

1 teaspoon thyme
1 bay leaf
Freshly ground pepper to taste
3–5 carrots, sliced
2 stalks celery, sliced
½ zucchini, sliced
½ cup onion, chopped
2 cups fresh spinach, chopped

Place barley, chicken stock, onion quarters, carrot thirds, celery slices, thyme, and bay leaf in a large soup pot and bring to a boil. Reduce heat, cover, and simmer for about 1 hour or until barley is tender.

Add sliced carrots, celery, zucchini, and chopped onion and cook until tender.

Add spinach a few minutes before serving.

Makes 9 one-cup servings
Per serving: 100 Total calories; trace Fat calories

CANTALOUPE SOUP

Cantaloupes are excellent sources of vitamins A and C and fiber as well as being just plain delicious. Combined with ginger, orange juice, and buttermilk, cantaloupe makes a refreshing and unusual summer soup.

2 cantaloupes, chilled if
    possible
¼ cup orange juice

1 teaspoon chopped ginger root
3 tablespoons sweet vermouth
½ cup buttermilk

Halve melons, discard seeds, scoop out meat, and place it in blender. Add orange juice, ginger, vermouth, and buttermilk, and blend. If cold, serve immediately. Otherwise, chill.

Makes 6 one-cup servings
Per serving: 80 Total calories; 4 Fat calories

CARROT SOUP

Carrot soup is a great spur-of-the-moment soup because it is simple to make and you probably have the ingredients on hand. It is thick and tasty — wonderful to warm the soul and body on a nippy winter day.

1 medium onion, chopped
3 small cloves garlic, minced
2 tablespoons margarine
1 teaspoon thyme
12 carrots, sliced (about 6
    cups)

2 potatoes, peeled and sliced
    (about 2 cups)
1 bay leaf
Freshly ground pepper to taste
2 cans (10¾ oz each) chicken
    broth, strained

In a soup pot or large casserole, sauté onion and garlic in margarine until soft.
Stir in thyme, carrots, potatoes, bay leaf, and pepper.
Add chicken broth and enough water to cover vegetables.
Bring soup to a boil. Reduce heat, cover, and simmer for 30 minutes.
Remove bay leaf and purée soup in blender.

Makes 11 one-cup servings
Per serving: 85 Total calories; 17 Fat calories

GINGER-CARROT SOUP

This soup can be eaten either cold or warm. The lime and ginger give it an interesting flavor.

1 tablespoon minced ginger root	2 cans (10¾ oz each) chicken broth, strained, + 1 can water
2 cloves garlic, minced	¼ cup fresh lime juice
½ cup chopped onion	(approximately)
2 tablespoons margarine	Nonfat yogurt, for garnish
5 cups sliced carrots	

In a soup pot or large casserole, sauté ginger, garlic, and onion in margarine until tender.

Stir in carrots.

Add chicken broth and water and simmer until carrots are tender (about 20 minutes).

Add lime juice and purée soup in blender until smooth.

Chill or serve warm. Top each bowl with a large dollop of yogurt.

Makes 10 one-cup servings
Per serving: 70 Total calories; 18 Fat calories

CUCUMBER SOUP

Cucumber soup gets a gold star for excellence. It is as refreshing as a dip in a cool lake on a hot day. It is simple, quick, and impressive.

2 cucumbers	1 clove garlic, crushed
2 cups nonfat yogurt	Walnuts, for garnish
1 can (10¾ oz) chicken broth, strained	

Peel cucumbers and cut into bite-size cubes. Salt heavily and set aside.

Spoon yogurt into a medium casserole and stir until smooth.

Stir in chicken broth.

Mix in garlic.

Rinse salt off cucumbers and add them to yogurt mixture.

Chill in refrigerator for several hours. Garnish with chopped walnuts.

Makes 5 one-cup servings
Per serving: 78 Total calories; 0 Fat calories
Per walnut half: 12 Total calories; 10 Fat calories

ORIENTAL NOODLE SOUP

Also a great last-minute soup. The dried Chinese noodles can be stored forever. The tofu and snow peas should be fresh.

2 cans chicken broth (10¾ oz each), strained, + 2 cans water
2 ounces cellophane noodles*
1 tablespoon soy sauce
¼ teaspoon white pepper
1 cake tofu,* cubed
1 green onion, sliced
10−15 snow peas

Bring broth and water to a boil in a soup pot. Add cellophane noodles.
Simmer about 10 minutes, until noodles are soft.
Add soy sauce and white pepper. Simmer a minute or two.
Add tofu, green onion, and snow peas and serve.

Makes 6 one-cup servings
Per serving: 64 Total calories; 8 Fat calories

SOUR CHERRY SOUP

Sour Cherry Soup is a sweet soup. It is ideal for a luncheon or dinner party and *very* simple to make. It has no fat but does have a lot of sugar.

2 cans (1 lb each) undrained sour cherries packed in water
¾ cup sugar
1 stick cinnamon
2 tablespoons unbleached white flour
6 tablespoons cold water
2 cups water

Remove about 12 cherries from one can and put aside for garnish. (Or buy another whole can of cherries.)
In a medium saucepan, cook cherries with their juice, sugar, and cinnamon stick for 10 to 15 minutes.
In a small bowl, mix flour and 3 tablespoons of the cold water until smooth. Blend in remaining 3 tablespoons cold water.
Remove cinnamon stick from cooked cherries and set aside.

---

*Available at Oriental food stores and some supermarkets.

Pour cherry mixture into blender. Add flour mixture and blend until soup is smooth.

Return soup to saucepan, add 2 cups water, and heat just to boiling.

Return cinnamon stick to soup and chill.

Garnish each bowl of soup with a few cherries before serving.

Makes 6 one-cup servings
Per serving: 165 Total calories; 0 Fat Calories

TARRAGON SQUASH SOUP

A rich, creamy soup that uses no cream. Puréed bread is the secret ingredient.

2 pounds butternut squash, peeled, seeded, and coarsely chopped

2 cloves garlic, peeled

1 teaspoon salt

2 cans (10¾ oz each) chicken broth, strained, + ½ cup water

2 slices stale bread, crusts removed

¼ teasoon freshly ground pepper

1 teaspoon dried tarragon, or

1 tablespoon fresh tarragon, chopped

In a large pot, combine squash, garlic, salt, chicken broth, and water and bring to a boil. Reduce heat and simmer until squash is tender (about 20–25 minutes).

Tear bread into small pieces and add to squash. Simmer for 3 minutes more.

Purée in blender or food processor.

Just before serving, stir in pepper and tarragon.

Makes 6 one-cup servings
Per serving: 122 Total calories; 4 Fat calories

TOMATO-RICE SOUP

If you hate wasting the juice that remains in the can after you have used only the tomatoes, this recipe will appeal to you. Each time you use canned tomatoes, accumulate their juice in a storage container in the freezer for future soups.

6 cups juice from canned
  tomatoes
1 tablespoon grated onion
1 pinch ground cloves

½ cup long-grain rice
1 cup frozen peas
1 cup frozen corn

Combine tomato juice, onion, cloves, and rice and bring to a boil. Reduce heat and simmer for about 25 minutes.

Add peas and corn and cook about 5 minutes more.

Makes 8 one-cup servings
Per serving: 93 Total calories; 0 Fat calories

TORTILLA SOUP

This is an instantaneous soup that always gets rave reviews.

6 corn tortillas*
1 medium onion, diced
3 cloves garlic, minced
1 tablespoon olive oil
2 tablespoons chili powder
1 teaspoon oregano
1 large can (28 oz) heavy
  concentrated crushed
  tomatoes

1 can (10¾ oz) chicken broth,
  strained, + 1 can water
1 green pepper, diced
1 cup frozen corn
Salt and pepper to taste

About 15 minutes before you serve soup, heat tortillas in a slow oven (325°F), until crisp.

In a soup pot, sauté onion and garlic in oil until soft.

Stir in chili powder and oregano.

Stir in tomatoes, chicken broth, and water.

---

*Corn tortillas can be found in the refrigerator section of most supermarkets. Be sure they contain no lard or other saturated fat.

Bring to a boil and simmer for a few minutes.

Add green pepper and corn.

Add salt and pepper to taste.

For each serving, break a tortilla into small pieces and place at the bottom of a soup bowl. Ladle soup over the tortilla and serve.

Makes 7 one-cup servings
Per serving: 155 Total calories; 36 Fat calories

VEGETABLE SOUP WITH SPINACH, POTATOES, RICE, AND CORN

2 cloves garlic, minced
1 tablespoon olive oil
5 ounces fresh spinach, torn
  into bite-size pieces
1 can chicken broth (10¾ oz),
  strained, + 2 cans water

½ teaspoon salt, optional
2 small potatoes, peeled and
  cubed
¼ cup long-grain rice
1 cup frozen corn

In soup pot, sauté garlic in oil until soft.

Stir in spinach and cook for about 1 minute.

Add broth, water, salt, potatoes, and rice, and bring to a boil.

Reduce to a simmer and cook for about 15 minutes or until potatoes are tender and rice is cooked.

Add corn and cook for about 1 minute.

Makes 5 one-cup servings
Per serving: 145 Total calories; 29 Fat calories

ZUCCHINI SOUP

One of the greatest recipes known to mankind. Hot or cold, summer or winter, for family or company, zucchini soup is delicious — and easy. You can even prepare it 20 minutes before you eat. If you want to make more and freeze it, just add a few more zucchini and more broth. This recipe is very flexible. Add more or less of any ingredient, and it will still taste superb.

3 large or 4 medium zucchini (or more or less), sliced
½ cup chopped onion
¼ cup long-grain rice
Chicken stock to cover zucchini, or 2 cans (10¾ oz each) chicken broth, strained, + water to cover zucchini

1 teaspoon salt
1 teaspoon curry powder (approximately)
1 teaspoon Dijon mustard (approximately)
½–1 cup nonfat yogurt

In a large soup pot, combine zucchini, onion, rice, chicken stock, water, and salt (add more water, if necessary, to cover zucchini).

Simmer for 15 minutes or until zucchini are tender.

Purée in blender, adding curry powder, mustard, and yogurt to taste. Eat warm or cool.

This soup freezes well. Reheat frozen soup for best results. Eat immediately or cool for later.

Makes 8 (approximately) one-cup servings
Per serving: 80 Total calories; 2 Fat calories

Poultry

APRICOT CHICKEN DIVINE

One-half cup of nonfat yogurt (0 fat calories, 55 total calories) replaces ½ cup of sour cream (217 fat calories, 247 total calories) to create this divine chicken.

1 tablespoon olive oil	⅓–½ cup apricot preserves
8 skinned chicken breast halves	1 tablespoon Dijon mustard
½ cup unbleached white flour	½ cup nonfat yogurt
1 teaspoon salt	2 tablespoons slivered almonds

Preheat oven to 375°F.

Cover bottom of a shallow baking pan with olive oil.

Meanwhile, shake chicken in a plastic bag filled with flour and salt until chicken is coated.

Place chicken in a single layer in the baking pan and bake for 25 minutes.

Combine apricot preserves, mustard, and yogurt.

Spread apricot mixture on chicken and bake for 30 minutes more or until done.

Just before serving, brown almonds lightly in toaster oven.

Sprinkle almonds over chicken and serve over rice.

Serves 8
Per serving: 243 Total calories; 39 Fat calories

CAJUN CHICKEN

1 tablespoon olive oil
8 boned and skinned chicken
  breast halves

½ cup unbleached white flour
½ teaspoon salt, optional

Seasoning Mix (Use more or less of the peppers for a hotter or milder taste.)

¾ teaspoon oregano
½ teaspoon thyme
½ teaspoon basil
½ teaspoon salt
½ teaspoon paprika

¼ teaspoon freshly ground black
  pepper
½ teaspoon cayenne pepper
¼ teaspoon white pepper

3 cloves garlic, minced
¾ cup chopped onion
2 stalks celery, diced
½ cup chopped green pepper
1 tomato, coarsely chopped
2 tablespoons olive oil

1 can (10¾ oz) chicken broth,
  strained
1 small can (8 oz) tomato sauce
1 potato, peeled and diced
2 bay leaves

Preheat oven to 350°F.

Cover bottom of a shallow baking pan with olive oil.

Shake chicken in a plastic bag filled with flour and salt until chicken is coated.

Place chicken in a single layer in baking pan and bake for 25 to 30 minutes until almost cooked through.

While chicken is baking, combine oregano, thyme, basil, salt, paprika, and peppers, and set aside.

In a large frying pan, sauté garlic, onion, celery, green pepper, and tomato in oil until soft.

Mix in seasoning mixture and let simmer for about a minute.

Mix in broth and tomato sauce. Bring to a boil, then simmer for 5 minutes.

Lower heat and add chicken breasts, potato, and bay leaves. Cook until potatoes are soft and chicken is done.

NOTE: If you find the finished dish too "hot" for your taste, dilute with an additional can of tomato sauce.

Serves 8
Per serving: 244 Total calories; 58 Fat calories

INDONESIAN CHICKEN WITH GREEN BEANS

A beautiful dish — green beans set against ochre-colored sauce — and very tasty. This is one of our all-time favorites.

1 pound green beans, washed and cut into bite-size pieces	1 small onion, chopped
6 boned and skinned chicken breast halves, cut into bite-size pieces	Juice of 1 lime (preferred) or lemon
	1 tablespoon double black soy sauce*
3 tablespoons olive oil	2 teaspoons brown sugar
10 cloves garlic, minced	2 teaspoons turmeric
1 tablespoon minced ginger root	1 teaspoon salt
	½ cup water

In a vegetable steamer or wok, steam green beans until tender but not overcooked. Set aside.

Sauté chicken in 2 tablespoons of the olive oil until chicken turns white and is cooked through. Set aside.

Heat the remaining 1 tablespoon of olive oil and sauté garlic, ginger, and onion until soft.

Stir in green beans.

Add lime juice, soy sauce, brown sugar, turmeric, salt, and ¼ cup of the water.

Slowly add remaining water, if necessary, but sauce should not be watery.

Add chicken pieces and stir until completely covered with sauce.

Serve over rice.

Serves 8
Per serving: 185 Total calories; 54 Fat calories

LEMON CHICKEN

A delicate blending of tart and sweet, Lemon Chicken can't help but become one of your most popular family or company dishes.

---

*Double black soy sauce is available at Oriental food stores and some supermarkets. You can make your own by mixing 2 teaspoons soy sauce with 1 teaspoon dark molasses.

8 boned and skinned chicken
  breast halves
Juice of 2½ lemons
1 tablespoon olive oil
1 cup unbleached white flour
1 teaspoon salt
½ teaspoon paprika

¼ teaspoon freshly ground
  pepper
2 tablespoons grated lemon peel
¼ cup brown sugar
2 tablespoons fresh lemon juice
  + 2 tablespoons water
1–2 lemons, sliced thin

Place chicken in a bowl or casserole. Cover with lemon juice and marinate in refrigerator for several hours or overnight, turning chicken periodically.

Preheat oven to 350°F.

Cover bottom of a shallow baking pan with olive oil.

Meanwhile, combine flour, salt, paprika, and pepper in plastic bag.

Remove chicken breasts from marinade and coat each with flour by shaking it in the plastic bag.

Place chicken in the baking pan in a single layer.

Either peel the yellow (zest) from two lemons and chop it fine with the brown sugar in a food processor, or grate the zest and mix it with the brown sugar.

Sprinkle the lemon zest–sugar mixture evenly over the chicken breasts. Combine lemon juice and water and sprinkle evenly over chicken.

Put 1 lemon slice on each chicken breast and bake chicken for 35 to 40 minutes or until it is cooked through.

Serves 8
Per serving: 200 Total calories; 29 Fat calories

BAR-B-QUE CHICKEN

1 tablespoon Dijon mustard
2 tablespoons vinegar
2 tablespoons molasses
¼ cup ketchup
½ teaspoon Worcestershire
  sauce

1 clove garlic, minced
Dash of Tabasco sauce
8 skinned chicken breast halves
  or thighs*

---

*For a barbecue, you may want greater quantities of chicken. Just double, triple, quadruple, etc., the recipe.

In a large bowl, mix together Dijon mustard, vinegar, molasses, ketchup, Worcestershire sauce, garlic, and Tabasco for marinade.

Marinate chicken for an hour (or less, if you haven't planned ahead).

Remove chicken and reserve remaining marinade.

Barbecue or broil chicken for 10 minutes.

Turn and coat chicken with marinade and continue cooking until done.

Heat reserved marinade to boiling, simmer for 2 minutes, and spoon over chicken before serving.

Serves 8

	Total calories	Fat calories
1 breast	165	13
1 thigh	150	24

CHICKEN MARRAKESH

8 boned and skinned chicken breast halves

⅓ cup fresh lemon juice

2 tablespoons grated lemon peel

1 clove garlic, minced

1–2 tablespoons thyme

1 teaspoon salt

1 teaspoon freshly ground pepper

2 lemons, thinly sliced (optional)

Place chicken in a bowl or casserole.

Mix together lemon juice, lemon peel, garlic, thyme, salt, and pepper and pour over chicken. Marinate chicken in refrigerator for at least 3 hours.

Preheat oven to 350°F.

Remove chicken from marinade and place in shallow baking dish.

Pour marinade over chicken and bake chicken for 30 to 45 minutes or until cooked through.

Garnish with lemon slices.

Serves 8
Per serving: 145 Total calories; 13 Fat calories

CHICKEN WITH RICE, TOMATOES, AND ARTICHOKES

4 boned and skinned chicken
  breast halves
2 cloves garlic, minced
½ cup chopped onion
2 tablespoons olive oil
1 large can (28 oz) tomatoes,
  chopped
2 cups water

½ teaspoon thyme
½ teaspoon oregano
1 teaspoon salt
¼ teaspoon freshly ground
  pepper
1 bay leaf
2 cups uncooked long-grain rice
1 jar (11½ oz) artichoke hearts,
  packed in water

Cut chicken into bite-size pieces and set aside.

In a large casserole, sauté garlic and onion in olive oil until soft.

Stir in tomatoes and their liquid, water, thyme, oregano, salt, pepper, and bay leaf and bring to a boil.

Add chicken and rice, cover casserole, and reduce heat to low.

Cook for 25 minutes or until rice is tender, most liquid is absorbed, and chicken is cooked through.

Stir in artichokes and serve.

Serves 8
Per serving: 320 Total calories; 39 Fat calories

TURKEY MEXIQUE

A great dish with a chili taste.

1 cup chopped onion
2 teaspoons minced garlic
1½ tablespoons olive oil
1–2 tablespoons chili powder
1 tablespoon cumin seed
½ teaspoon salt
1 tablespoon unbleached white
  flour

1½ cups chicken broth, strained
3 tablespoons tomato paste
3 cups diced cooked turkey breast
1 green pepper, diced
¼ cup stuffed green olives, sliced

In a large skillet, sauté onion and garlic in olive oil until soft.

Stir in chili powder, cumin seed, salt, and flour.

Add chicken broth and tomato paste and blend well.
Cook for 5 minutes over low heat.
Stir in turkey, green pepper, and olives and heat through.
Serve over rice.

Serves 6
Per serving: 170 Total calories; 40 Fat calories

Fish and Shellfish

BROILED GINGER FISH

1 cup flour
1 teaspoon salt
½ teaspoon freshly ground
  pepper
4 six-ounce fish fillets
  (monkfish, haddock, etc.)

4 teaspoons margarine
4 teaspoons diced ginger root
Lemon slices to cover fillets

Set oven to broil and grease broiler pan with oil.
Combine flour, salt, and pepper on a large plate.
Dredge fillets in flour, covering both sides.
Dot fillets with margarine, sprinkle them with ginger, and cover with lemon slices.
Broil for 5 to 15 minutes or until fish flakes easily.

Serves 4
Per serving: 209 Total calories; 50 Fat calories

FISH BAKED IN OLIVE, CHILI PEPPER, AND TOMATO SAUCE

¾ cup chopped onion
2 cloves garlic, minced
1 tablespoon olive oil
1 tablespoon cornstarch
1 can (16 oz) tomatoes,
  chopped, juice reserved
⅓ cup sliced stuffed green
  olives

1 teaspoon chopped red or green
  chili pepper
1½ pounds flounder fillets (or
  other mild fish)
Salt to taste
1 tablespoon fresh lemon juice

Preheat oven to 375°F.

In a medium skillet, sauté onion and garlic in olive oil until soft.

Mix in cornstarch.

Add tomatoes and their juice and mix until well blended.

Cook over medium-high heat until sauce thickens.

Stir in olives and chili pepper.

Spoon half the sauce into a baking pan large enough to hold the fillets in one layer. Place fillets over sauce.

Salt fillets and sprinkle them with lemon juice.

Cover fillets with remaining sauce and bake for 10 minutes or until they flake easily.

Serves 6
Per serving: 163 Total calories; 34 Fat calories

SCALLOP OR SHRIMP CREOLE

2 green peppers, chopped
1 cup chopped onion
2 cloves garlic, minced
1½ tablespoons olive oil
1 teaspoon brown sugar
¼ teaspoon freshly ground
  pepper
½ teaspoon thyme
¼ teaspoon cayenne pepper
1 bay leaf

½ teaspoon salt
2 large cans (28 oz each)
  tomatoes, drained, juiced, and
  chopped
½ cup sliced celery
1½ cups sliced mushrooms
3 tablespoons chopped parsley
1 pound bay scallops or shrimp,
  shelled and deveined

Sauté green peppers, onion, and garlic in olive oil until soft.

Add brown sugar, pepper, thyme, cayenne pepper, bay leaf, and salt and stir well.

Stir in tomatoes and cook over low heat for 30 minutes or until sauce is thick.

Add celery and mushrooms and cook for a few minutes more.

Mix in parsley and scallops or shrimp and cook for 5 to 10 minutes or until shellfish is cooked through.

Serve immediately so shellfish will not overcook.

Serve over rice.

Serves 6
Per serving: 199 Total calories
                          Fat calories
   with shrimp   45
   with scallops   35

SCALLOP OR SHRIMP CURRY

Delight your guests or family with this unusual curry. The apples and lime create a unique combination of sweet and sour tastes.

1 cup chopped onion
1 apple, peeled, cored, and
  chopped
2 cloves garlic, minced
1 tablespoon curry powder
2 tablespoons margarine
¼ cup unbleached white flour
½ teaspoon salt
¼ teaspoon cardamom

¼ teaspoon freshly ground
  pepper
1 can (10¾ oz) chicken broth,
  strained
1 tablespoon fresh lime juice
1¼ pounds bay scallops or
  shrimp, shelled and deveined
1 cup sliced mushrooms
10–15 snow peas (optional)

In a large skillet, sauté onion, apple, garlic, and curry powder in margarine until tender.

Remove skillet from heat and blend in flour, salt, cardamom, and pepper.

Stir in chicken broth and lime juice until curry sauce is well blended.

Bring curry sauce to a boil, reduce heat, and simmer, uncovered, for about 5 minutes. Stir occasionally.

Meanwhile, place scallops or shrimp in a pot of boiling water and cook until just tender (5–10 minutes). Drain and set aside.

When curry sauce is finished cooking, add shellfish and mushrooms and serve over rice.

Serves 6
Per serving: 197 Total calories
                          Fat calories
   with shrimp   46
   with scallops   35

Vegetables

INDIAN VEGETABLES

This recipe makes a large pot of colorful, tasty vegetables, which may be eaten warm or cold. Try it as a main dish served over rice.

2 tablespoons olive oil
1 teaspoon black mustard
 seeds*
3 cloves garlic, chopped
1 medium onion, chopped
1 green pepper, chopped
2–3 potatoes, peeled and
 cubed
1 small eggplant, peeled and
 cubed
1½ teaspoons turmeric
1 teaspoon salt
¼ cup water
1 teaspoon cumin
1 teaspoon coriander

1 teaspoon garam masala*
Any vegetables, for example:
 1 head broccoli, cut into
  flowerets (about 3 cups)
 1 cup or more cauliflower
  flowerets
 6 carrots, sliced
 1 cup or more green beans, cut
  in half
 1 cup sliced celery
 1 zucchini, sliced
1 cup water

In a large pot, heat olive oil and add black mustard seeds.

When the mustard seeds begin to pop, add garlic, onion, and green pepper and cook until soft.

Stir in potatoes and eggplant.

Add turmeric and salt and mix until vegetables are covered with turmeric sauce.

---

*Available at Indian or Oriental food stores

163

Add ¼ cup water, reduce heat to low, cover the pot, and cook for 10 minutes.

Stir in cumin, coriander, garam marsala, and vegetables.

Add 1 cup water and increase heat to medium.

After 10 minutes, lower heat and cook until vegetables are tender.

Serves 12
Per serving: 96 Total calories; 20 Fat calories

HOT AND GARLICKY EGGPLANT

1 medium eggplant (about 1 pound)
5 small, dried black Chinese mushrooms*
1 tablespoon chili paste with garlic*
1 tablespoon vinegar
½ tablespoon soy sauce
½ tablespoon double black soy sauce*
2 tablespoons dry sherry
½ teaspoon sugar
1 large green pepper, chopped
1 tablespoon olive oil
½ cup water

Slice eggplant into bite-size pieces. Salt generously and set aside for about 20 minutes.

Meanwhile, place mushrooms in a small bowl and cover them with boiling water.

After about 15 minutes, remove mushrooms. Squeeze out the excess water and discard stems. Slice mushrooms and set aside.

Wash off the salt and bitter juices of the eggplant. In a vegetable steamer, cook eggplant until soft. Set aside.

Combine chili paste with garlic, vinegar, soy sauces, sherry, and sugar and set aside.

In a large skillet, sauté green pepper and mushrooms in oil until tender.

Stir in eggplant.

Mix in soy sauce mixture until vegetables are covered and then stir in water.

Simmer for about 5 minutes.

Makes 8 half-cup servings
Per serving: 35 Total calories; 15 Fat calories

---

*Available at Oriental food stores

POTATO SKINS

Leslie Goodman-Malamuth of the Center for Science in the Public Interest devised this recipe as a substitute for the high-fat potato skins you often find in restaurants. Not only is this recipe quick and easy, the resulting potatoes are scrumptious.

4 large potatoes
1 tablespoon* olive oil

Paprika to taste

Preheat oven to 450°F.
Scrub potatoes well, cut them lengthwise into six wedges the size and shape of dill pickle spears, and dry them on a paper towel.
In a large bowl, toss potato spears with olive oil until they are well covered.
Spread potatoes on a baking sheet, dust them with paprika, and bake for 20 to 30 minutes or until fork-tender.

Serves 6 (So good, 2 people can easily finish them off!)
Per serving: 79 Total calories; 20 Fat calories

SWEET POTATOES WITH ORANGES, APPLES, AND SWEET WINE

8 cups sweet potatoes cut into
  ½-inch slices
1 cup diced apple
1 orange, cut into bite-size
  pieces

2 tablespoons fresh lemon juice
1 tablespoon brown sugar
½ cup plum wine or other sweet
  wine
5 whole cloves

Preheat oven to 375°F.
Place sweet potato slices in a saucepan with water to cover. Bring to a boil. Reduce heat, cover, and simmer until just tender.
Drain sweet potatoes and place in a casserole.
Mix apple, orange, lemon juice, brown sugar, wine, and cloves.
Pour mixture over sweet potatoes.
Bake, covered, for 30 minutes or until apples are tender.

Serves 12
Per serving: 123 Total calories; 0 Fat calories

---

*Reduce to 1 teaspoon to decrease fat calories to 7 per serving.

STEAMED ZUCCHINI MATCHSTICKS

So light, so tasty — you don't even need to add salt, spices, or fat. But you may want to crush garlic into one teaspoon of melted margarine and combine it with the vegetables.

2 small zucchini (or ½ small zucchini per person)	1 thick carrot, peeled 1 teaspoon margarine (optional) 1 clove garlic (optional)

Cut zucchini and carrot into 2-inch lengths.

Place a zucchini section on a cutting surface, skin-side down.

Holding the sides of the section, slice lengthwise at ⅛-inch intervals. Hold the slices together.

Roll the section one-quarter turn, making sure the slices stay together.

Again, make parallel slices, ⅛ inch apart lengthwise.

Result: zucchini matchsticks.

Repeat for remaining sections of zucchini and carrot.

Place zucchini sticks on top of carrot sticks in a vegetable steamer and steam until just tender (about 1 or 2 minutes).

Serves 4

	Total calories	Fat calories
Per serving	17	0
with margarine	24	7

Pizza, Chili, Pasta, and Rice

FOCACCIA

The whole-wheat flour in this pizza not only makes it healthier but also gives it a toasty taste and crunchy texture. Try it! It is easy and makes great snacks. Freeze it in snack-size slices.

Dough

1½ teaspoons dry active yeast	2½ cups whole-wheat flour
½ teaspoon honey	¾ teaspoon salt
1 cup warm water	1 tablespoon olive oil

Tomato Sauce

1 large can (28 oz) tomatoes, or 3 large tomatoes	½ teaspoon oregano
2 cloves garlic, minced	¼ teaspoon basil
1 small onion, chopped	Ground hot cherry peppers (optional)
1 tablespoon olive oil	

The Dough

Place yeast, honey, and warm water in food processor or large bowl. Let proof.

Add flour, salt, and olive oil and process or knead until smooth and elastic, adding flour if needed.

Place dough in an oiled bowl, cover with a towel, and let rise in a warm place for about 1 hour.

Punch down dough and let it rest on floured counter for 10 minutes.

Preheat oven to 400°F and grease a 10 × 15–inch cookie sheet with oil.

Roll dough out (or press with your hands) onto the cookie sheet.

Pinch a rim around the edge. Cover with a towel and let rise for 30 minutes.

Meanwhile, make the tomato sauce.

The Tomato Sauce

If using canned tomatoes, drain liquid and chop tomatoes. If using whole tomatoes, chop fine.

In a medium skillet, sauté garlic and onion in olive oil until tender.

Stir in tomatoes, oregano, and basil and let simmer until thick (about 10–15 minutes).

Let cool.

Spread the sauce over the dough.

Add hot cherry peppers, if desired.

Bake for 20 to 25 minutes.

Makes 12 pieces
Per piece: 120 Total calories; 24 Fat calories

ASPARAGUS PASTA

Asparagus pasta makes a delightful luncheon dish, first course for an elegant meal, or light dinner. No one consuming this dish will believe how incredibly simple it is to make.

1–2 pounds aparagus, sliced on the diagonal into 1-inch pieces	4 anchovy fillets, chopped
¼ cup Dijon mustard	½ teaspoon thyme
2 tablespoons olive oil	¼ cup chopped parsley
½ cup thinly sliced shallots	1 pound very thin spaghetti or pasta of your choice
2 cloves garlic, minced	Salt and pepper to taste

In a large pot of boiling water, cook asparagus until tender and still bright green (about 3 minutes).

Combine mustard, olive oil, shallots, garlic, anchovies, thyme, and parsley. Set aside.

Cook pasta. Drain, but reserve 1 cup of the cooking water.

Combine pasta with dressing and asparagus and mix well. Add some of the cooking water if too dry. Add salt and pepper to taste.

Serves 8
Per serving: 250 Total calories; 38 Fat calories

Variation: Follow the above recipe but halve all ingredients and add two boned and skinned chicken breast halves that have been steamed and cut into bite-size pieces.

Serves 4
Per serving: 287 Total calories; 52 Fat calories

CHILI NON CARNE

This is one of the best chili recipes we have ever tasted. It is filled with nutritious vegetables that provide texture but do not interfere with the delicious chili taste. Eat it hot in a bowl mixed with chopped onion, tomatoes, and lettuce, or spoon it into pita bread with chopped onion, lettuce, and tomatoes. Dried beans such as kidney beans and navy beans have been shown to be effective in lowering blood cholesterol.

¾ cup chopped onion
2 cloves garlic, minced
2 tablespoons olive oil
2 tablespoons chili powder
¼ teaspoon basil
¼ teaspoon oregano
¼ teaspoon cumin
2 cups finely chopped zucchini
1 cup finely chopped carrot
1 large can (28 oz) tomatoes
+ 1 small can (14½ oz)
    tomatoes, drained and
    chopped

1 can (15 oz) kidney beans,
    undrained
2 cans (15 oz each) kidney beans,
    drained and thoroughly rinsed
Chopped onions, tomatoes,
    lettuce, or green peppers, for
    garnish

In a large pot, sauté onion and garlic in olive oil until soft.
Mix in chili powder, basil, oregano, and cumin.
Stir in zucchini and carrots until well blended. Cook for about 1 minute over low heat, stirring occasionally.

Stir in chopped tomatoes, undrained kidney beans, and drained kidney beans.

Bring to a boil. Reduce heat and simmer for 30 to 45 minutes or until thick.

Top with chopped onions, tomatoes, and lettuce or green peppers.

Makes 8 one-cup servings
Per serving: 142 Total calories; 30 Fat calories

EASY SPAGHETTI SAUCE À LA SICILIA

Make a basic tomato sauce and add steamed eggplant and mushrooms for an appetizing spaghetti sauce that needs no ground meat.

1 small eggplant, peeled and cubed	2 cups sliced mushrooms
6 cups Basic Tomato Sauce (see below)	12 ounces spaghetti

Prepare eggplant and steam until tender. Set aside.

In a medium saucepan, heat 6 cups of tomato sauce.

Stir in eggplant and mushrooms, cook 5 minutes more.

While spaghetti sauce is cooking, prepare spaghetti according to package directions.

Pour tomato sauce over spaghetti and serve.

Serves 6
Per serving: 285 Total calories; 24 Fat calories

Basic Tomato Sauce

1 cup chopped onion	1 can (6 oz) tomato paste
1 tablespoon olive oil	2 teaspoons basil
4 large cans (28 oz each) tomatoes, drained	1 teaspoon salt

In a large saucepan, cook onion in olive oil until soft.

Chop tomatoes and stir in tomato paste. (Tomatoes can easily be chopped and tomato paste blended in a food processor.)

Add to onions.

Stir in basil and salt.
Simmer until thick (at least 1 hour).
This tomato sauce freezes well.

Makes 8 cups
Per cup: 74 Total calories; 15 Fat calories

INDIAN RICE

1 tablespoon olive oil
2 cloves garlic, minced
1 tablespoon minced ginger
  root
¾ cup chopped onion
¼ teaspoon cardamom
¼ teaspoon caraway seeds

1 teaspoon coriander
¼ teaspoon cinnamon
¼ teaspoon ground cloves
¼ teaspoon salt
1½ cups long-grain rice
3¾ cups water

In a medium saucepan, heat olive oil.
Add garlic, ginger, and onion and cook until soft.
Mix in cardamom, caraway seeds, coriander, cinnamon, cloves, salt, and rice and blend well.
Add water, cover, and bring to a boil. Reduce heat and cook until all water is absorbed (about 25 minutes).

Makes 12 half-cup servings
Per serving: 97 Total calories; 10 Fat calories

Salads

DIJON CHICKEN-RICE SALAD

3¾ cups water
1½ cups long-grain rice
½ teaspoon salt
2 tablespoons Dijon mustard
2 tablespoons white vinegar
2 tablespoons olive oil

½–1 cup diced green and/or red
   pepper
¼ cup pitted black olives, sliced
¼ cup sliced green onion
2 cooked chicken breast halves,
   diced

In a medium saucepan, bring water to a boil.

Add rice and salt, reduce heat, cover, and simmer for 20 to 25 minutes or until water is absorbed.

Place rice in a bowl.

Combine mustard, vinegar, and olive oil and mix into rice.

Add green pepper, olives, green onion, and chicken and mix well.

Tastes best when tepid.

Serves 6
Per serving: 265 Total calories; 51 Fat calories

CUCUMBER SALAD

2 cucumbers, peeled and sliced
   thin
1 medium onion, sliced thin
1 teaspoon salt

1 teaspoon sugar
1 teaspoon dill weed
1 cup white vinegar

Mix cucumbers and onion together in a ceramic or glass bowl.
Add salt, sugar, and dill weed to vinegar and pour over cucumbers
and onion.
Chill 1 hour.

Serves 6
Per serving: 20 Total calories; 0 Fat calories

FRUIT SALAD WITH COTTAGE CHEESE OR YOGURT

This high-protein, low-fat dish makes a filling lunch. Round it off
with a piece of Anadama Bread (page 177) and, for dessert, home-
popped popcorn.

Spring or Summer Fruits

¼ cantaloupe   1 peach
½ cup blueberries   ⅙ honeydew melon

Fall or Winter Fruits

½ Golden Delicious apple   ½ Bosc pear
1 kiwi   ½ orange

½ cup low-fat (1%) cottage
   cheese or nonfat yogurt

Cut fruit into bite-size pieces and place in bowl.
Mix in cottage cheese or yogurt.

Serves 1

	Total calories	Fat calories
Spring or summer salad:		
with cottage cheese	280	10
with nonfat yogurt	250	0
Fall or winter salad:		
with cottage cheese	270	10
with nonfat yogurt	245	0

POTATO SALAD

4–5 Russet (red) potatoes
½ cup nonfat yogurt
3 tablespoons reduced-
   calorie mayonnaise

1 teaspoon tarragon
1 tablespoon white vinegar
1 teaspoon Dijon mustard
½ teaspoon salt

Scrub potatoes thoroughly. Steam until tender.
Meanwhile, combine remaining ingredients. Set aside.
Cut potatoes into chunks (do not remove skin).
Pour sauce over potatoes so they are thoroughly coated.
Serve warm or cold.

Serves 6
Per serving: 105 Total calories; 22 Fat calories

CURRIED TUNA SALAD WITH PEARS

3 tablespoons reduced-calorie
   mayonnaise
1½ tablespoons nonfat yogurt
¾–1 teaspoon curry powder

2 cans (6½ oz each) water-
   packed tuna, drained
3 tablespoons diced pear
Lettuce

Combine mayonnaise, yogurt, and curry powder.
Mix into tuna fish.
Stir in pear.
Serve over lettuce.

Serves 3
Per serving: 220 Total calories; 49 Fat calories

Dips

CHICKPEA SANDWICH OR DIP

1 can chickpeas
2 cloves garlic
⅓ cup parsley
1 tablespoon tahini (sesame
  seed paste)*
Juice of 1 lemon (about ¼
  cup)

4 six-inch whole-wheat pita
  bread pockets
Chopped tomatoes, green onions,
  and lettuce, for garnish

Drain chickpeas. Reserve liquid. In blender or food processor, chop garlic and parsley.

Add chickpeas, tahini, and lemon juice.

Blend until smooth, adding more chickpea liquid if spread is too stiff.

Make sandwiches by spooning chickpea spread into pita bread pockets.

Garnish with chopped tomatoes, green onions, and lettuce.

Makes 4 sandwiches

Use as a dip for vegetables, crackers, squares of pita, etc.

Makes about 1½ cups

	Total calories	Fat calories
Per sandwich	195	39
Per tablespoon	20	5

---

*Available at Mideast food shops and many supermarkets

BABA GHANOUSH

1 medium eggplant	1–2 cloves garlic
¼ cup or more fresh lemon	¼ cup chopped parsley
juice	Salt to taste
3 tablespoons tahini (sesame	
seed paste)	

Peel eggplant, cut into bite-size pieces, and salt heavily. Set aside for 15 minutes. Rinse and squeeze eggplant and steam in vegetable steamer until soft.

Purée eggplant in food processor or blender.

Blend in lemon juice and tahini.

Just before you serve, crush garlic into purée and mix in parsley and salt.

Taste. Add more lemon juice if you wish.

Serve with whole-wheat or plain pita bread cut into pieces.

Makes about 2 cups
Per tablespoon: 12 Total calories; 7 Fat calories

Breads, Muffins, and Waffles

ANADAMA BREAD

This version of the New England bread has whole-wheat flour added to it to make it healthier while retaining its wonderful taste and texture.

1 tablespoon active dry yeast
Pinch of sugar
¼ cup warm water
¾ cup corn meal
1 ½ cups whole-wheat flour
1 ½ cups unbleached white
    flour (approximately)

1–1 ½ teaspoons salt
2 tablespoons olive oil
1 cup water
3 tablespoons molasses

Dissolve yeast with pinch of sugar in ¼ cup warm water in a large bowl or a food processor. Let proof.

Mix in corn meal, whole-wheat flour, 1 cup of the white flour, and salt.

Stir in olive oil, 1 cup warm water, and molasses.

Knead dough 10 minutes or process 15 seconds or until dough is smooth and elastic, adding more white flour if necessary.

Place dough in a large oiled bowl, cover with a towel, and let rise in a warm place for 1 hour or until doubled in bulk.

Form into a loaf and place in a loaf pan greased with margarine. Cover and let rise for 1 hour or until doubled in bulk.

Preheat oven to 400°F.

Bake loaf for 15 minutes.

Reduce heat to 350°F and bake about 30 minutes more or until loaf is golden brown and sounds hollow when tapped.

Makes 1 loaf

	Total calories	Fat calories
Per ½-inch slice	110	15
Per loaf	1861	257

CARDAMOM BREAD

1 tablespoon active dry yeast	1 teaspoon salt
2 tablespoons brown sugar	¼–½ teaspoon cardamom*
¼ cup warm water	2 tablespoons olive oil
2–4 cups unbleached white flour	1 cup skim milk

Combine yeast, brown sugar, and water in a large bowl or a food processor. Let proof.

Add 2 cups flour, salt, and cardamom and mix.

Add skim milk and olive oil and mix.

Knead dough 10 minutes or process 15 seconds or until dough is smooth and elastic, adding more flour if necessary.

Place dough in a large oiled bowl, cover with a towel, and let rise in warm place for 1 hour or until doubled in bulk.

Roll into loaf and place in loaf pan greased with margarine.

Cover with a towel and let rise for 1 hour or until doubled in bulk.

Preheat oven to 425°F.

Bake loaves for 10 minutes.

Reduce heat to 350°F and bake for 30 minutes more or until loaves are golden brown and sound hollow when tapped.

Makes 1 loaf

	Total calories	Fat calories
Per ½-inch slice	95	15
Per loaf	1605	255

---

*For a totally different taste, substitute 1 teaspoon cinnamon.

ONION FLAT BREAD

1 tablespoon active dry yeast	1 teaspoon + a few shakes salt
1 pinch sugar	1 teaspoon margarine
1 cup warm water	1 cup chopped onions
2½–3 cups unbleached white flour*	1 teaspoon paprika

Place yeast, sugar, and water in a large bowl or a food processor. Let proof.

Mix in 2 cups flour and salt. Knead for 10 minutes or process for 15 seconds, until smooth and elastic, adding flour if necessary.

Place dough in an oiled bowl, cover with a towel, and let rise in a warm place for an hour or until doubled in bulk.

Punch dough down and split in half. Let rest for 5 minutes.

Meanwhile, grease two 9-inch cake pans with margarine.

Melt the teaspoon of margarine.

Press dough into cake pans.

Spread margarine over the tops and press onion into the surface.

Let rise about 45 minutes or until doubled in bulk.

Preheat oven to 450°F.

Sprinkle tops with paprika and a few shakes of salt.

Bake 20–25 minutes, until lightly browned.

Makes 2 loaves, 8 slices per loaf
Per loaf: 667 Total calories; 56 Fat calories
Per slice: 83 Total calories; 7 Fat calories

SESAME BREADSTICKS

Beware! These breadsticks are habit-forming.

1 teaspoon active dry yeast	⅔ cup nonfat skim milk
¼ cup warm water	1 tablespoon olive oil
⅔ cup whole-wheat flour	1 egg white
2 or more cups unbleached white flour	2 teaspoons water
1 teaspoon salt, optional	1 tablespoon sesame seeds

*For a slightly different taste, use 1 cup of whole-wheat flour, along with 1½–2 cups unbleached white flour.

Place yeast and warm water in a large bowl or a food processor. Let proof.

Mix in flours and salt.

Add milk and olive oil, and knead for 10 minutes or process until dough is smooth and elastic, adding more flour if necessary.

Place dough in a bowl, cover with a towel, and let rise 1 hour.

Preheat oven to 400°F.

On a lightly floured surface, roll the dough into a quarter-inch-thick rectangle.

Cut the dough into half-inch strips. (If you prefer thicker breadsticks, cut the dough into one-inch strips.)

Roll each strip in your palms to make a breadstick and lay it on an ungreased baking sheet. Place the sticks about a half inch apart.

Beat the egg white and water together and brush onto breadsticks.

Sprinkle sesame seeds evenly over breadsticks.

Count the breadsticks so you can calculate their fat calories.

Bake for 20 to 30 minutes or until golden brown. Cool on a rack.

Makes about 35 six-inch sticks
To determine the total calories and fat calories for each breadstick, divide the number of breadsticks into the following numbers:
Total calories: 1343   Fat calories: 196
For example, 196 fat calories divided by 35 breadsticks = 6 fat calories each.

BRAN MUFFINS

Wheat bran, made from the outer coverings of wheat kernels, is rich in vitamins, minerals, and insoluble dietary fiber. Insoluble dietary fiber promotes regularity and is believed to protect against colon cancer.

1 cup whole-wheat flour	1 cup buttermilk
1 cup wheat bran	1 egg, beaten
3 tablespoons brown sugar	3 tablespoons molasses
¼ teaspoon salt	2 tablespoons olive or sunflower
1 teaspoon baking soda	oil
½ teaspoon baking powder	⅓ cup raisins

Preheat oven to 400°F. Grease a 12-cup muffin tin with margarine.

Combine whole-wheat flour, wheat bran, brown sugar, salt, baking soda, and baking powder. Set aside.

In a mixing bowl, mix buttermilk, egg, molasses, and oil.
Add dry ingredients and mix until just moistened.
Fold in raisins.
Fill muffin tin and bake for about 15 minutes or until golden brown and a cake tester comes out clean.

Makes 12 muffins
Per muffin: 116 Total calories; 23 Fat calories

APPLE OAT MUFFINS

1½ cups oat bran
½ cup whole-wheat flour
3 tablespoons brown sugar
2 teaspoons baking powder
½ teaspoon salt
1 teaspoon cinnamon
½ cup apple juice
¼ cup skim milk

1 egg
2 tablespoons olive or sunflower
   oil
2 tablespoons honey
1 cup apples, peeled, cored, and
   diced
2 tablespoons raisins

Preheat oven to 400°F. Grease a 12-cup muffin tin with margarine.
Combine oat bran, flour, brown sugar, baking powder, salt, and cinnamon and set aside.
In a large mixing bowl, combine apple juice, skim milk, egg, oil, and honey.
Add flour mixture, apples, and raisins and combine until just moistened.
Fill muffin tin and bake at 400°F for about 20 minutes or until golden brown and a cake tester comes out clean.

Makes 12 muffins
Per muffin: 125 Total calories; 32 Fat calories

APRICOT OAT MUFFINS

Yet another oat muffin. Healthy and delicious — a good snack or breakfast on the run.

½ cup orange juice
1 cup dried apricots, chopped
  (easily done in food
  processor)
¼ cup brown sugar
1 cup oat bran
¼ cup wheat germ

¾ cup whole-wheat flour
2 teaspoons baking powder
2 tablespoons olive or sunflower
  oil
½ cup skim milk
1 egg

Preheat oven to 400°F. Grease a 12-cup muffin tin with margarine.

In a small saucepan, heat orange juice until boiling. Mix in apricots and brown sugar.

Remove saucepan from heat and cool apricot mixture slightly.

In a medium bowl, combine oat bran, wheat germ, whole-wheat flour, and baking powder. Set aside.

In a mixing bowl, beat together oil, skim milk, and egg.

Add dry ingredients and apricot-orange juice mixture to milk mixture and mix until just moistened.

Fill muffin tin and bake for 15 minutes or until golden brown and a cake tester comes out clean.

Makes 12 muffins
Per muffin: 135 Total calories; 32 Fat calories

CINNAMON FRENCH TOAST

2 egg whites
3 tablespoons skim milk
½ teaspoon vanilla
½ teaspoon ground cinnamon

Pinch of grated nutmeg
3 slices whole-wheat bread or
  French bread
2 teaspoons margarine

In a shallow dish, mix egg whites, skim milk, vanilla, cinnamon, and nutmeg.

Soak both sides of bread in mixture.

In a large frying pan, melt margarine over high heat.

Add bread. Reduce heat to medium.
Turn bread after 2 minutes. Cook until golden brown and crispy.

Serves 3
Per serving: 106 Total calories; 29 Fat calories

BUTTERMILK WAFFLES

1 egg white at room temperature	½ teaspoon salt
1 cup whole-wheat flour	1 cup buttermilk
1 cup unbleached white flour	1 cup skim milk
2 teaspoons baking powder	3 tablespoons olive or sunflower oil

Preheat waffle iron.
Beat egg white until stiff but not dry. Set aside.
In a medium bowl, combine whole-wheat flour, white flour, baking powder, and salt.
Add buttermilk and skim milk. *Do not overmix.*
Fold in egg white. Fold in oil.
Place batter on waffle iron in amounts specified by your waffle iron instructions. Cook accordingly.

Makes 8 Belgian waffles

	Total calories	Fat calories
Total batter	1381	379
Per square*	173	47

---

*Because waffle irons come in many sizes, this recipe may make more or fewer than 8 waffle squares. Divide 1381 by the number of waffle squares you make to figure out the total calories per square (for example, 1381 ÷ 8 = 172.6). Divide 379 by the number of waffle squares to figure out the fat calories per square (for example, 379 ÷ 8 = 47.4).

Desserts

TANTE NANCY'S APPLE CRUMB CAKE

Apple Crumb Cake is our first choice. The crust is thick, crunchy, and sweet. The slightly tart apples melt in your mouth. Luscious.

2–2½ pounds tart apples*
(about 6–7 large), peeled,
cored, and sliced
⅓ cup water
¼ cup sugar

2 cups unbleached white flour
¾ cup sugar
1½ teaspoons baking powder
½ cup margarine
1 egg yolk

Preheat oven to 350°F. Grease an 8-inch springform pan with margarine.

In a large pot, cook apple slices with water and ¼ cup sugar until apples are tender but not mushy. Drain and reserve.

In a small bowl, mix flour, ¾ cup sugar, and baking powder.

With a pastry blender, cut in ½ cup margarine.

Cut in egg yolk.

Reserve 1 cup of flour mixture for the topping. Press remainder into bottom and sides of pan.

Spoon drained apples into pan.

Cover with reserved topping.

Bake for about 1 hour or until crust is golden brown.

Makes 12 slices
Per slice: 220 Total calories; 66 Fat calories

---

*You can use as few as 5 large apples, but more is better. Or substitute 2–2½ pounds peaches or 4 cups blueberries.

GRAHAM CRACKER CRUST

Not only do Honey Graham Crackers make a delicious cookie, Honey Graham Cracker crumbs make a delicious pie crust, particularly for lemon meringue or Key lime pie. Make your own graham cracker crumbs and graham cracker crust using the Honey Graham Crackers recipe on page 188.

8 homemade graham cracker crumbs (1¼ cups)	1 teaspoon sugar
	2 tablespoons margarine

Preheat oven to 375°F.
In food processor or blender, crush 8 graham crackers into fine crumbs.
Combine crumbs and sugar and pour into pie plate.
Melt margarine and mix into crumbs.
Press crumbs into pie plate to make a crust.
Bake 8 minutes, or until lightly browned.

Makes one pie crust
Per crust: 690 Total calories; 276 Fat calories

KEY LIME PIE

This pie is as pretty to look at as it is delightful to eat. It never fails to wow guests and please the most discriminating palate. Many Key lime pies call for 3 egg yolks, but you will use only 1 to create this divine dessert. You can use lemon juice instead of lime juice and call this Lemon Meringue Pie.

Graham Cracker Crust (see above)

Filling

¾ cup sugar	½–⅔ cup fresh lime juice +
¼ cup unbleached white flour	water to equal 2¼ cups
3 tablespoons cornstarch	1 egg yolk
¼ teaspoon salt	1 teaspoon margarine

Meringue

5 egg whites, at room temperature	¼ teaspoon cream of tartar
	½ cup + 2 tablespoons sugar

The Filling

In a medium saucepan, thoroughly mix sugar, flour, cornstarch, and salt.

Add ¼ cup lime water and blend into a smooth paste.

Add remaining lime water and mix until smooth.

Stir filling over medium heat until it begins to boil and thicken. Remove saucepan from heat.

In a small bowl, combine egg yolk with a small amount of filling and blend until smooth. Mix back into filling in saucepan. (This step is important. If you were to add the egg yolk directly into the hot filling, the egg yolk would curdle.) Stir margarine into the filling and pour into crust. Cool until filling gels.

The Meringue

Preheat oven to 375°F.

Whip egg whites with cream of tartar until stiff but not dry.

Add sugar and continue beating until whites form stiff peaks.

Gently cover lime filling with egg whites, making sure whites cover pie completely.

Bake for 8 to 10 minutes or until meringue is golden brown.

Cool at room temperature.

Makes 10 slices
Per slice, with Graham Cracker Crust:* 210 Total calories; 36 Fat calories

PINEAPPLE POUND CAKE

2½ cups unbleached white
    flour
1½ teaspoons baking soda
½ teaspoon salt
½ cup margarine
¾ cup sugar
3 egg whites

1 tablespoon grated orange peel
1 teaspoon vanilla
1 cup nonfat yogurt
1 cup pineapple chunks, drained
¼ cup pineapple or orange juice
¼ cup sugar

Preheat oven to 375°F. Grease a 10-inch tube pan with margarine.

Mix flour, baking soda, and salt and set aside.

---

*Based on the Graham Cracker Crust, page 185.

Cream margarine and sugar.

Add egg whites, orange peel, and vanilla and beat well.

Add flour mixture and yogurt alternately to sugar mixture and mix well.

Pour half the batter into pan. Spread pineapple evenly over batter. Cover with remaining batter.

Bake for 40 minutes or until a cake tester comes out clean.

Let the cake cool for 5 minutes.

Meanwhile, in a small saucepan, combine juice and sugar.

Bring to a boil, reduce heat, and simmer for 3 to 5 minutes.

Remove cake from pan. Pierce it with a fork and spoon juice mixture into holes and over the top of the cake.

Makes 16 slices
Per slice: 177 Total calories; 47 Fat calories

CINNAMON SWEET CAKES

A family favorite that can be made on the spur of the moment.

¼ cup olive oil
1 egg
½ cup skim milk
½ cup sugar

¾ cup whole-wheat flour
¾ cup unbleached white flour
2 teaspoons baking powder
½ teaspoon salt

Topping

½ cup brown sugar
½ cup chopped walnuts
1 tablespoon unbleached white
   flour

1 tablespoon margarine
1 teaspoon cinnamon

Preheat oven to 375°F. Grease an 8 × 8–inch baking pan with margarine.

In a large mixing bowl, beat together oil, egg, and skim milk.

Add sugar, whole-wheat flour, white flour, baking powder, and salt and beat until smooth.

Spoon batter into baking pan. (Batter will be thick.)

To make the topping, combine brown sugar, walnuts, flour, and cinnamon in a small bowl.

Melt margarine and stir into mixture.

Sprinkle topping evenly over batter.

Bake for about 25 minutes or until a cake tester comes out clean.

Makes 16 squares
Per square: 148 Total calories; 61 Fat calories

MANDELBROT

These cookies are addictive. Thank you, Esther Krashes!

⅔ cup sugar

¼ cup olive oil

3 egg whites

1 egg

1½ cups unbleached white flour

1 teaspoon baking powder

½ cup coarsely ground almonds

1 teaspoon orange extract

Preheat oven to 350°F.

Lightly grease a cookie sheet with margarine or olive oil.

In a large mixing bowl, cream sugar and olive oil.

Mix in egg whites and egg.

Add flour and baking powder and mix until smooth.

Stir in almonds and orange extract.

Pour onto cookie sheet. Spread into rectangle (8″ × 10″), about ½ inch thick.

Bake for 20 minutes or until lightly browned.

Remove cookie sheet from oven.

Cut dough into strips about 3 inches wide and then score (do not cut through) into bars about ¾ inch wide.

Turn strips over and bake 10 more minutes or until crisp.

Break into bars.

Makes 4 dozen bars
Per bar: 46 Total calories; 18 Fat calories

HONEY GRAHAM CRACKERS

1 cup whole-wheat flour

½ cup unbleached white flour

½ teaspoon baking powder

¼ teaspoon baking soda

Pinch of salt

2 tablespoons margarine

2 tablespoons light brown sugar

2 tablespoons honey

½ teaspoon vanilla

2 tablespoons skim milk

Preheat oven to 350°F and grease a cookie sheet with margarine.
Combine flours, baking powder, baking soda, and salt, and set aside.
Cream margarine, sugar, and honey in an electric mixer.
Mix in vanilla.
Add flour mixture and milk.
Gather dough together (add a drop of milk if too dry) and knead into a ball.
Roll dough onto cookie sheet into a rectangle, ⅛ inch thick.
If dough is too sticky, sprinkle it with flour.
Without moving dough, cut into 3-inch squares.
Lightly score a line through the center of each square and pierce each side several times with a fork.
Bake 10 to 15 minutes, until edges brown. Remove crackers and cool on a wire rack.
Crackers will become crisp as they cool.

Makes 18 crackers
Per cracker: 58 Total calories; 12 Fat calories

OATMEAL COOKIES

¼ cup olive or sunflower oil	2 cups rolled oats
⅓ cup brown sugar	⅓ cup unbleached white flour
2 tablespoons sugar	⅓ cup whole-wheat flour
1 egg white	¼ teaspoon salt
¾ teaspoon vanilla	½ teaspoon baking soda
3 tablespoons water	1 teaspoon cinnamon

Preheat oven to 350°F. Grease a cookie sheet with margarine.
Cream oil and sugars.
Mix in egg white, vanilla, and water.
Add oats, white flour, whole-wheat flour, salt, baking soda, and cinnamon and mix until blended. Do not overmix or you will lose the texture of the oats.
Drop batter by teaspoonfuls onto cookie sheet and bake for 10 to 15 minutes.

Makes 2 dozen cookies
Per cookie: 75 Total calories; 25 Fat calories

FOOD TABLES

Food Tables

CONTENTS

BEVERAGES

FOOD	AMOUNT	TOTAL CALORIES	FAT CALORIES
Alcoholic			
Beer			
regular	12 fl oz	150	0
light	12 fl oz	100	0
Gin, rum, vodka, whiskey			
80 proof	1.5 fl oz	95	0
86 proof	1.5 fl oz	105	0
90 proof	1.5 fl oz	110	0
Other			
brandy Alexander	3 fl oz	254	52
Irish coffee	1 average	188	65
piña colada	6 fl oz	392	103
eggnog	8 fl oz	342	171

Food tables are based on U.S. Department of Agriculture data. See References, Chapter 3.

193

BEVERAGES

FOOD	AMOUNT	TOTAL CALORIES	FAT CALORIES
Wine			
dessert	3.5 fl oz	140	0
table	3.5 fl oz	75	0
Carbonated			
Club soda	12 fl oz	0	0
Cola, regular	12 fl oz	160	0
Cola, diet (artificially sweetened)	12 fl oz	trace	0
Ginger ale	12 fl oz	125	0
Lemon-lime	12 fl oz	150	0
Orange, grape	12 fl oz	180	0
Other Beverages			
Cocoa			
Hershey's made w/whole milk	6 fl oz	90	55
Hershey's made w/skim milk	6 fl oz	38	3
Swiss Miss made w/water	6 fl oz	110	27
Coffee	8 fl oz	trace	0
Fruit drinks, noncarbonated			
canned	6 fl oz	85–100	0
frozen	6 fl oz	80	trace
Tea	8 fl oz	trace	trace

Milk beverages: see **DAIRY PRODUCTS AND EGGS** and **FAST FOODS**.

Fruit juices: see **FRUITS AND FRUIT JUICES**.

DAIRY PRODUCTS AND EGGS

FOOD	AMOUNT	TOTAL CALORIES	FAT CALORIES
Butter	1 pat	36	36
	1 tbsp	100	100

For margarine and other butter substitutes, see **FATS AND OILS**.

Cheese			
American	1 oz	106	80
Blue	1 oz	100	73
Camembert	1 oz	85	62
Cheddar	1 oz	114	85

DAIRY PRODUCTS AND EGGS

FOOD	AMOUNT	TOTAL CALORIES	FAT CALORIES
Colby	1 oz	112	82
Cottage cheese			
creamed	½ cup	117	43
2% fat	½ cup	102	20
1% fat	½ cup	82	10
Cream cheese			
regular	1 tbsp	52	48
whipped	1 tbsp	37	34
Edam	1 oz	101	71
Feta	1 oz	75	54
Gouda	1 oz	101	70
Gruyère	1 oz	117	83
Limburger	1 oz	93	69
Monterey Jack	1 oz	106	77
Mozzarella			
whole milk	1 oz	80	55
part skim milk	1 oz	72	41
Muenster	1 oz	104	77
Parmesan	1 tbsp	23	14
Provolone	1 oz	100	68
Ricotta			
whole milk	½ cup	216	145
part skim milk	½ cup	171	88
Romano	1 oz	110	69
Roquefort	1 oz	105	78
Swiss	1 oz	107	70
Cheese, Reduced-Calorie or Light			
American flavor (Lite-line)	1 oz	50	18
Lo-Chol (Dorman's)	1 oz	70	45
Low Sodium Slices (Weight Watchers)	1 oz	50	18
Mild Cheddar flavor (Lite-line)	1 oz	50	18
Monterey Jack flavor (Lite-line)	1 oz	50	18
Mozzarella (Lite-line)	1 oz	50	18
Muenster flavor (Lite-line)	1 oz	50	18
Sharp Cheddar flavor (Lite-line)	1 oz	50	18
Slices (Weight Watchers)	1 oz	45	18
Slim Jack (Dorman's)	1 oz	90	63
Swiss flavor (Lite-line)	1 oz	50	18
Swiss flavor slices (Weight Watchers)	1 oz	50	18

DAIRY PRODUCTS AND EGGS

FOOD	AMOUNT	TOTAL CALORIES	FAT CALORIES
Reduced Calorie Mini Bonbel (Laughing Cow)	¾ oz	45	27
Reduced Calorie Wedge (Laughing Cow)	¾ oz	35	18
Cheese Spreads			
Pimento (Kraft)	1 oz	70	45
Pineapple (Kraft)	1 oz	70	45
Cream			
Half-and-half	1 tbsp	20	15
Light or table	1 tbsp	29	26

For coffee whiteners, see **Imitation Dairy Products.**

FOOD	AMOUNT	TOTAL CALORIES	FAT CALORIES
Sour cream	1 tbsp	26	23
	1 cup	493	433
Sour cream, imitation (coconut, palm oil)	1 tbsp	30	25
Whipping, heavy, fluid	1 cup	821	792
Whipping, light, fluid	1 cup	699	665
whipped	½ cup	210	198
Whipped cream topping, pressurized	1 tbsp	10	8
	1 cup	154	120
Whipped cream, imitation Cool Whip	1 tbsp	12	9
	½ cup	96	72

Frozen Desserts (See also SWEETS, Frozen Novelties)
Frozen Yogurt

FOOD	AMOUNT	TOTAL CALORIES	FAT CALORIES
Colombo			
regular	4 fl oz	149	21
Lite (nonfat)	4 fl oz	95	0
Dannon	4 fl oz	107	18
Edy's	4 fl oz	107	18
Honey Hill			
regular	4 fl oz	107	24
nonfat	4 fl oz	80	0
ICBIY			
regular	4 fl oz	144	32
nonfat	4 fl oz	80	0

DAIRY PRODUCTS AND EGGS

FOOD	AMOUNT	TOTAL CALORIES	FAT CALORIES
TCBY			
regular	4 fl oz	140	36
nonfat	4 fl oz	100	0
Yoplait	4 fl oz	90	27
Ice cream			
Light			
Breyers praline almond crunch, fudge toffee parfait	1 cup	260	90
Breyers strawberry	1 cup	220	54
Breyers vanilla, chocolate fudge, fudge twirl	1 cup	240	72
Lucerne cookies and cream	1 cup	270	72
Lucerne rocky road	1 cup	260	72
Lucerne vanilla	1 cup	220	54
Regular			
Breyers butter pecan	1 cup	360	216
Breyers chocolate	1 cup	320	144
Breyers strawberry	1 cup	260	108
Breyers vanilla	1 cup	300	144
Rich	1 cup	349	213
Ben & Jerry's	1 cup	587	324
Häagen-Dazs, chocolate	1 cup	500	306
Häagen-Dazs, Vanilla Swiss Almond	1 cup	600	396
Klondike, chocolate	1 bar	300	207
Soft serve	1 cup	377	203
Others			
Ice Milk, vanilla	1 cup	184	51
Sherbet	1 cup	270	34
Tofutti, chocolate (nondairy)	1 cup	420	234
Milk			
Buttermilk	1 cup	99	0–36
Canned			
condensed, sweetened	1 tbsp	62	15
evaporated			
skim	1 tbsp	13	0
	1 cup	200	5
whole	1 tbsp	21	11
	1 cup	340	172

DAIRY PRODUCTS AND EGGS

FOOD	AMOUNT	TOTAL CALORIES	FAT CALORIES
Chocolate			
2% milk	1 cup	179	45
whole milk	1 cup	208	76
Low-fat, 1%	1 cup	104	23
Low-fat, 2%	1 cup	121	42
Nonfat			
dry	¼ cup	109	2
instant	3.2 oz (envelope for 1 qt)	326	6
Skim	1 cup	86	4
Whole	1 cup	150	73
Whole, dry	¼ cup	159	77

Milk Shake (See also FAST FOODS)

Chocolate, thick	10.6 oz	356	73
Vanilla, thick	11 oz	350	85

Yogurt
Custard-style

Whitney's 100% Natural			
lemon or vanilla	6 oz	200	54
tropical fruits	6 oz	200	54
other fruit flavors	6 oz	200	45
Yoplait			
fruit flavors	6 oz	190	36
vanilla	6 oz	180	36

French-style

La Yogurt			
fruit flavors	6 oz	190	36
vanilla	6 oz	160	36
Yoplait	6 oz	190	36

Low-fat

Dannon			
coffee, lemon, vanilla, fresh fruit flavors	8 oz	200	36
fruit on the bottom	8 oz	240	27
mini-pack fruit flavors	4.4 oz	130	18
Light n' Lively	6 oz	180	18

Nonfat

Colombo			
plain Lite	8 oz	110	0

DAIRY PRODUCTS AND EGGS

FOOD	AMOUNT	TOTAL CALORIES	FAT CALORIES
Colombo (*cont.*)			
fruit flavors Lite	8 oz	190	<9
vanilla Lite	8 oz	160	<9
Weight Watchers, fruit flavors	8 oz	150	9
Yoplait 150, fruit flavors	6 oz	150	0
Whole Milk			
Colombo, French vanilla	8 oz	210	72
Drinks			
Dannon Dan-Ups	8 oz	190	36
Imitation Dairy Products			
Coffee Whiteners			
Frozen			
liquid (soy oil)	1 tbsp	20	14
liquid (coconut, palm oils)	1 tbsp	20	14
Rich's Coffee Rich	1 tbsp	20	18
Rich's Poly Rich	1 tbsp	20	18
Powdered			
coconut, palm oils	1 tsp	11	6
Coffee-mate	1 tsp	10	8
Cremora	1 tsp	12	9
Other			
Imitation sour cream (coconut, palm oil)	1 tbsp	30	25
Imitation whipped cream			
Cool Whip	1 tbsp	12	9
Tofutti, chocolate (nondairy)	1 cup	420	234
Tofutti, vanilla	1 cup	320	144
Eggs, Chicken			
Large, fresh	1 egg	79	50
white	1 white	16	0
yolk	1 yolk	63	50
Large, cooked			
fried in 2 tsp butter	1 egg	146	117
scrambled in milk and butter	2 eggs	260	182
Egg Substitutes			
Egg Beaters (Fleishmann's)	¼ cup	25	0
Egg substitute, frozen	¼ cup	96	60

DAIRY PRODUCTS AND EGGS

FOOD	AMOUNT	TOTAL CALORIES	FAT CALORIES
Mixed Dairy Dishes			
See also **FROZEN AND MICROWAVE FOODS.**			
Macaroni and cheese			
canned	1 cup	230	90
homemade	1 cup	430	198
Quiche Lorraine	⅛ pie	600	432

FAST FOODS

FOOD	AMOUNT	TOTAL CALORIES	FAT CALORIES
Enchilada	1	235	144
Taco	1	195	99
Arby's			
Apple turnover	1	310	189
Arby's sub (no dressing)	1	484	144
Bac'n Cheddar deluxe roast beef	1	561	306
Bacon and egg croissant	1	420	225
Baked potato, superstuffed, broccoli and Cheddar	1	541	198
Baked potato, superstuffed, deluxe	1	648	342
Baked potato, superstuffed, mushroom and cheese	1	506	198
Baked potato, superstuffed, taco	1	619	243
Beef 'n Cheddar	1	490	189
Blueberry turnover	1	340	180
Butter croissant	1	220	90
Cherry turnover	1	320	180
Chicken breast sandwich	1	592	243
Chicken breast, roasted	1	254	63
Chicken club sandwich	1	621	288
Chicken salad croissant	1	460	324
Chicken salad sandwich	1	386	180
Chocolate shake	10.6 fl oz	384	99
French dip roast beef sandwich	1	386	108
French fries	1 serving	211	72
Ham and Swiss croissant	1	330	135
Ham n' cheese sandwich	1	353	117

FAST FOODS

FOOD	AMOUNT	TOTAL CALORIES	FAT CALORIES
Horsey sauce	1 oz	120	54
Jamocha shake	10.8 fl oz	424	90
Junior roast beef	1	218	72
King roast beef	1	467	171
Mushroom and Swiss croissant	1	340	162
Potato cakes	1 serving	201	126
Regular roast beef	1	353	135
Sausage and egg croissant	1	499	297
Super roast beef	1	501	198
Turkey deluxe	1 serving	375	153
Vanilla shake	8.8 fl oz	295	90
Arthur Treacher's			
Chicken, fried	1 serving	369	198
Chicken sandwich	1	413	171
Chips (French fries)	1 serving	276	117
Chowder	1 serving	112	45
Coleslaw	1 serving	123	72
Fish, broiled	5 oz	245	126
Fish, fried	2 pieces	355	180
Krunch Pup (batter-fried hot dog)	1	203	135
Lemon Luv (fried pie)	1 serving	276	126
Shrimp, fried	1 serving	381	216
Burger King			
Apple pie	1	305	108
Bacon double cheeseburger	1	510	279
Bacon, egg, and cheese croissan'wich	1	355	216
Cheeseburger	1	317	135
Chicken tenders	6 pieces	204	90
Chocolate shake	10 fl oz	374	99
Double beef Whopper	1	887	513
Double beef Whopper with cheese	1	970	576
Double cheeseburger	1	478	243
Double hamburger	1	394	189
French fries, regular	1 serving	227	117
Hamburger	1	275	108
Hash browns	1 serving	162	99
Onion rings, regular	1 serving	274	144
Scrambled egg platter (eggs, crois-sant, hash browns)	1 serving	468	270

FAST FOODS

FOOD	AMOUNT	TOTAL CALORIES	FAT CALORIES
Specialty chicken sandwich	1	688	360
Specialty ham and cheese sandwich	1	471	216
Vanilla shake	10 fl oz	321	90
Whaler sandwich	1	488	243
Whaler sandwich with cheese	1	530	270
Whopper	1	626	342
Whopper with cheese	1	709	405
Whopper Jr.	1	322	153
Whopper Jr. with cheese	1	364	180

Church's Fried Chicken

Apple pie	3 oz	300	171
Catfish, fried	3 pieces	201	108
Chicken breast, fried	1 serving	278	153
Chicken leg, fried	1 serving	147	81
Chicken thigh, fried	1 serving	305	198
Chicken wing, fried	1 serving	303	180
Chicken nuggets, regular	6 pieces	330	171
Chicken nuggets, spicy	6 pieces	312	153
Coleslaw	1 serving	83	63
Corn on the cob, buttered	9 oz	165	27
Dinner roll	1	83	18
French fries, regular	3 oz	256	117
Hushpuppy	1 serving	78	27
Pecan pie	1 serving	367	180

Dairy Queen

Banana split	1	540	99
Buster bar	1	460	261
Chicken sandwich	1	670	369
Chocolate malt, large	20 fl oz	1060	225
Chocolate malt, regular	14 fl oz	760	162
Chocolate malt, small	10 fl oz	520	117
Chocolate shake, large	20 fl oz	990	234
Chocolate shake, regular	14 fl oz	710	171
Chocolate shake, small	10 fl oz	490	117
Chocolate sundae, large	8.4 fl oz	440	90
Chocolate sundae, regular	6 fl oz	310	72
Chocolate sundae, small	3.5 fl oz	190	36
Dilly bar	1	210	117
Dipped chocolate cone, large	1	510	216
Dipped chocolate cone, regular	1	340	144

FAST FOODS

FOOD	AMOUNT	TOTAL CALORIES	FAT CALORIES
Dipped chocolate cone, small	1	190	81
Double Delight	1 serving	490	180
Double hamburger	1	530	252
Double hamburger with cheese	1	650	333
DQ sandwich	1	140	36
Fish sandwich, fried	1	400	153
Fish sandwich with cheese	1	440	189
Float	1	410	63
Freeze	1	500	108
French fries, regular	1 serving	200	90
French fries, large	1 serving	320	144
Hot dog	1	280	144
Hog dog with cheese	1	330	189
Hot dog with chili	1	320	180
Hot fudge brownie delight	1	600	225
Mr. Misty float	1	390	63
Mr. Misty freeze	1	500	108
Mr. Misty kiss	1	70	0
Mr. Misty, large	1	340	0
Mr. Misty, regular	1	250	0
Mr. Misty, small	1	190	0
Onion rings	3 oz	280	144
Parfait	1 serving	430	72
Peanut Buster parfait	1 serving	740	306
Single hamburger	1	360	144
Single hamburger with cheese	1	410	180
Soft ice cream, without cone	4 oz	180	54
Soft ice cream cone, large	1	340	90
Soft ice cream cone, regular	1	240	63
Soft ice cream cone, small	1	140	36
Strawberry shortcake	1 serving	540	99
Super hot dog	1	520	243
Super hot dog with cheese	1	580	306
Super hot dog with chili	1	570	288
Triple hamburger	1	710	405
Triple hamburger with cheese	1	820	450

Domino's Pizza

FOOD	AMOUNT	TOTAL CALORIES	FAT CALORIES
12" cheese pizza	2 slices	340	54
12" pepperoni pizza	2 slices	394	108
16" cheese pizza	2 slices	400	72
16" pepperoni pizza	2 slices	454	126

FAST FOODS

FOOD	AMOUNT	TOTAL CALORIES	FAT CALORIES
Hardee's			
Apple turnover	1	282	126
Bacon cheeseburger	1	556	297
Big Cookie Treat	1	278	138
Big Country Breakfast Bacon	1	761	452
Big Country Breakfast Ham	1	665	343
Big Country Breakfast Sausage	1	849	630
Big Deluxe Burger	1	503	261
Biscuit	1	257	112
Bacon and egg	1	410	234
Canadian Sunrise	1	482	270
Cheese	1	304	142
Cinnamon 'n Raisin	1	276	146
Country Ham	1	323	162
Egg	1	336	168
Gravy	1 serving	401	198
Ham	1	300	130
Sausage	1	426	255
Sausage and egg	1	503	311
Steak	1	491	255
Cheeseburger	1	327	134
Cheeseburger, ¼ lb	1	511	254
Chef salad	1 serving	309	117
Fisherman's fillet sandwich	1	469	181
French fries, large	1 serving	438	207
French fries, regular	1 serving	252	112
Ham 'n cheese sandwich	1	316	86
Hamburger	1	244	83
Hash rounds potatoes	1 serving	249	146
Hot dog	1	285	128
Milkshake, chocolate	11 fl oz	390	94
Mushroom 'n Swiss hamburger sandwich	1	509	208
Roast beef sandwich, regular	1	312	112
Big roast beef	1	440	194
Shrimp 'n pasta salad	1 serving	362	261
Turkey club sandwich	1	426	201
Jack-in-the-Box			
Ham and Swiss burger	1	638	351
Hamburger	1	276	108
Jumbo Jack	1	485	234
Jumbo Jack with cheese	1	630	315

FAST FOODS

FOOD	AMOUNT	TOTAL CALORIES	FAT CALORIES
Moby Jack	1	444	225
Mushroom burger	1	477	243
Onion rings	1 serving	382	207
Pancake breakfast with bacon and syrup	1 serving	630	243
Pasta seafood salad	1 serving	394	198
Sausage crescent	1	584	387
Scrambled eggs breakfast	1 serving	720	396
Sirloin steak dinner	1	699	243
Strawberry shake	11 fl oz	320	63
Supreme crescent	1	547	360
Supreme nachos	1 serving	718	360
Swiss and bacon burger	1	643	387
Taco, regular	1 serving	191	99
Taco salad	1 serving	377	216
Taco, super	1 serving	288	153
Vanilla shake	10.7 fl oz	320	54

Kentucky Fried Chicken

FOOD	AMOUNT	TOTAL CALORIES	FAT CALORIES
Biscuit	1	269	126
Coleslaw	1 serving	105	54
Corn on the cob	1 serving	176	27
Extra Crispy or Spicy			
breast	1 piece	354	216
drumstick	1 piece	173	99
thigh	1 piece	371	234
wing	1 piece	201	122
Extra Crispy special dinner			
wing + breast	1 dinner	755	383
drumstick + thigh	1 dinner	765	483
wing + thigh	1 dinner	902	434
Kentucky fries	1 serving	268	117
Kentucky nuggets	6 pieces	276	153
Original Recipe			
breast	1 piece	276	153
drumstick	1 piece	147	81
thigh	1 piece	278	171
wing	1 piece	181	108
Original Recipe dinner			
wing + breast	1 dinner	604	289
drumstick + thigh	1 dinner	643	317
wing + thigh	1 dinner	661	340

FAST FOODS

FOOD	AMOUNT	TOTAL CALORIES	FAT CALORIES
Long John Silver			
Apple pie	1 serving	280	99
Batter-fried fish	1 piece	202	108
Batter-fried shrimp dinner	1 serving	711	405
Batter-fried shrimp	1 piece	47	27
Breaded clams	1 order	526	279
Breaded oyster	1 piece	60	27
Breaded shrimp platter	1 order	962	513
Breaded shrimp	1 order	388	207
Cherry pie	1 serving	294	99
Chicken nuggets dinner	6 pieces	699	405
Chicken Plank	1 piece	152	72
Chicken Planks Dinner	3 pieces	885	459
Chicken Planks Dinner	4 pieces	1037	531
Clam chowder	1 serving	128	45
Clam dinner	1 order	955	522
Crackers	4	50	18
Fish and chicken	1 order	935	495
Fish and Fryes, 2 pieces fish	1 order	651	324
Fish and Fryes, 3 pieces fish	1 order	853	432
Fish dinner, fried, 3-piece	1 order	1180	630
Fish sandwich platter	1 order	835	378
Fryes	1 order	247	108
Hushpuppies	2 pieces	145	63
Kitchen-breaded fish	1 piece	122	54
Kitchen-breaded fish dinner, 2-piece	1 order	818	414
Kitchen-breaded fish dinner, 3-piece	1 order	940	468
Ocean Chef Salad	1 order	229	72
Oyster dinner	1 order	789	405
Pumpkin pie	1 piece	251	99
Scallop dinner	1 order	747	405
Seafood platter	1 order	976	522
Seafood salad	1 order	426	270
Tartar sauce	1 serving	119	99
McDonald's			
Apple pie, 3 oz	1 pie	253	126
Big Mac	1	570	315
Biscuit	1	330	162
with bacon, egg, and cheese	1 order	483	288

FAST FOODS

FOOD	AMOUNT	TOTAL CALORIES	FAT CALORIES
Biscuit (*cont.*)			
with sausage	1 order	467	279
with sausage and egg	1 order	585	360
Caramel sundae	1 order	361	90
Cheeseburger	1	318	144
Cherry pie, 3 oz	1 pie	260	126
Chicken McNuggets	6 pieces	323	180
Chocolate shake	10.2 fl oz	383	81
Chocolaty Chip cookies	1 box	342	144
Egg McMuffin	1 order	340	144
English muffin with butter	1 order	186	45
Filet-o-Fish	1 order	435	234
Fries, regular	1 order	220	108
Hamburger	1	263	99
Hash brown potatoes	1 order	144	81
Hot fudge sundae	1 order	357	99
Hotcakes with syrup and butter	1 order	500	90
McD.L.T.	1 order	680	396
McDonaldland cookies	1 serving	308	99
Quarter Pounder	1	427	216
Quarter Pounder with cheese	1	525	288
Sausage	1 serving	210	171
Sausage McMuffin	1 serving	427	234
Sausage McMuffin with egg	1 serving	517	297
Scrambled eggs	1 serving	180	117
Soft serve cone	1 serving	189	45
Strawberry shake	10.2 fl oz	362	81
Strawberry sundae	1 serving	320	81
Vanilla shake	10.2 fl oz	352	72
Pizza Hut			
Supreme medium pizza	¼ pizza	506	145
Roy Rogers			
Apple Danish	1	249	108
Bacon bits	1 tsp	24	9
Bacon cheeseburger	1	581	351
Baked potato			
bacon 'n cheese	1	397	198
broccoli 'n cheese	1	376	162
with margarine	1	274	63
plain	1	211	trace
sour cream 'n chives	1	408	189

FAST FOODS

FOOD	AMOUNT	TOTAL CALORIES	FAT CALORIES
Baked potato (*cont.*)			
taco beef 'n cheese	1	463	198
Biscuit	1	231	108
Breakfast crescent sandwich	1	401	243
with bacon	1	431	270
with ham	1	557	378
with sausage	1	449	261
Brownie	1 serving	264	99
Caramel sundae	1 serving	293	72
Cheddar cheese	¼ cup	112	81
Cheese Danish	1	271	108
Cheeseburger	1	563	333
Cherry Danish	1	271	126
Chicken breast	1 serving	324	171
Chicken breast and wing	1 serving	466	261
Chicken leg	1 serving	117	63
Chicken thigh	1 serving	282	180
Chicken thigh and leg	1 serving	399	234
Chicken wing	1 serving	142	90
Chinese noodles	¼ cup	55	27
Chocolate shake	11.25 fl oz	358	90
Coleslaw	1 serving	110	63
Crescent roll	1	287	162
Egg and biscuit platter	1 serving	394	243
with bacon	1 serving	435	270
with ham	1 serving	442	261
with sausage	1 serving	550	369
French fries, large	1 serving	357	162
French fries, regular	1 serving	268	126
Hamburger	1	456	252
Hot chocolate	6 fl oz	123	18
Macaroni	1 serving	186	99
Pancake platter with syrup and			
butter	1 serving	452	135
with bacon	1 serving	493	162
with ham	1 serving	506	153
with sausage	1 serving	608	270
Potato salad	1 serving	107	54
Roast beef sandwich	1	317	90
with cheese	1	424	171
Roast beef sandwich, large	1	360	108
with cheese	1	467	189

FAST FOODS

FOOD	AMOUNT	TOTAL CALORIES	FAT CALORIES
RR Bar burger	1	611	351
Strawberry shake	11 fl oz	315	90
Strawberry shortcake	1 serving	447	171
Strawberry sundae	1 serving	216	63
Vanilla shake	10.8 fl oz	306	99
Wendy's			
Bacon cheeseburger	1	460	252
Baked potato	1	250	18
with bacon and cheese	1	570	270
with broccoli and cheese	1	500	225
with cheese	1	590	306
with chicken à la king	1	350	54
with chili and cheese	1	510	180
with sour cream and chives	1	460	216
with sour cream and Stroganoff	1	490	189
Chicken sandwich	1	320	90
Chili	8 oz	260	72
Chow mein noodles	¼ cup	60	27
Coleslaw	½ cup	90	72
Danish	1	360	162
Double cheeseburger	1	630	360
Double hamburger	1	560	306
French fries, regular	1 serving	280	126
French toast	2 slices	400	171
Frosty dairy dessert, small	12 fl oz	400	126
Fruit-flavored drink	12 fl oz	110	0
Hamburger, kid's meal	1 serving	200	72
Hamburger	1	350	162
Home fries	1 serving	360	198
Hot chocolate	6 fl oz	100	27
Omelet 1, ham and cheese	1 serving	250	153
Omelet 2, ham, cheese, and mush-room	1 serving	290	189
Omelet 3, ham, cheese, onion, and green pepper	1 serving	280	171
Omelet 4, mushroom, onion, and green pepper	1 serving	210	135
Pasta salad	½ cup	134	54
Pick-up-window side salad	1 serving	110	54
Sausage	1 patty	200	162
Scrambled eggs	1 serving	190	108

FAST FOODS

FOOD	AMOUNT	TOTAL CALORIES	FAT CALORIES
Sunflower seeds and raisins	1¼ oz	180	117
Taco salad	1 serving	390	162
Toast with margarine	2 slices	250	81
Triple cheeseburger	1 order	1040	612
Turkey ham	¼ cup	46	18

FATS AND OILS

FOOD	AMOUNT	TOTAL CALORIES	FAT CALORIES
Animal Fats			
Beef tallow	1 tbsp	116	116
Butter			
regular	1 pat	36	36
	1 tbsp	100	100
whipped	1 tbsp	67	67
Chicken fat	1 tbsp	115	115
Lard (pork)	1 tbsp	116	116
Margarines			
Butter blends	1 tbsp	100	100
Butter Buds Sprinkles	½ tsp (1 g)	4	0
Diet or reduced-calorie	1 tbsp	50	50
Molly McButter	½ tsp	4	0
Regular			
Promise	1 tbsp	90	90
All other regular	1 tbsp	100	100
Whipped, soft			
Blue Bonnet, Fleishmann's, Chiffon, Mrs. Filbert's, Family Spread, Shedd's Spread	1 tbsp	70	70
Oils			
Canola (Puritan)	1 tbsp	120	120
Coconut	1 tbsp	120	120
Corn	1 tbsp	120	120
Cottonseed	1 tbsp	120	120
Olive	1 tbsp	119	119
Palm	1 tbsp	120	120
Palm kernel	1 tbsp	120	120
Peanut	1 tbsp	119	119

FATS AND OILS

FOOD	AMOUNT	TOTAL CALORIES	FAT CALORIES
Safflower	1 tbsp	120	120
Sesame	1 tbsp	120	120
Soybean	1 tbsp	120	120
Sunflower	1 tbsp	120	120
Walnut	1 tbsp	120	120
Salad Dressings and Spreads			
Blue cheese	1 tbsp	77	72
nonfat (Estée)	1 tbsp	2	0
Caesar (Pfeiffer)	1 tbsp	80	54
French			
regular	1 tbsp	67	58
low-calorie	1 tbsp	22	8
nonfat (Estée)	1 tbsp	2	0
nonfat (Kraft)	1 tbsp	25	0
nonfat (Pritikin)	1 tbsp	10	0
Italian			
regular	1 tbsp	69	64
low-calorie	1 tbsp	16	14
nonfat (Estée)	1 tbsp	2	0
nonfat (Herb Magic)	1 tbsp	4	0
nonfat (Kraft)	1 tbsp	10	0
nonfat (Pritikin)	1 tbsp	6	0
Mayonnaise			
soybean	1 tbsp	99	99
reduced-calorie	1 tbsp	45	45
imitation (soybean)	1 tbsp	64	64
Mayonnaise-type			
Miracle Whip			
Light reduced calorie salad dressing	1 tbsp	45	36
Salad Dressing	1 tbsp	70	63
Red wine vinegar and oil (Pfeiffer)	1 tbsp	10	9
Russian			
regular	1 tbsp	76	70
low-calorie	1 tbsp	23	6
Thousand Island			
regular	1 tbsp	59	50
low-calorie	1 tbsp	24	14
nonfat	1 tbsp	30	0
Shortenings			
Crisco	1 tbsp	113	113

FISH AND SHELLFISH

Unless otherwise noted, fish is baked, steamed, or broiled with *no added fat.* If fish is baked in butter or margarine, for each teaspoon of butter or margarine, add 33 to the total calories and 33 to the fat calories. See also **FROZEN AND MICRO-WAVE FOODS.**

*Remember that most of the following calorie figures are for **only 1 ounce** of fish!*

FOOD	AMOUNT	TOTAL CALORIES	FAT CALORIES
Abalone			
raw	1 oz	30	2
fried	1 oz	54	17
Anchovy			
raw	1 oz	37	12
canned in oil, drained	5 anchovies	42	17
	1 oz	60	25
Bass			
Black Sea, baked and stuffed	1 oz	73	40
freshwater, raw	1 oz	32	9
	1 fillet	90	26
striped, raw	1 oz	27	6
	1 fillet	154	33
Bluefish			
raw	1 oz	35	11
	1 fillet	186	57
baked or broiled, with butter or margarine	1 oz	45	14
fried	1 oz	58	25
striped, oven-fried	1 oz	56	22
Burbot, raw	1 oz	25	2
	1 fillet	104	8
Butterfish, raw	1 oz	41	20
	1 fillet	47	23
Carp			
raw	1 oz	36	14
	1 fillet	276	110
cooked, dry heat	1 oz	46	18
	1 fillet	276	110
Catfish, channel			
raw	1 oz	33	11
	1 fillet	92	30
breaded and fried	1 oz	65	34
	1 fillet	199	104
Caviar, black and red	1 tbsp	40	26
	1 oz	71	45

FISH AND SHELLFISH

FOOD	AMOUNT	TOTAL CALORIES	FAT CALORIES
Cisco (lake herring)			
raw	1 oz	28	5
	1 fillet	78	14
smoked	1 oz	50	30
Clams			
raw, cherrystones or littlenecks	9 large or 20 small	133	16
	1 oz	23	3
breaded and fried	1 oz	57	28
	20 small clams	379	189
canned, drained solids	1 oz	42	5
	½ cup	118	14
cooked, moist heat	1 oz	42	5
	20 small clams	133	16
fritters	1 fritter	124	54
Commercial products			
Mrs. Paul's deviled	1 cake	180	86
Mrs. Paul's fried	2.5 oz	270	114
Mrs. Paul's Cake Thins	2	310	124
Mrs. Paul's sticks	5	240	55
Cod, Atlantic			
raw	1 oz	23	2
	1 fillet	190	14
canned	1 oz	30	2
baked	1 oz	30	2
	1 fillet	189	14
dried and salted	1 oz	81	6
Cod, Pacific, raw	1 oz	23	2
	1 fillet	95	7
Crab			
Alaska king			
raw	1 oz	24	2
	1 leg	144	9
cooked, moist heat	1 oz	27	4
	1 leg	129	19
Alaska king, imitation, made from surimi	1 oz	29	3
Blue, raw	1 oz	25	3
	1 crab	18	2
canned	1 oz	28	3
	½ cup	67	7

FISH AND SHELLFISH

FOOD	AMOUNT	TOTAL CALORIES	FAT CALORIES
Crab (cont.)			
cooked, moist heat	1 oz	29	5
	½ cup	69	11
Chesapeake Bay Deluxe Crab			
Cakes, frozen	1 oz	65	41
Commercial products			
Mrs. Paul's Cake Thins	2	320	129
Mrs. Paul's Deviled	1 cake	160	63
Nutri Sea Crab Sticks	1 oz	29	3
Nutri Sea King Crab	1 oz	31	3
Sea Legs Crabmeat, Salad			
Style	1 oz	27	3
Crab cakes	1 cake	93	41
	1 oz	44	19
Dungeoness, raw	1 oz	24	2
Crayfish			
raw	1 oz	25	3
	8 crayfish	24	2
steamed	1 oz	32	3
Croaker, Atlantic			
raw	1 oz	30	8
	1 fillet	83	22
breaded and fried	1 oz	63	32
	1 fillet	192	99
Cusk, raw	1 oz	25	2
Cuttlefish, raw	1 oz	22	2
Dolphin fish, raw	1 oz	24	2
	1 fillet	174	13
Drum, fresh water, raw	1 oz	34	13
	1 fillet	236	88
Eel			
raw	1 oz	52	30
baked	1 oz	67	38
	1 fillet	375	214
Fish, frozen			
Mrs. Paul's au Gratin	1 serving (5 oz)	250	104
Mrs. Paul's Buttered	1 fillet	155	115
Mrs. Paul's Cakes	1 cake	105	36
Mrs. Paul's Cake Thins	1 thin	160	80
Mrs. Paul's Fried	1 fillet	110	40
Mrs. Paul's light batter	1 fillet	140	56
Mrs. Paul's Sticks	1 stick	38	11
Mrs. Paul's sticks, light batter	1 stick	58	23

FISH AND SHELLFISH

FOOD	AMOUNT	TOTAL CALORIES	FAT CALORIES
Fish, frozen (*cont.*)			
Mrs. Paul's Fish 'n Chips, light			
batter	1 oz	53	20
Van de Kamp's fish fillets	1 oz	20	3
Flounder			
raw	1 oz	26	3
	1 fillet	149	17
baked or steamed	1 oz	33	4
	1 fillet	148	17
Mrs. Paul's fried fillets	1 fillet	110	44
Gefilte fish	1 piece	35	7
	1 oz	24	4
Grouper			
raw	1 oz	26	3
	1 fillet	238	24
baked or steamed	1 oz	33	3
	1 fillet	238	24
Haddock			
raw	1 oz	25	2
	1 fillet	168	12
baked or steamed	1 oz	32	2
	1 fillet	168	12
Mrs. Paul's fried fillets	1 fillet	115	40
oven-fried	1 fillet	182	31
smoked	1 oz	33	2
Halibut, Atlantic and Pacific			
baked or steamed	1 oz	40	7
	½ fillet	223	42
Herring, Atlantic			
raw	1 oz	45	23
	1 fillet	291	150
baked or steamed	1 oz	57	30
canned	1 oz	59	35
canned in tomato sauce	1 herring	97	52
pickled	1 oz	65	39
	1 herring	112	68
	1 piece	33	21
smoked, kippered	1 oz	60	33
	1 fillet	87	45
Herring, Pacific, raw	1 oz	55	35
Lobster, northern			
raw	1 oz	26	2
	1 whole	136	12

FISH AND SHELLFISH

FOOD	AMOUNT	TOTAL CALORIES	FAT CALORIES
Lobster (*cont.*)			
cooked, moist heat	1 oz	28	2
	1 cup	142	8
Newburg (with butter, eggs, sherry, cream)	1 cup	485	239
salad (with mayonnaise)	½ cup or 4 oz	286	149
Lox (smoked salmon)	1 oz	33	11
Mackerel, Atlantic			
raw	1 oz	58	35
	1 fillet	229	140
baked or steamed	1 oz	74	45
	1 fillet	231	141
Mackerel, jack, canned	1 cup	296	108
Mackerel, king, raw	1 oz	30	9
	½ fillet	207	36
Mackerel, Pacific and jack, raw	1 oz	44	20
	1 fillet	353	160
Mackerel, Spanish			
raw	1 oz	39	16
	1 fillet	260	106
baked or steamed	1 oz	45	16
	1 fillet	230	83
Milkfish, raw	1 oz	42	17
Monkfish, raw	1 oz	21	4
Mullet, striped			
raw	1 oz	33	10
	1 fillet	139	41
baked	1 oz	42	12
	1 fillet	139	41
Mussels, blue			
raw	1 oz	24	6
	1 cup	129	30
cooked, moist heat	1 oz	49	11
Ocean perch, Atlantic			
raw	1 oz	27	4
	1 fillet	60	9
baked	1 oz	34	5
	1 fillet	60	9
breaded and fried	1 fillet	185	99
Octopus, raw	1 oz	23	3
Oysters, eastern			
raw	6 medium	58	19
	1 cup	170	55

FISH AND SHELLFISH

FOOD	AMOUNT	TOTAL CALORIES	FAT CALORIES
Oysters, eastern (*cont.*)			
breaded and fried	1 oz	56	32
	6 medium	173	100
canned	1 oz	19	6
	½ cup	85	28
steamed	1 oz	39	13
	6 medium	58	19
stew (2 parts milk, 1 part oyster)	1 cup	233	139
Oysters, Pacific, raw	1 oz	23	6
	1 medium	41	10
Pike, northern			
raw	1 oz	25	2
	½ fillet	175	12
baked	1 oz	32	2
	½ fillet	176	12
Pike, walleye, raw	1 oz	26	3
	1 fillet	147	17
Pollock, Atlantic, raw	1 oz	26	2
	½ fillet	177	17
Pollock, walleye			
raw	1 oz	23	2
	1 fillet	62	6
baked	1 oz	32	3
	1 fillet	68	6
Pompano, Florida			
raw	1 oz	47	24
	1 fillet	184	95
baked	1 oz	60	31
	1 fillet	185	96
Pout, ocean, raw	1 oz	22	2
	½ fillet	140	14
Rockfish, Pacific			
raw	1 oz	27	4
	1 fillet	180	27
baked	1 oz	34	5
	1 fillet	180	27
Roughy, orange, raw	1 oz	36	18
Sablefish			
raw	1 oz	55	39
	½ fillet	377	266
smoked	1 oz	72	51
Salmon, Atlantic, raw	1 oz	40	16

FISH AND SHELLFISH

FOOD	AMOUNT	TOTAL CALORIES	FAT CALORIES
Salmon, Chinook			
raw	1 oz	51	27
smoked	1 oz	33	11
Salmon, Chum			
raw	1 oz	34	10
canned, drained	1 oz	40	14
Salmon, coho			
raw	1 oz	41	15
steamed	1 oz	52	19
Salmon, pink			
raw	1 oz	33	9
canned	1 oz	39	15
Salmon, smoked (see lox)			
Salmon, sockeye			
raw	1 oz	48	22
baked	1 oz	61	28
canned, drained	1 oz	43	19
Sardines, Atlantic, canned in oil, drained	1 oz	59	29
	2 sardines	50	25
	1 can (3.25 oz)	192	95
Sardines, Pacific, canned in tomato sauce, drained	1 oz	51	31
	1 sardine	68	41
Scallops			
raw	1 oz	25	2
	2 large or 5 small	26	2
breaded, fried	1 oz	61	28
	2 large	67	31
steamed	1 oz	32	4
Scup, raw	1 oz	30	7
	1 fillet	67	16
Sea bass			
raw	1 oz	27	5
	1 fillet	125	23
baked	1 oz	35	7
	1 fillet	125	23
Sea trout, raw	1 oz	29	9
	1 fillet	248	77
Shad			
raw	1 oz	56	35
	1 fillet	362	228

FISH AND SHELLFISH

FOOD	AMOUNT	TOTAL CALORIES	FAT CALORIES
Shad (*cont.*)			
baked	1 oz	57	29
Shark			
raw	1 oz	37	11
batter-dipped, fried	1 oz	65	35
Sheepshead			
raw	1 oz	31	6
	1 fillet	257	52
baked	1 oz	36	4
	1 fillet	234	27
Shrimp			
raw	1 oz	30	4
	4 large shrimp	30	4
breaded, fried	1 oz	69	31
	4 large shrimp	73	33
Mrs. Paul's Cake Thins	1 thin	155	60
Mrs. Paul's Crepes	1 serving (5.5 oz)	250	105
canned	1 oz	34	5
	½ cup	77	11
steamed	1 oz	28	3
	4 large shrimp	22	2
Smelt, rainbow			
raw	1 oz	28	6
baked	1 oz	35	8
Snapper			
raw	1 oz	28	3
	1 fillet	217	26
baked	1 oz	36	4
	1 fillet	217	26
Sole			
raw	1 oz	26	3
	1 fillet	149	17
baked or steamed	1 oz	33	4
	1 fillet	148	17
Spiny lobster, raw	1 oz	32	4
	1 whole	233	28
Spot, raw	1 oz	35	12
	1 fillet	79	28
Squid			
raw	1 oz	26	4
fried	1 oz	50	19
Sturgeon			
raw	1 oz	30	10

FISH AND SHELLFISH

FOOD	AMOUNT	TOTAL CALORIES	FAT CALORIES
Sturgeon (*cont.*)			
baked	1 oz	38	13
smoked	1 oz	48	11
Sucker, white, raw	1 oz	26	6
	1 fillet	147	33
Sunfish, pumpkinseed, raw	1 oz	25	2
	1 fillet	43	3
Surimi	1 oz	28	2
Swordfish			
raw	1 oz	34	10
baked	1 oz	44	13
Tilefish			
raw	1 oz	27	6
	½ fillet	184	40
baked	1 oz	42	12
	½ fillet	220	63
Trout, rainbow			
raw	1 oz	33	9
	1 fillet	93	24
baked	1 oz	43	11
	1 fillet	94	24
Tuna			
raw	1 oz	41	12
baked	1 oz	52	16
canned			
solid white, oil	1 oz	65	36
solid white, water, drained	1 oz	30	5
chunk light, oil, drained	1 oz	56	21
Tuna salad	½ cup	190	85
Turbot, European, raw	1 oz	27	8
	½ fillet	194	54
Whelk			
raw	1 oz	39	1
steamed	1 oz	78	2
Whitefish			
raw	1 oz	38	15
	1 fillet	266	104
smoked	1 oz	30	2
Whiting			
raw	1 oz	26	3
	1 fillet	83	11
baked	1 oz	33	4
	1 fillet	83	11

FISH AND SHELLFISH

FOOD	AMOUNT	TOTAL CALORIES	FAT CALORIES
Wolf fish, Atlantic, raw	1 oz	27	6
	½ fillet	147	33
Yellowtail, raw	1 oz	41	13
	½ fillet	273	88

FROZEN AND MICROWAVE FOODS

FOOD	AMOUNT	TOTAL CALORIES	FAT CALORIES
Breakfast Foods			
Aunt Jemima			
Blueberry Waffles	2 waffles	180	54
Buttermilk Waffles	2 waffles	190	54
Cinnamon French Toast	2 slices (3 oz)	210	63
French toast	2 slices (3 oz)	170	45
Microwave Lite Buttermilk Pancakes	3 (4-inch diam) pancakes	140	27
Microwave pancakes, original flavor	3 (4-inch diam) pancakes	210	36
Microwave pancakes, buttermilk	3 (4-inch diam) pancakes	210	27
Original Waffles	2 waffles	190	54
Toaster Browns, original flavor	1.75 oz	100	54
Whole-Grain Waffles	2 waffles	180	63
Belgian Chef Waffles	1 waffle	90	18
Golden Cheese Blintz	1 blintz	110	<9
Hormel Canadian Bacon, Egg and Cheese Biscuit	1	350	144
Kellogg's			
Eggo Homestyle Waffles	1 waffle	120	45
Nutri·Grain Waffles from Eggo	1 waffle	130	45
Morningstar Farms			
Breakfast Links	3 links	180	108
Breakfast Patties	2 patties	190	99
Breakfast Strips	3 strips	80	54
Scramblers	½ carton (2 oz)	60	27
Nabisco Egg Beaters	¼ cup	25	0
Pet			
Downyflake Jumbo Size Waffles	2 waffles	170	36

FROZEN AND MICROWAVE FOODS

FOOD	AMOUNT	TOTAL CALORIES	FAT CALORIES
Pet *(cont.)*			
Downyflake Multigrain Waffles	2 waffles	230	117
Pillsbury			
Microwave Blueberry Pancakes	3 pancakes	260	36
Microwave Buttermilk Pancakes	3 pancakes	260	36
Roman Meal waffles	2 waffles	280	126
Sara Lee			
All Butter Cinnamon Rolls	1 roll (2.5 oz)	230	99
All Butter Croissants	1 croissant (1.5 oz)	170	81
All Butter Petite Croissants	1 croissant (1 oz)	120	54
Apple Cinnamon Coffee Cake Snacks	1 cake	290	117
Apple Spice Muffins	1 muffin (2.5 oz)	220	72
Blueberry Muffins	1 muffin	200	72
Butter Streusel Coffee Cake	⅛ cake	160	63
Butter Streusel Coffee Cake Snacks	1 (2 oz)	230	108
Coffee Cake Pecan	⅛ cake	160	72
Corn Muffins	1 muffin	250	117
Raisin Bran Muffins	1 muffin	220	63
Swanson, Great Starts			
Breakfast Sandwiches			
Beefsteak, Egg, and Cheese on a Muffin	1	400	216
Egg, Cheese, and Bacon on a Biscuit	1	340	135
Sausage, Egg, and Cheese on a Biscuit	1	520	288
Cinnamon Swirl French Toast with Sausage	1 package	480	252
Country Sausage and Buttermilk Biscuits	1 biscuit	170	126
Scrambled Eggs and Home Fried Potatoes (Budget Breakfast)	1 package	230	180
Scrambled Eggs, Home Fried Potatoes, and 3 Bacon Slices	1 package	400	324
Scrambled Eggs and Sausage with Hashed Brown Potatoes	1 package	430	315
6 Silver Dollar Pancakes with Sausage (Budget Breakfast)	1 package	290	108
Pancakes with Sausage	1 package	470	198

FROZEN AND MICROWAVE FOODS

FOOD	AMOUNT	TOTAL CALORIES	FAT CALORIES
Desserts (see also **SWEETS, Frozen Novelties, Cakes, and Pastries)**			
Cool Whip, regular	1 tbsp	12	9
Cool Whip, extra creamy	1 tbsp	16	9
Pillsbury			
All Ready Pie Crust, 2 (9-inch)			
crusts	⅛ of 2 crusts	240	135
Microwave Bundt Tunnel of			
Fudge	⅛ cake	290	153
Microwave Fudge Brownie Mix	1 brownie	180	81
Milk Chocolate Frosting Supreme	1/12 cake	150	54
Sara Lee			
Cheese Cake Snacks	1 (2 oz)	200	126
Chocolate Mousse	1/10 mousse	200	126
Deluxe Carrot Cake Snacks	1 (1.8 oz)	180	63
Fudge Cake Snacks	1 (1.6 oz)	190	90
Pound Cake	1/10 cake	130	63
Strawberry French Cheese Cake	1/10 cake	200	99
Weight Watchers			
Apple Pie	1 serving (2.5 oz)	190	45
Apple Sweet Roll	1 serving (2.5 oz)	180	36
Black Forest cake	1 serving (3 oz)	180	45
Chocolate Brownies	1 brownie	100	36
Chocolate Cake	1 serving (2.5 oz)	180	54
Strawberry Cheese Cake	1 serving (3.9 oz)	180	45
Dinners			
Armour Classics Lite			
Baby Bay Shrimp	1 package	250	54
Chicken Burgundy	1 package	210	18
Chicken Cacciatore	1 package	250	36
Chicken Marsala	1 package	270	63
Salisbury Steak	1 package	270	117
Seafood with Natural Herbs	1 package	220	18
Steak Diane	1 package	270	81
Sweet and Sour Chicken	1 package	240	18
Armour Dinner Classics			
Boneless Beef Short Ribs	1 package	390	171
Chicken Fricassee	1 package	310	90
Chicken with Wine and Mush-			
room Sauce	1 package	320	144
Salisbury Steak	1 package	430	189

FROZEN AND MICROWAVE FOODS

FOOD	AMOUNT	TOTAL CALORIES	FAT CALORIES
Armour Dinner Classics (*cont.*)			
Sirloin Roast	1 package	250	72
Sirloin Tips	1 package	290	99
Veal Parmigiana	1 package	430	225
Budget Gourmet Slim Selects			
Chicken Enchilada Suiza	1 package	270	81
Fettucini and Meat Sauce Parmesan	1 package	290	90
Glazed Turkey	1 package	270	45
Linguini with Scallops and Clams	1 package	280	99
Mandarin Chicken	1 package	290	54
Oriental Beef	1 package	290	81
Sirloin of Beef in Herb Sauce	1 package	290	108
Celeste			
Vegetable Pizza (large size)	¼ pizza	310	144
Gorton's			
Breaded Fish Sticks	4 sticks	210	81
Crispy Batter Dipped Fish Fillets	2 fillets	300	180
Crispy Batter Dipped Fish Sticks	4 sticks	220	108
Crunch Fish Fillets	2 fillets	350	234
Crunchy Fish Sticks	4 sticks	220	135
Crunchy Fried Clam Strips	½ package	310	207
Microwave Crunchy Fish Fillets	2 fillets	350	234
Microwave Crunchy Fish Sticks	6 sticks	340	198
Minced and Chopped Clams	½ can	70	9
New England Clam Chowder	¼ can	140	45
Potato Crisp Fish Fillets	2 fillets	340	216
Potato Crisp Fish Sticks	4 sticks	260	144
Gorton's Fishmarket Fresh			
Cod	5 oz	110	9
Flounder	5 oz	110	9
Haddock	5 oz	110	9
Ocean perch	5 oz	140	27
Sole	5 oz	110	9
Gorton's Light Recipe			
Baked Stuffed Scrod	1 package	250	126
Filet of Haddock with Lemon Butter Sauce	1 package	250	117
Filet of Sole with Lemon Butter Sauce	1 package	250	126
Lightly Breaded Fish Fillets	1 fillet	170	63
Shrimp Scampi	1 package	350	216

FROZEN AND MICROWAVE FOODS

FOOD	AMOUNT	TOTAL CALORIES	FAT CALORIES
Gorton's Light Recipe (cont.)			
Stuffed Flounder	1 package	260	126
Tempura Batter Fish Fillets	1 fillet	190	108
Gorton's Seafood Lover's Fillets			
Baked Scrod	1 package	320	162
Fillets Amandine	1 package	230	126
Fillets in Herb Butter	1 package	220	126
Salmon in Dill Sauce	1 package	410	297
Seafood Stuffed Fillets	1 package	260	117
Sole in Wine Sauce	1 package	140	36
Healthy Choices			
Breast of Turkey	1 package	270	45
Chicken and Pasta Divine	1 package	310	36
Chicken Oriental	1 package	220	18
Chicken Parmigiana	1 package	280	27
Oriental Pepper Steak	1 package	270	45
Salisbury Steak	1 package	300	63
Sirloin Tips	1 package	290	54
Sole au Gratin	1 package	280	45
Sweet and Sour Chicken	1 package	280	18
Lean Cuisine			
Beef and Pork Cannelloni	1 package	270	90
Breast of Chicken Marsala	1 package	190	45
Cheese Cannelloni	1 package	270	90
Chicken à l'Orange	1 package	270	45
Chicken and Vegetables with Vermicelli	1 package	270	63
Chicken Cacciatore with Vermicelli	1 package	280	90
Chicken Chow Mein with Rice	1 package	250	45
Filet of Fish Divan	1 package	270	81
Filet of Fish Florentine	1 package	240	81
Filet of Fish Jardinière with Souffléed Potatoes	1 package	280	90
Glazed Chicken with Vegetable Rice	1 package	270	72
Herbed Lamb with Rice	1 package	280	72
Lasagna with Meat and Sauce	1 package	270	72
Linguini with Clam Sauce	1 package	260	63
Meatball Stew	1 package	250	90
Oriental Beef	1 package	270	72
Oriental Scallops	1 package	220	27

FROZEN AND MICROWAVE FOODS

FOOD	AMOUNT	TOTAL CALORIES	FAT CALORIES
Lean Cuisine (*cont.*)			
Rigatoni Bake	1 package	260	90
Salisbury Steak	1 package	270	117
Shrimp and Chicken Cantonese	1 package	270	81
Sliced Turkey Breast in Mushroom Sauce	1 package	220	45
Spaghetti with Beef and Mushroom Sauce	1 package	280	63
Stuffed Cabbage with Meat in Tomato Sauce	1 package	220	81
Tuna Lasagna	1 package	280	90
Turkey Dijon	1 package	280	90
Veal Lasagna	1 package	280	72
Vegetable and Pasta Mornay with Ham	1 package	280	117
Zucchini Lasagna	1 package	260	63
Le Menu			
Beef Sirloin Tips	1 package	420	171
Chicken à la King	1 package	490	207
Chicken Parmigiana	1 package	400	180
Ham Steak	1 package	310	99
Sliced Turkey Breast	1 package	270	54
Yankee Pot Roast	1 package	360	135
Le Menu Light Style			
Glazed Chicken Breast	1 package	270	54
Salisbury Steak	1 package	220	63
Morningstar Farms			
Country Crisps	3 oz	250	144
Mrs. Paul's			
Batter Dipped Fish Fillets	2 fillets	320	117
Crispy Crunchy Fish Fillets	2 fillets	310	153
Crispy Crunchy Fish Sticks	4 sticks	200	90
Crispy Crunchy Natural Fish Fillets	2 fillets	230	135
Crunchy Batter Haddock Fillets	2 fillets	330	153
Deviled Crab Miniatures	½ package	250	108
Deviled Crabs	½ package	170	63
Fried Clams	½ package	240	117
Mrs. Paul's Light Entrée			
Fish Dijon	1 package	220	81
Shrimp and Clams	1 package	280	81
Mrs. Paul's Light Fillets			
Farm-raised Catfish	½ package	250	90

FROZEN AND MICROWAVE FOODS

FOOD	AMOUNT	TOTAL CALORIES	FAT CALORIES
Mrs. Paul's Light Fillets (*cont.*)			
Flounder	½ package	260	99
Haddock	½ package	220	45
Pillsbury Microwave Classic			
Casserole Breast of Chicken	1 package	400	198
Stouffer's Dinner Supreme			
Baked Chicken Breast with			
Gravy	1 package	300	99
Beef Rib Tips Bourguignonne	1 package	390	207
Chicken Florentine	1 package	420	171
Chicken Parmigiana	1 package	390	153
Glazed Ham Steak in Sauce	1 package	380	135
Roast Turkey Breast with Gravy			
and Dressing	1 package	330	90
Veal Parmigiana	1 package	370	135
Swanson Dinners			
Beans and Franks	1 package	440	180
Chopped Sirloin Beef	1 package	380	180
Fried Chicken (White Portions)	1 package	650	297
Meat Loaf	1 package	430	198
Salisbury Steak	1 package	410	162
Turkey (Mostly White Meat)	1 package	350	99
Veal Parmigiana	1 package	450	198
Swanson Home Style			
Breaded Veal Parmigiana	1 package	280	135
Chicken and Noodles	1 package	400	144
Fish 'n' Chips	1 package	350	153
Fried Chicken and Whipped			
Potatoes	1 package	300	189
Lasagna with Meat Sauce	1 package	400	153
Macaroni and Cheese	1 package	400	189
Salisbury Steak in Gravy with			
Macaroni and Cheese	1 package	410	288
Turkey (Mostly White Meat) in			
Gravy with Dressing and			
Whipped Potatoes	1 package	320	117
Swanson Hungry Man			
Beef Pot Pie	1 package (16 oz)	700	324
Chicken Pot Pie	1 package (16 oz)	740	369
Turkey Pot Pie	1 package (16 oz)	740	378
Swanson Original Style			
Beef Pot Pie	1 package (7 oz)	390	189
Chicken Pot Pie	1 package (7 oz)	410	216

FROZEN AND MICROWAVE FOODS

FOOD	AMOUNT	TOTAL CALORIES	FAT CALORIES
Swanson Original Style (*cont.*)			
Turkey Pot Pie	1 package (7 oz)	410	198
Tyson Gourmet Selection			
Breast of Turkey with Dressing	1 package	380	99
Chicken Francais	1 package	270	108
Chicken Marsala	1 package	300	117
Van de Kamp's			
Breaded Fish Sticks	4 sticks	270	171
Fish Fillets in Batter	1 fillet	180	90
Microwave Crispy Breaded Fish Fillets	1 fillet	130	63
Weight Watchers			
Baked Cheese Ravioli	1 package	300	108
Beef Enchiladas Ranchero	1 package	310	117
Beef Steak Burritos	1 burrito	310	117
Broccoli and Cheese Baked Potato	1 package	280	63
Cheese Enchiladas Ranchero	1 package	360	189
Cheese Manicotti	1 package	320	126
Chicken Divan Baked Potato	1 package	280	36
Chicken Enchiladas Suiza	1 package	350	153
Deluxe Combination Pizza	1 package	280	54
Imperial Chicken	1 package	220	45
Italian Cheese Lasagna	1 package	360	144
Lasagna with Meat Sauce	1 package	330	117
Oven Fried Fish	1 package	220	108
Pasta Primavera	1 package	290	108
Pasta Rigati	1 package	290	72
Pepperoni Pizza	1 package	320	81
Sausage Pizza	1 package	290	54
Seafood Linguini	1 package	220	63
Southern Fried Chicken Patty	1 package	270	144
Spaghetti with Meat Sauce	1 package	290	72
Stuffed Turkey Breast	1 package	260	90
Veal Patty Parmigiana	1 package	220	81

Sandwiches

FOOD	AMOUNT	TOTAL CALORIES	FAT CALORIES
Morningstar Farms			
Grillers	1 patty	180	108
Sara Lee			
Le Sanwich Croissants, ham and Swiss cheese	1 croissant	340	162

FROZEN AND MICROWAVE FOODS

FOOD	AMOUNT	TOTAL CALORIES	FAT CALORIES
Snacks			
Celeste			
Vegetable pizza, large size	¼ pizza	310	144

FRUITS AND FRUIT JUICES

FOOD	AMOUNT	TOTAL CALORIES	FAT CALORIES
Apples			
raw			
unpeeled	1 (3/lb)	81	trace
peeled	1 (3/lb)	72	trace
boiled			
peeled	½ cup slices	46	trace
canned, sweetened	½ cup slices	68	trace
Apple juice	1 cup	115	trace
Applesauce			
unsweetened	½ cup	53	trace
sweetened	½ cup	97	trace
Apricots			
fresh	3 (12/lb)	50	trace
	1 cup halves	74	trace
dried			
raw	10 halves	83	trace
	1 cup halves	310	trace
cooked	1 cup halves	210	trace
Avocado, fresh			
California	1	305	270
Florida	1	340	243
Bananas, whole	1	105	5
Blackberries, fresh	½ cup	37	trace
Blueberries, fresh	1 cup	80	trace
Boysenberries, canned in heavy syrup	½ cup	113	trace
Cantaloupe	½ melon	95	7
	1 cup cubes	57	trace
Cherries, sour red			
fresh			
pitted	1 cup	77	trace
unpitted	1 cup	51	trace

FRUITS AND FRUIT JUICES

FOOD	AMOUNT	TOTAL CALORIES	FAT CALORIES
Cherries, sour red (*cont.*)			
canned			
in light syrup	½ cup	94	trace
in heavy syrup	½ cup	116	trace
Cherries, sweet			
fresh	10	50	6
canned	1 cup	104	12
in light syrup	½ cup	85	trace
in heavy syrup	½ cup	107	trace
Cranberries, fresh	1 cup whole	46	trace
Cranberry juice cocktail, sweetened	1 cup	145	trace
Cranberry sauce, sweetened	½ cup	210	trace
Dates			
whole, pitted	10	230	trace
chopped	1 cup	490	7
Figs			
fresh	1 medium	37	trace
	1 large	47	trace
dried, raw	10	475	20
	1 cup	508	21
dried, cooked	1 cup	279	11
Fruit cocktail, canned			
in water	1 cup	79	trace
in juice	1 cup	115	trace
in light syrup	1 cup	110	trace
in heavy syrup	1 cup	185	trace
Grapefruit, fresh	½ fruit	38	trace
	1 cup sections	74	trace
Grapefruit juice			
fresh	½ cup	47	trace
canned			
unsweetened	½ cup	47	trace
sweetened	½ cup	57	trace
Grapes, Thompson seedless, fresh	10	35	trace
	1 cup	97	trace
Grape juice, canned or bottled	1 cup	155	trace
Guava, fresh	1	45	trace
Honeydew	⅟₁₀ melon	46	trace
	1 cup cubes	60	trace
Kiwis, fresh	1 medium	46	trace
	1 large	55	trace

FRUITS AND FRUIT JUICES

FOOD	AMOUNT	TOTAL CALORIES	FAT CALORIES
Kumquats, fresh	1	12	0
Lemons, fresh, peeled	1 medium	17	trace
	1 large	25	trace
Lemon juice, fresh	1 tbsp	4	0
	1 cup	60	0
Limes, fresh	1	20	trace
Lime juice, fresh	1 tbsp	4	0
	1 cup	65	trace
Mangos, fresh	1	135	trace
	1 cup slices	108	trace
Mixed fruit, dried	11-oz package	712	13
Mulberries, fresh	10	7	trace
	1 cup	61	trace
Nectarines, fresh	1	67	trace
	1 cup slices	68	trace
Oranges, fresh	1	60	trace
Orange juice	juice from 1 fruit	39	trace
	1 cup	111	trace
Papayas			
fresh	1	117	trace
	1 cup cubes	54	trace
Peaches			
fresh	1 (4/lb)	37	trace
canned			
in water	1 cup halves	58	trace
in juice, halves	1 cup	109	trace
in light syrup, halves	1 cup	136	trace
in heavy syrup, halves	1 cup	190	trace
dried			
raw, halves	10	311	9
	1 cup	383	11
cooked, halves			
unsweetened	1 cup	198	6
sweetened	1 cup	278	5
Pears			
fresh	1	98	trace
canned, halves			
in water	1 cup	71	trace
in juice	1 cup	125	trace
in light syrup	1 cup	144	trace
in heavy syrup	1 cup	190	trace

FRUITS AND FRUIT JUICES

FOOD	AMOUNT	TOTAL CALORIES	FAT CALORIES
Pears (*cont.*)			
dried, halves			
raw, halves	10	459	10
	1 cup	472	10
cooked, halves			
unsweetened	1 cup	325	7
sweetened	1 cup	392	7
Pineapple			
fresh	1 slice (¾- inch thick)	42	trace
	1 cup diced	75	trace
canned			
in water	1 cup tidbits	79	trace
in juice	1 cup chunks or tidbits	150	trace
in light syrup	1 cup slices	131	trace
in heavy syrup	1 cup slices	199	trace
Pineapple juice, unsweetened	1 cup	140	trace
Plantains			
raw	1	220	trace
cooked, slices	1 cup	180	trace
Plums, fresh	1	36	trace
	1 cup slices	91	9
Prunes			
canned in heavy syrup	5	90	trace
	1 cup	245	trace
dried			
raw	10	201	trace
	1 cup	385	7
cooked			
unsweetened	1 cup	225	trace
sweetened	1 cup	295	trace
Prune juice	1 cup	180	trace
Raisins, seedless	1 cup packed	494	7
	1 packet (½ oz)	40	trace
Raspberries, fresh	1 cup	60	trace
Rhubarb, fresh, diced	1 cup	26	trace
Strawberries			
fresh	1 cup	45	trace
canned in heavy syrup	1 cup	234	trace
Tangerines, fresh	1	35	trace
	1 cup sections	86	trace

FRUITS AND FRUIT JUICES

FOOD	AMOUNT	TOTAL CALORIES	FAT CALORIES
Watermelon	$\frac{1}{16}$ melon	152	4
	1 cup diced	50	trace

GRAIN PRODUCTS

FOOD	AMOUNT	TOTAL CALORIES	FAT CALORIES
Breads			
Bagels, plain or water, enriched	1 (3.5-inch diam)	200	18
Lender's			
egg, plain, or onion	1 (2 oz)	150	9
Raisin 'n Honey	1 (2.5 oz)	200	9
Wheat 'n Raisin	1 (2.5 oz)	190	9
Plain Bagelette	2 (1.8 oz)	140	9
Sara Lee, Cinnamon and Raisin, plain, or poppyseed	1 (3 oz)	240	18
Biscuits (baking powder)	1 (2-inch diam)	95	27
Arnold Old Fashioned Buttermilk	2 (1.3 oz)	120	45
Boston brown	½-inch slice	95	9
Cracked wheat	1 slice (18/loaf)	65	9
Crumbs			
dry	1 cup	390	45
soft	1 cup	120	18
Croissant	1 (4½ × 4 × 1¾ in)	235	108
English muffin	1 muffin	140	9
French, enriched	1 loaf (1 lb)	1270	0–162
	1-inch slice	100	0–9
French toast	1 slice	155	63
Honey Granola (Pepperidge Farm)	1 slice	65	18
Italian, enriched	1 loaf (1 lb)	1255	36
	¾-inch slice	85	trace
Mixed-grain, enriched	1 slice (18/loaf)	65	9
Muffins			
blueberry	1 medium	140	45
	1 large	290	99
bran	1 medium	140	36

GRAIN PRODUCTS

FOOD	AMOUNT	TOTAL CALORIES	FAT CALORIES
Muffins (*cont.*)			
corn	1 medium	145	54
oat bran			
A&P, Waldbaum's, Food			
Emporium	1 (4–4.5 oz)	340	63
David's Cookies	1 (2–2.5 oz)	78	9
Grand Union	1 (3.5 oz)	363	63
Macy's	1 (5.5 oz)	468	144
Natural Source	1 (5.75 oz)	670	261
The Greatest Cookie, Whole			
Earth Bakery	1 (6–6.75 oz)	524	216
Zaro's	1 (6.5 oz)	553	162
Oat and Honey Granola (Pepperidge Farm)	1 slice	70	18
Oatmeal, enriched	1 slice (18/loaf)	65	9
Pita, white	1 (6½-inch diam)	125	9
Pumpernickel	1 slice (15/loaf)	80	9
Raisin, enriched	1 slice (18/loaf)	65	9
Rolls			
dinner	1 (2 × 2½-inch diam)	85	18
hot dog or hamburger	1	115	18
hard	1 (2 × 3¾-inch diam)	155	18
submarine	1 (11½ × 3 × 2½-inch)	400	72
Rye, light	1 slice (18/loaf)	65	9
Stuffing mix			
dry	1 cup	500	279
moist	1 cup	420	234
Pepperidge Farm Distinctive Stuffing Mix			
Country Garden Herb	1 oz	110	27
Wild Rice and Mushroom	1 oz	100	18
Stove Top			
dry mix	1 serving	110	9
prepared with butter or margarine	1 serving	180	81
Stove Top One Step Stuffing Mix			
Cornbread dry mix	1 serving	130	27
prepared with butter or margarine	1 serving	180	81

GRAIN PRODUCTS

FOOD	AMOUNT	TOTAL CALORIES	FAT CALORIES
Vienna, enriched	1 loaf (1 lb)	1270	162
	½-inch slice	70	9
Wheat, enriched	1 slice (18/loaf)	65	9
White, enriched	1 slice (18/loaf)	65	9
	1 slice (22/loaf)	55	9
Whole-wheat, enriched	1 slice (16/loaf)	70	9

Breakfast Cereals, Cold

IMPORTANT: For all cereals, add 73 calories of fat per cup of whole milk; 42 per cup of 2% milk; 23 per cup of 1% milk; 4 per cup of skim milk.

FOOD	AMOUNT	TOTAL CALORIES	FAT CALORIES
All-Bran (Kellogg's)	⅓ cup (1 oz)	70	9
Fruit & Almonds	⅔ cup (1.3 oz)	100	18
with Extra Fiber	½ cup (1 oz)	60	9
Almond Delight (Ralston)	¾ cup (1 oz)	110	18
Alpha Bits (Post)	1 cup (1 oz)	110	<9
Apple Bran Granola	1 oz	120	63
Apple Cinnamon Squares			
(Kellogg's)	½ cup (1 oz)	90	0
Apple Jacks (Kellogg's)	1 cup (1 oz)	110	0
Apple Raisin Crisp (Kellogg's)	⅔ cup (1.3 oz)	130	0
100% Bran (Nabisco)	½ cup (1 oz)	70	18
Bran Chex (Ralston)	⅔ cup (1 oz)	90	0
Bran Flakes (Kellogg's)	⅔ cup (1 oz)	90	0
Cap'n Crunch (Quaker)	¾ cup (1 oz)	120	27
Cap'n Crunch's Peanut Butter			
Crunch	1 cup	154	41
Cheerios (General Mills)	1¼ cups (1 oz)	110	18
Cinnamon Life (Quaker)	⅔ cup (1 oz)	110	18
Clusters (General Mills)	½ cup (1 oz)	100	27
Cocoa Krispies (Kellogg's)	¾ cup (1 oz)	110	0
Cocoa Puffs (General Mills)	1 cup (1 oz)	110	9
Cookie Crisp, Chocolate Chip			
Flavor (Ralston)	1 cup (1 oz)	110	9
Corn Bran (Quaker)	⅔ cup (1 oz)	110	<9
Corn Chex (Ralston)	1 cup (1 oz)	110	0
Corn Flakes (Kellogg's)	1 cup (1 oz)	110	0
Corn Pops (Kellogg's)	1 cup (1 oz)	110	0
Count Chocula (General Mills)	1 cup (1 oz)	110	9
Crispix (Kellogg's)	¾ cup (1 oz)	110	0

GRAIN PRODUCTS

FOOD	AMOUNT	TOTAL CALORIES	FAT CALORIES
Crispy Critters Low in Sugar (Post)	1 cup (1 oz)	110	9
Crispy Wheats 'n Raisins (General Mills)	¾ cup (1 oz)	110	9
Double Chex (Ralston)	⅔ cup (1 oz)	100	0
Familia, Swiss Mixed Cereal	¼ cup (1 oz)	110	18
Fiber One (General Mills)	½ cup (1 oz)	60	9
Froot Loops (Kellogg's)	1 cup (1 oz)	110	9
Frosted Flakes (Kellogg's)	¾ cup (1 oz)	110	0
Frosted Mini-Wheats (Kellogg's)	4 biscuits (1 oz)	100	0
Fruit & Fibre Dates, Raisins & Walnuts (Post)	½ cup (1 oz)	90	<9
Fruit & Fibre Harvest Medley (Post)	½ cup (1 oz)	90	9
Fruit & Fibre Peaches, Raisins & Almonds (Post)	½ cup (1 oz)	90	9
Fruit & Fibre Tropical Fruit	½ cup (1 oz)	90	9
Fruit Wheats (Nabisco)	½ cup (1 oz)	100	0
Fruit Wheats Strawberry (Nabisco)	½ cup (1 oz)	100	0
Fruitful Bran (Kellogg's)	⅔ cup (1.3 oz)	120	0
Fruity Marshmallow Krispies (Kellogg's)	1¼ cups (1.3 oz)	140	0
Fruity Pebbles (Post)	⅞ cup (1 oz)	110	9
Golden Grahams (General Mills)	¾ cup (1 oz)	110	9
Granola (homemade)	¼ cup (1 oz)	138	69
Grape-Nuts (Post)	¼ cup (1 oz)	110	<9
Grape-Nuts Flakes (Post)	⅞ cup (1 oz)	100	<9
Honey and Nut Corn Flakes (Kellogg's)	⅔ cup (1 oz)	110	9
Honeycomb (Post)	1⅓ cups (1 oz)	110	<9
Honey Graham Chex (Ralston)	⅔ cup (1 oz)	110	9
Honey Nut Cheerios (General Mills)	¾ cup (1 oz)	110	9
Honey Smacks (Kellogg's)	¾ cup (1 oz)	110	0
Just Right with Fruit and Nuts (Kellogg's)	¾ cup (1.3 oz)	130	9
with Fiber Nuggets	⅔ cup (1 oz)	100	0
Kix (General Mills)	1½ cups (1 oz)	110	9
Life (Quaker)	⅔ cup (1 oz)	110	18
Lucky Charms (General Mills)	1 cup (1 oz)	110	9
Most (Kellogg's)	½ cup (1 oz)	95	<9
Natural Bran Flakes (Post)	⅔ cup (1 oz)	90	<9

GRAIN PRODUCTS

FOOD	AMOUNT	TOTAL CALORIES	FAT CALORIES
100% Natural (Quaker)	¼ cup (1 oz)	140	54
100% Natural Raisin & Date (Quaker)	¼ cup (1 oz)	130	45
Natural Cereal (Heartland)	¼ cup (1 oz)	123	40
with coconut	¼ cup (1 oz)	125	41
Nature Valley Granola	⅓ cup (1 oz)	126	44
Nutrific (Kellogg's)	1 cup (1.4 oz)	130	18
Nutri·Grain (Kellogg's)			
Corn	½ cup (1 oz)	100	9
Nuggets	¼ cup (1 oz)	100	9
Wheat	⅔ cup (1.4 oz)	130	0
Wheat and Raisins	⅔ cup (1.4 oz)	130	0
Oatmeal Raisin Crisp (General Mills)	½ cup (1 oz)	110	18
Pac-Man (General Mills)	1 cup (1 oz)	110	9
Product 19 (Kellogg's)	1 cup (1 oz)	100	0
Pro Grain (Kellogg's)	¾ cup (1 oz)	100	0
Puffed Rice (Quaker)	1 cup (½ oz)	60	<9
Puffed Wheat (Quaker)	1 cup (½ oz)	50	<9
Quisp (Quaker)	1 cup (1 oz)	124	20
Raisin Bran			
Kellogg's	¾ cup (1.4 oz)	120	9
Post	½ cup (1 oz)	90	<9
Raisin Nut Bran (General Mills)	½ cup (1 oz)	110	27
Raisin Squares (Kellogg's)	½ cup (1 oz)	90	0
Rice Chex (Ralston)	1⅛ cups (1 oz)	110	0
Rice Krispies (Kellogg's)	1 cup (1 oz)	110	0
Shredded Wheat (Nabisco)	1 biscuit (⅚ oz)	90	9
Shredded Wheat 'n Bran (Nabisco)	⅔ cup (1 oz)	110	9
S'mores Crunch (General Mills)	¾ cup (1 oz)	120	18
Special K (Kellogg's)	1 cup (1 oz)	110	0
Spoon Size Shredded Wheat (Nabisco)	⅔ cup (1 oz)	110	0
Strawberry Squares (Kellogg's)	½ cup (1 oz)	90	0
Super Golden Crisp (Post)	⅞ cup (1 oz)	110	<9
Team Flakes (Nabisco)	1 cup (1 oz)	110	9
Toasted Wheat & Raisins (Nabisco)	¾ cup (1.4 oz)	140	9
Total (General Mills)	1 cup (1 oz)	110	9
Trix (General Mills)	1 cup (1 oz)	110	9
Wheat Chex (Ralston)	⅔ cup (1 oz)	100	<9

GRAIN PRODUCTS

FOOD	AMOUNT	TOTAL CALORIES	FAT CALORIES
Wheat germ (Kretschmer)	¼ cup (1 oz)	110	27
Wheaties (General Mills)	1 cup (1 oz)	110	9

Most other ready-to-eat cereals have fewer than 9 calories of fat per cup; for actual fat content, check boxes and multiply grams by 9 to get calories of fat. Remember to add the calories of fat in the milk you use.

Breakfast Cereals, Hot
Hot breakfast cereals contain fewer than 10 calories of fat per serving; add 36 calories of fat per pat of butter or margarine and 100 per tablespoon. If you use milk, add calories of fat, depending on type of milk (see *Breakfast Cereals, Cold*).

FOOD	AMOUNT	TOTAL CALORIES	FAT CALORIES
Corn (hominy) grits, cooked			
regular and quick	1 cup	145	trace
instant, plain	1 packet	80	trace
Cream of Rice (Nabisco)	1 oz dry	100	0
Cream of Wheat (Nabisco)			
regular, quick, instant, cooked	1 cup	140	trace
Mix 'n Eat, plain, cooked	1 packet (1 oz)	100	trace
Farina (Pillsbury)	⅔ cup	80	9
Malt-O-Meal, cooked	1 cup	120	trace
Maypo	1 oz dry	100	9
Oat Bran (Quaker)	⅓ cup dry	110	18
Oatmeal or rolled oats			
regular, quick (Quaker)	⅔ cup (⅓ cup dry)	110	18
instant, plain (Quaker)	1 packet	110	18
Ralston High Fiber, uncooked	¼ cup	80	<9
Wheatena	½ cup	100	9

Crackers
FOOD	AMOUNT	TOTAL CALORIES	FAT CALORIES
American Heritage Wheat (Sunshine)	4 crackers	60	27
Better Cheddars Low Salt (Nabisco)	10 crackers	70	36
Breadsticks (Stella D'oro, Dietetic)			
plain	3 pieces	130	36
sesame	3 pieces	170	63
Cheddar (Estée)	.5 oz	70	36
Cheese and Peanut Butter (Austin)	6 crackers	200	99
Cheese Nips (Nabisco)	13 crackers	70	27

GRAIN PRODUCTS

FOOD	AMOUNT	TOTAL CALORIES	FAT CALORIES
Cheez-It (Sunshine)	12 crackers	70	36
Chex-Snack Mix, Sour Cream and Onion (Ralston)	1 oz	130	45
Chicken in a Biskit Flavored (Nabisco)	7 crackers	70	36
English Water Biscuit (Pepperidge Farm)	4 crackers	70	9
Escort (Nabisco)	3 crackers	80	36
Fiber with Sesame Seeds (Ideal)	2 crackers	40	0
Goldfish (Pepperidge Farm)			
Cheddar	22 crackers	70	27
Original Salted	22 crackers	70	36
Parmesan	22 crackers	70	27
Pizza	22 crackers	70	36
Pretzel	22 crackers	60	18
Graham, plain (Sunshine)	4 scored sections	60	18
Harvest Wheats (Keebler)	3 crackers	70	36
Hearty Wheat (Pepperidge Farm)	3 crackers	80	27
Hi-Ho (Sunshine)	4 crackers	80	45
Krispy Saltines (Sunshine)	5 crackers	60	9
Matzo (Manischewitz)			
American	1 piece	120	18
Egg and Onion	1 piece	110	<9
Plain Miniatures	5 crackers	45	<9
Thin Tea	1 piece	100	<9
Thins	1 piece	90	<9
Unsalted	1 piece	110	<9
Melba Rounds (Devonsheer)	4 rounds	50	0
Melba Toast (Devonsheer)	3 slices	50	0
Ocean Crisp (FFV)	1 cracker	40	9
Oyster and Chowder (OTC)	2 crackers	50	9
Oyster and Soup (Sunshine)	16 crackers	60	9
Oysterettes, Soup and Oyster (Nabisco)	18 crackers	60	9
Premium Low Salt (Nabisco)	5 crackers	60	18
Premium Unsalted Tops (Nabisco)	5 crackers	60	18
Quackers, Cheddar Cheese (Nabisco)	28 ducks	70	27
Rice cakes	1 cake	35	0
Ritz (Nabisco)	4 crackers	70	36
Ritz Low Salt (Nabisco)	4 crackers	70	27

GRAIN PRODUCTS

FOOD	AMOUNT	TOTAL CALORIES	FAT CALORIES
Ritz Bits (Nabisco)	22 crackers	80	45
Ry-Krisp			
Original	2 triple crackers	40	0
Seasoned	2 triple crackers	45	9
Rye wafers	2 wafers (1⅞ × 3½ inch)	55	9
Saltines	5 crackers	60	9
Sesame (Estée)	.5 oz	70	36
Sesame (Pepperidge Farm)	3 crackers	60	18
Sesame Crisp (FFV)	1 cracker	50	9
Sesame Crisp Wafers (FFV)	4 wafers	60	18
Snack, standard	1 round cracker	15	9
Snack Sticks (Pepperidge Farm)			
Cheese	4 crackers	70	27
Pumpernickel	4 crackers	70	18
Sesame	4 crackers	70	27
Sociables (Nabisco)	6 crackers	70	27
Stone Creek Cracked Wheat (Keebler)	4 crackers	60	18
Tam Tams (Manischewitz)			
No Salt	5 crackers	70	36
Onion	5 crackers	80	36
Plain	5 crackers	70	36
Wheat	5 crackers	80	36
Thin Butter (Pepperidge Farm)	4 crackers	80	27
Town House, Low Salt (Keebler)	5 crackers	80	45
Triscuit Wafers (Nabisco)	3 crackers	60	18
Tuc (Keebler)	3 crackers	70	36
Uneeda Biscuits, Unsalted Tops (Nabisco)	3 crackers	60	18
Vegetable, No Salt Added (Hain)	5 crackers	70	27
Vegetable Thins (Nabisco)	7 crackers	70	36
Waldorf, Low Sodium (Keebler)	4 crackers	60	18
Wasa Crispbread	1 cracker	45	0
Wheat Rye, No Salt Added (Hain)	5 crackers	60	18
Wheat Thins (Nabisco)	8 crackers	70	27
Wheat Wafers (Estée)	10 wafers	60	18
Wheat Wafers (Sunshine)	8 wafers	80	36
Wheatsworth Stone Ground Wheat (Nabisco)	5 crackers	70	27
Zwieback Toast (Nabisco)	2 crackers	50	9

GRAIN PRODUCTS

FOOD	AMOUNT	TOTAL CALORIES	FAT CALORIES
Flour			
Buckwheat flour, light	1 cup	340	9
Corn meal			
whole-ground, dry	1 cup	435	45
degermed			
dry	1 cup	500	18
cooked	1 cup	120	trace
Cornstarch	1 tbsp	29	trace
Wheat flour			
cake or pastry, sifted	1 cup	350	7
self-rising, unsifted	1 cup	440	12
white (unbleached)			
sifted	1 cup	420	11
unsifted	1 tbsp	26	1
	1 cup	455	12
whole-wheat	1 cup	400	21
Grains (Cereal Grasses)			
Barley, pearl, light, uncooked	1 cup	700	18
Bulgur, uncooked	1 cup	600	27
Rice			
brown			
raw	1 cup	666	32
cooked	1 cup	230	9
white			
raw	1 cup	670	6
cooked	1 cup	224	trace
instant	1 cup	180	trace
parboiled	1 cup	185	2
Wheat bran	1 oz	60	12
	1 cup	90	18
Wheat germ	¼ cup	110	27
	1 tbsp	23	6
Miscellaneous			
French toast	1 slice	155	63
Pancakes			
buckwheat	1 (4-inch diam)	55	18
plain, from mix	1 (4-inch diam)	60	18
Tortillas, corn	1	65	9
Tostitos (tortilla chips)	1 oz	140	72
Waffles, from mix	1 (7-inch diam)	205	72

GRAIN PRODUCTS

FOOD	AMOUNT	TOTAL CALORIES	FAT CALORIES
Pastas			
Chow mein (La Choy)	1 cup	320	144
Fettucine Alfredo	1 cup	880	610
Lasagna	1/12 casserole, 9 × 12 inches	570	210
Macaroni (macaroni, linguini, etc.)			
dry	1 oz	110	<9
cooked	1 cup	155	9
Noodles, egg, cooked	1 cup	200	18
Pasta dinners, Kraft			
American Style Spaghetti	1 cup	310	72
Macaroni and Cheese	¾ cup	290	117
Noodle with Chicken	¾ cup	240	81
Ragu Pasta Meals			
Mini Lasagna in Sauce	¾ cup	160	9
Spaghetti in Sauce	¾ cup	170	9
Twists in Sauce	¾ cup	160	9
Spaghetti			
dry	8 oz	838	25
cooked	1 cup	155	9
Pastries (See also **SWEETS***)*			
Breakfast bars			
Carnation Breakfast Bars, peanut butter with chocolate chip	1 bar (1.4 oz)	200	99
Kudo chocolate and granola snacks	1 bar (1.26 oz)	190	108
Nature Valley Granola Bars, oats and honey	1 bar (.83 oz)	120	45
Quaker Chewy Granola Bars, peanut butter and chocolate chip	1 bar (1 oz)	130	45
Danish pastry			
plain, without fruit or nuts			
packaged ring	1 ring (12 oz)	1305	639
round piece	1 (1 × 4¼-inch diam)	220	108
fruit, round	1	235	117
Doughnuts			
cake-type, plain	1	210	108
yeast-leavened, glazed	1	235	117

GRAIN PRODUCTS

FOOD	AMOUNT	TOTAL CALORIES	FAT CALORIES
Pop Tarts (Kellogg's), Frosted			
Dutch Apple	1 pastry	210	54
Toaster pastries	1	210	54
***Snack Foods (See also* SWEETS)**			
Bugles (General Mills)	1 oz	150	72
Cheese Twists	1 oz	140	63
Chee-tos (Nabisco)	1 oz	150	90
Corn chips	1 oz	155	81
Cornuts	1 oz	120	36
Fritos	1 oz	150	81
Jax (Bachman)	1 oz	150	72
Popcorn			
air-popped, no fat added	1 cup popped	30	trace
air-popped, fat added (Bachman All Natural)	1 oz popped (5.5 cups)	160	99
candied (Cracker Jack)	⅔ cup (1 oz)	120	27
microwave			
butter flavor (General Mills)	1 cup popped	60	36
butter flavor (Orville Redenbacher's)	1 cup popped	30	18
butter flavor (Pillsbury)	1 cup popped	70	36
natural flavor (General Mills)	1 cup popped	60	27
natural flavor (Orville Redenbacher's)	1 cup popped	30	18
natural flavor (Pillsbury)	1 cup popped	70	36
popped in vegetable oil	1 cup popped	55	27
Potato chips	10	105	64
Potato sticks	1 oz	148	88
Pretzels			
sticks	10 (2-inch)	10	trace
twisted, Dutch	1	65	9
twisted, thin	1	24	2

MEATS (BEEF, LAMB, PORK, VEAL, AND GAME)

See also **SAUSAGES AND LUNCHEON MEATS** for cold cuts made from beef and pork products and **FROZEN AND MICROWAVE FOODS.**

Beef
*Remember that the following calorie figures are for **only 1 ounce** of beef!*

FOOD	AMOUNT	TOTAL CALORIES	FAT CALORIES
Arm pot roast, braised			
lean and fat	1 oz	99	66
lean only	1 oz	65	25
Bottom round steak, braised			
lean and fat	1 oz	74	38
lean only	1 oz	67	25
Brain			
pan-fried	1 oz	56	40
simmered	1 oz	45	32
Brisket, flat half, braised			
lean and fat	1 oz	116	89
lean only	1 oz	74	40
Chuck steak, braised			
lean and fat	1 oz	108	78
lean only	1 oz	77	39
Club steak, broiled			
lean and fat	1 oz	129	104
lean only	1 oz	69	33
Flank steak, braised			
lean and fat	1 oz	73	39
lean only	1 oz	69	35
Ground beef			
raw			
extra lean	1 oz	66	44
lean	1 oz	75	53
regular	1 oz	88	68
broiled, medium			
extra lean	1 oz	72	42
lean	1 oz	77	47
regular	1 oz	82	53
pan-fried, medium			
extra lean	1 oz	72	42
lean	1 oz	78	49
regular	1 oz	87	58
Liver			
braised	1 oz	46	12
pan-fried	1 oz	61	20

MEATS (BEEF, LAMB, PORK, VEAL, AND GAME)

FOOD	AMOUNT	TOTAL CALORIES	FAT CALORIES
Liver (*cont.*)			
fine paté	½ cup	289	204
Porterhouse steak, broiled			
lean and fat	1 oz	85	54
lean only	1 oz	62	28
Rib roast			
lean and fat	1 oz	108	81
lean only	1 oz	68	35
Round, broiled			
lean and fat	1 oz	78	47
lean only	1 oz	55	20
Rump roast			
lean and fat	1 oz	98	70
lean only	1 oz	59	24
Shortribs, braised			
lean and fat	1 oz	133	107
lean only	1 oz	84	46
Sirloin steak, broiled			
lean and fat	1 oz	79	46
lean only	1 oz	59	22
Sweetbreads (pancreas)			
braised	1 oz	77	44
T-bone steak, broiled			
lean and fat	1 oz	92	63
lean only	1 oz	61	26
Tenderloin steak, broiled			
lean and fat	1 oz	75	44
lean only	1 oz	58	24
Tongue, simmered	1 oz	81	53
Top round, broiled			
lean and fat	1 oz	60	22
lean only	1 oz	54	16
Tripe, raw	1 oz	28	10

Mixed Beef Dishes (*See also* FROZEN AND MICROWAVE FOODS)

FOOD	AMOUNT	TOTAL CALORIES	FAT CALORIES
Beef and vegetable stew	1 cup	220	99
Beef potpie (9-inch diam)	⅓ pie	515	270
Chili con carne with beans			
canned	1 cup	340	144
Lasagna (9 x 13–inch casserole)	1/12 casserole	570	210
Spaghetti with meatballs and			
tomato sauce, canned	1 cup	260	90

MEATS (BEEF, LAMB, PORK, VEAL, AND GAME)

FOOD	AMOUNT	TOTAL CALORIES	FAT CALORIES
Lamb			
Remember that the following calorie figures are for **only 1 ounce** *of lamb!*			
Foreshank, braised			
lean and fat	1 oz	69	34
lean only	1 oz	53	15
Leg, whole (shank and sirloin), roasted			
lean and fat	1 oz	73	42
lean only	1 oz	54	20
Leg, shank half, roasted			
lean and fat	1 oz	64	32
lean only	1 oz	51	17
Leg, sirloin half, roasted			
lean and fat	1 oz	83	53
lean only	1 oz	58	23
Loin			
broiled			
lean and fat	1 oz	89	59
lean only	1 oz	61	25
roasted			
lean and fat	1 oz	88	60
lean only	1 oz	57	25
Rib			
broiled			
lean and fat	1 oz	102	75
lean only	1 oz	67	33
roasted			
lean and fat	1 oz	102	76
lean only	1 oz	66	34
Shoulder, whole (arm and blade)			
braised			
lean and fat	1 oz	97	63
lean only	1 oz	80	40
roasted			
lean and fat	1 oz	78	51
lean only	1 oz	58	27
Shoulder, arm			
braised			
lean and fat	1 oz	98	61
lean only	1 oz	79	36
roasted			
lean and fat	1 oz	79	52
lean only	1 oz	54	24

MEATS (BEEF, LAMB, PORK, VEAL, AND GAME)

FOOD	AMOUNT	TOTAL CALORIES	FAT CALORIES
Shoulder, blade			
braised			
lean and fat	1 oz	98	63
lean only	1 oz	82	42
broiled			
lean and fat	1 oz	79	51
lean only	1 oz	60	29
Cubed lamb for stew or kabob (leg			
and shoulder), lean only			
braised	1 oz	63	22
broiled	1 oz	53	19
Ground lamb, broiled	1 oz	80	50

Pork
Pork Products, Fresh
*Remember that most of the following calorie figures are for **only 1 ounce** of pork product!*

FOOD	AMOUNT	TOTAL CALORIES	FAT CALORIES
Ham (leg), roasted			
lean and fat	1 oz	83	53
lean only	1 oz	62	28
Liver, braised	1 oz	47	11
country paté	½ cup	430	357
Loin			
whole, broiled			
lean and fat	1 oz	98	69
lean only	1 oz	73	39
blade, pan-fried			
lean and fat	1 oz	117	94
lean only	1 oz	80	51
center loin, braised			
lean and fat	1 oz	100	65
lean only	1 oz	77	35
center rib, broiled			
lean and fat	1 oz	97	67
lean only	1 oz	73	38
sirloin, broiled			
lean and fat	1 oz	94	64
lean only	1 oz	69	35
tenderloin, roasted			
lean only	1 oz	47	12
top loin, pan-fried			
lean and fat	1 oz	111	85
lean only	1 oz	73	39

MEATS (BEEF, LAMB, PORK, VEAL, AND GAME)

FOOD	AMOUNT	TOTAL CALORIES	FAT CALORIES
Shoulder			
whole, roasted			
lean and fat	1 oz	92	65
lean only	1 oz	69	38
arm picnic, roasted			
lean and fat	1 oz	94	67
lean only	1 oz	65	32
blade, Boston, roasted			
lean and fat	1 oz	91	64
lean only	1 oz	73	43
Spareribs, braised			
lean and fat	1 oz	113	77
Pork Variety Meats and By-Products			
Backfat, raw	1 oz	230	226
Chitterlings, simmered	1 oz	86	73
Feet, simmered	1 oz	55	49
Pork Products, Cured			
Bacon, cooked	1 strip	36	28
Breakfast strips, cooked	1 strip	52	37
Canadian bacon, grilled	1 slice	43	18
Salt pork, raw	1 oz	212	205

For cold cuts made from pork products, see **SAUSAGES AND LUNCHEON MEATS.**

Veal
*Remember that the following calorie figures are for **only 1 ounce** of veal!*

FOOD	AMOUNT	TOTAL CALORIES	FAT CALORIES
Breast, lean and fat, braised	1 oz	86	54
Cutlet, lean and fat, braised	1 oz	61	27
Leg (top round)			
braised			
lean and fat	1 oz	60	16
lean only	1 oz	57	13
pan-fried, breaded			
lean and fat	1 oz	65	23
lean only	1 oz	58	16
pan-fried, not breaded			
lean and fat	1 oz	60	21
lean only	1 oz	52	12

MEATS (BEEF, LAMB, PORK, VEAL, AND GAME)

FOOD	AMOUNT	TOTAL CALORIES	FAT CALORIES
Leg (*cont.*)			
roasted			
lean and fat	1 oz	45	12
lean only	1 oz	43	9
Loin			
braised			
lean and fat	1 oz	81	44
lean only	1 oz	64	23
roasted			
lean and fat	1 oz	61	31
lean only	1 oz	50	18
Rib			
braised			
lean and fat	1 oz	71	32
lean only	1 oz	62	20
roasted			
lean and fat	1 oz	65	36
lean only	1 oz	50	19
Shoulder, whole (arm and blade)			
braised			
lean and fat	1 oz	65	26
lean only	1 oz	56	16
roasted			
lean and fat	1 oz	52	21
lean only	1 oz	48	17
Shoulder, arm			
braised			
lean and fat	1 oz	67	26
lean only	1 oz	57	14
roasted			
lean and fat	1 oz	52	21
lean only	1 oz	46	15
Shoulder, blade			
braised			
lean and fat	1 oz	64	26
lean only	1 oz	56	17
roasted			
lean and fat	1 oz	53	22
lean only	1 oz	49	18
Sirloin			
braised			
lean and fat	1 oz	72	34
lean only	1 oz	58	17

MEATS (BEEF, LAMB, PORK, VEAL, AND GAME)

FOOD	AMOUNT	TOTAL CALORIES	FAT CALORIES
Sirloin (*cont.*)			
roasted			
lean and fat	1 oz	57	27
lean only	1 oz	48	16
Cubed veal for stew (leg and shoulder), lean only, braised	1 oz	53	11
Ground veal, broiled	1 oz	49	19

Game Meats

*Remember that the following calorie figures are for **only 1 ounce** of game!*

FOOD	AMOUNT	TOTAL CALORIES	FAT CALORIES
Antelope, roasted	1 oz	42	7
Bear, simmered	1 oz	73	34
Beaver, roasted	1 oz	47	14
Beefalo, composite of cuts, roasted	1 oz	53	16
Bison, roasted	1 oz	41	6
Boar, wild, roasted	1 oz	45	11
Buffalo, water, roasted	1 oz	37	5
Caribou, roasted	1 oz	47	11
Deer, roasted	1 oz	45	8
Elk, roasted	1 oz	41	5
Goat, roasted	1 oz	41	8
Horse, roasted	1 oz	50	15
Moose, roasted	1 oz	38	2
Muskrat, roasted	1 oz	52	23
Opossum, roasted	1 oz	63	26
Rabbit, domesticated, composite of cuts			
roasted	1 oz	44	16
stewed	1 oz	58	21
Rabbit, wild, stewed	1 oz	49	9
Raccoon, roasted	1 oz	72	37
Squirrel, roasted	1 oz	39	9

NUTS AND SEEDS

FOOD	AMOUNT	TOTAL CALORIES	FAT CALORIES
Nuts			
Almonds, shelled			
slivered	1 cup	795	630
whole, dry-roasted	1 oz (24 nuts)	165	132
Almond butter			
plain	1 tbsp	101	85
honey-cinnamon	1 tbsp	96	75
Almond paste	1 oz	127	69
	1 cup	1012	556
Beechnuts, dried	1 oz	164	128
Brazil nuts, shelled, dried	1 oz (8 med)	186	169
Butternuts, dried	1 oz	174	146
Cashew nuts			
dry-roasted	1 oz (18 med)	163	118
	1 cup	785	572
oil-roasted	1 oz (18 med)	163	123
	1 cup	750	564
Cashew butter, plain	1 tbsp	94	71
	1 oz	167	126
Chestnuts, Chinese			
raw	1 oz	64	3
dried	1 oz	103	5
boiled and steamed	1 oz	44	2
roasted	1 oz	68	3
Chestnuts, European			
raw, unpeeled	1 oz	60	6
raw, peeled	1 oz	56	3
dried			
unpeeled	1 oz	106	11
peeled	1 oz	105	10
boiled and steamed	1 oz	37	4
roasted	1 oz (3 nuts)	70	6
	1 cup	350	28
Chestnuts, Japanese			
raw	1 oz	44	1
dried	1 oz	102	3
boiled and steamed	1 oz	16	1
roasted	1 oz	57	2
Coconut meat			
raw, shredded or grated	1 oz	101	86
	1 cup	283	241

NUTS AND SEEDS

FOOD	AMOUNT	TOTAL CALORIES	FAT CALORIES
Coconut meat (*cont.*)			
dried			
creamed	1 oz	194	177
sweetened, flaked	1 oz	126	82
	1 cup	341	220
toasted	1 oz	168	120
Coconut cream			
fresh	1 tbsp	49	47
	1 cup	792	749
canned	1 tbsp	36	30
	1 cup	568	472
Coconut milk			
fresh	1 tbsp	35	32
	1 cup	552	515
canned	1 tbsp	30	29
	1 cup	445	434
frozen	1 tbsp	30	28
	1 cup	486	449
Filberts or hazelnuts			
dried	1 oz	180	160
	1 cup, chopped kernels	725	648
dry-roasted	1 oz	188	169
oil-roasted	1 oz	187	163
Hickory nuts, dried	1 oz	187	165
Macadamia nuts			
dried	1 oz	199	188
oil-roasted	1 oz (24 halves)	204	196
	1 cup	960	923
Mixed nuts			
dry-roasted, with peanuts	1 oz	169	131
	1 cup	814	634
oil-roasted, with peanuts	1 oz	175	144
	1 cup	876	720
oil-roasted, without peanuts	1 oz	175	144
	1 cup	886	728
Peanuts, shelled			
dry-roasted	1 oz (35 kernels)	161	126
	1 cup	827	646
oil-roasted	1 oz (35 kernels)	165	126
	1 cup	840	642

NUTS AND SEEDS

FOOD	AMOUNT	TOTAL CALORIES	FAT CALORIES
Peanut butter, smooth	1 tbsp	95	74
Pecans			
dried	1 oz	190	173
dry-roasted	1 oz (14 halves)	187	165
oil-roasted	1 oz	195	182
Pistachio nuts			
dried	1 oz	164	124
dry-roasted	1 oz (47 kernels)	172	135
Walnuts, black, dried	1 oz (14 halves)	172	145
	1 cup	760	637
Walnuts, English or Persian, dried	1 oz (14 halves)	182	158
	1 cup	770	668

Seeds

FOOD	AMOUNT	TOTAL CALORIES	FAT CALORIES
Poppy Seeds	1 tsp	15	11
	1 tbsp	66	51
Pumpkin and squash			
whole, roasted	1 oz	127	50
kernels, dried	1 oz	154	117
kernels, roasted	1 oz	148	108
Sesame, kernels, dried	1 tbsp	47	39
	1 cup	882	739
Sunflower			
in shell, roasted	1 oz	86	59
shelled			
dried	1 oz	162	127
dry-roasted	1 oz	165	127
	1 tbsp	46	36
	1 cup	745	574
oil-roasted	1 oz	175	147
	1 cup	830	698
toasted	1 oz	176	145
	1 cup	829	685
Tahini	1 tbsp	90	72

POULTRY

For cold cuts made from poultry products, see **SAUSAGES AND LUNCHEON MEATS** and **FROZEN AND MICROWAVE FOODS.**

FOOD	AMOUNT	TOTAL CALORIES	FAT CALORIES
Chicken			
Back			
meat and skin			
raw	½ back (3.5 oz)	316	256
	1 oz	90	73
fried, batter-dipped	½ back (4.2 oz)	397	237
	1 oz	94	56
fried, flour-coated	½ back (2.5 oz)	238	134
	1 oz	94	53
roasted	½ back (1.9 oz)	159	100
	1 oz	85	54
meat only			
raw	½ back (1.8 oz)	70	27
	1 oz	39	15
fried	½ back (2 oz)	167	80
	1 oz	82	39
roasted	½ back (1.4 oz)	96	47
	1 oz	68	34
Breast			
meat and skin			
raw	½ breast (5.1 oz)	250	121
	1 oz	49	24
fried, batter-dipped	½ breast (4.9 oz)	364	166
	1 oz	74	34
fried, flour-coated	½ breast (3.4 oz)	218	78
	1 oz	63	23
roasted	½ breast (3.4 oz)	193	69
	1 oz	56	20
meat only			
raw	½ breast (4.2 oz)	129	13
	1 oz	31	3
fried	½ breast (3 oz)	161	36
	1 oz	53	12
roasted	½ breast (3 oz)	142	28
	1 oz	47	9
Drumstick			
meat and skin			
raw	1 drumstick (2.6 oz)	117	57

POULTRY

FOOD	AMOUNT	TOTAL CALORIES	FAT CALORIES
Drumstick (*cont.*)			
	1 oz	46	22
fried, batter-dipped	1 drumstick		
	(2.5 oz)	193	102
	1 oz	76	40
fried, flour-coated	1 drumstick		
	(1.7 oz)	120	60
	1 oz	69	35
roasted	1 drumstick		
	(1.8 oz)	112	52
	1 oz	61	28
meat only			
raw	1 drumstick		
	(2.2 oz)	74	19
	1 oz	34	9
fried	1 drumstick		
	(1.5 oz)	82	31
	1 oz	55	21
roasted	1 drumstick		
	(1.6 oz)	76	22
	1 oz	49	14
Gizzard			
raw	1 gizzard (1.3 oz)	44	14
	1 oz	33	11
simmered	1 cup	222	48
	1 oz	43	9
Leg			
meat and skin			
raw	1 leg (5.9 oz)	312	182
	1 oz	53	31
fried, batter-dipped	1 leg (5.6 oz)	431	230
	1 oz	77	41
fried, flour-coated	1 leg (4 oz)	285	145
	1 oz	72	37
roasted	1 leg (4 oz)	265	138
	1 oz	66	34
meat only			
raw	1 leg (4.6 oz)	156	45
	1 oz	34	10
fried	1 leg (3.3 oz)	195	79
	1 oz	59	24
roasted	1 leg (3.4 oz)	182	72
	1 oz	54	22

POULTRY

FOOD	AMOUNT	TOTAL CALORIES	FAT CALORIES
Liver			
raw	1 liver (1.1 oz)	40	11
	1 oz	35	10
simmered	1 cup	219	69
	1 oz	44	14
chopped chicken livers	1 tbsp	28	17
pâté, canned	1 tbsp	26	15
	1 oz	57	33
Neck			
meat and skin			
raw	1 neck (1.8 oz)	148	118
	1 oz	84	67
fried, batter-dipped	1 neck (1.8 oz)	172	110
	1 oz	94	60
fried, flour-coated	1 neck (1.3 oz)	119	76
	1 oz	94	60
simmered	1 neck (1.3 oz)	94	62
	1 oz	70	46
meat only			
raw	1 neck (.7 oz)	31	16
	1 oz	44	22
fried	1 neck (.8 oz)	50	23
	1 oz	65	30
simmered	1 neck (.6 oz)	32	13
	1 oz	51	21
Thigh			
meat and skin			
raw	1 thigh (3.3 oz)	199	129
	1 oz	60	39
fried, batter-dipped	1 thigh (3 oz)	238	128
	1 oz	78	42
fried, flour-coated	1 thigh (2.2 oz)	162	84
	1 oz	74	38
roasted	1 thigh (2.2 oz)	153	86
	1 oz	70	40
meat only			
raw	1 thigh (2.4 oz)	82	24
	1 oz	34	10
fried	1 thigh (1.8 oz)	113	48
	1 oz	62	26
roasted	1 thigh (1.8 oz)	109	51
	1 oz	59	28

POULTRY

FOOD	AMOUNT	TOTAL CALORIES	FAT CALORIES
Wing			
meat and skin			
raw	1 wing (1.7 oz)	109	70
	1 oz	63	41
fried, batter-dipped	1 wing (1.7 oz)	159	96
	1 oz	92	56
fried, flour-coated	1 wing (1.1 oz)	103	64
	1 oz	91	57
roasted	1 wing (1.2 oz)	99	60
	1 oz	82	50
meat only			
raw	1 wing (1 oz)	36	9
	1 oz	36	9
fried	1 wing (.7 oz)	42	16
	1 oz	60	23
roasted	1 wing (.74 oz)	43	15
	1 oz	58	21

Mixed Chicken Dishes (See also FROZEN AND MICROWAVE FOODS)

FOOD	AMOUNT	TOTAL CALORIES	FAT CALORIES
Chicken à la king	1 cup	470	306
Chicken and noodles	1 cup	365	162
Chicken potpie (9-inch diam)	⅓ pie	545	279
Chicken salad	½ cup	252	141

Duck, Domesticated

FOOD	AMOUNT	TOTAL CALORIES	FAT CALORIES
Meat and skin			
raw	½ duck (22.4 oz)	2561	2245
	1 oz	115	100
roasted	½ duck (13.5 oz)	1287	975
	1 oz	96	72
Meat only			
raw	½ duck (10.7 oz)	399	162
	1 oz	37	15
roasted	½ duck (7.8 oz)	445	223
	1 oz	57	29
Liver, raw	1 liver (1.6 oz)	60	18
	1 oz	39	12

Duck, Wild

FOOD	AMOUNT	TOTAL CALORIES	FAT CALORIES
Meat and skin, raw	½ duck (9.5 oz)	571	369
	1 oz	60	39
breast meat only, raw	½ breast (2.9 oz)	102	32
	1 oz	35	11

POULTRY

FOOD	AMOUNT	TOTAL CALORIES	FAT CALORIES
Goose, Domesticated			
Meat and skin			
raw	½ goose		
	(46.5 oz)	4893	3991
	1 oz	105	86
roasted	½ goose		
	(27.3 oz)	2362	1527
	1 oz	86	56
Meat only			
raw	½ goose (27 oz)	1237	492
	1 oz	46	18
roasted	½ goose		
	(20.8 oz)	1406	674
	1 oz	67	32
Liver, raw	1 liver (3.3 oz)	125	36
pâté, smoked, canned	1 tbsp	60	51
	1 oz	131	112
Pheasant			
Meat and skin, raw	½ pheasant		
	(14.1 oz)	723	335
	1 oz	51	24
Meat only, raw	½ pheasant		
	(12.4 oz)	470	115
	1 oz	38	9
Breast meat only, raw	½ breast (6.4 oz)	243	53
	1 oz	38	8
Leg meat only, raw	1 leg (3.8 oz)	143	41
	1 oz	38	11
Quail			
Meat and skin, raw	1 quail (3.8 oz)	210	118
	1 oz	54	31
Meat only, raw	1 quail (3.2 oz)	123	38
	1 oz	38	12
Breast meat only, raw	1 breast (2 oz)	69	15
	1 oz	35	8
Squab (Pigeon)			
Meat and skin, raw	1 squab (7 oz)	584	426
	1 oz	83	61

POULTRY

FOOD	AMOUNT	TOTAL CALORIES	FAT CALORIES
Meat only, raw	1 squab (5.9 oz)	239	113
	1 oz	40	19
Breast meat only, raw	1 breast (3.6 oz)	135	41
	1 oz	38	12

Turkey
Back
meat and skin

raw	½ back (6.5 oz)	275	120
	1 oz	43	18
roasted	½ back (4.6 oz)	265	120
	1 oz	58	26

meat only

raw	½ back (5.3 oz)	180	47
	1 oz	34	9
roasted	½ back (3.4 oz)	164	49
	1 oz	48	14

Breast
meat and skin

raw	½ breast (15.3 oz)	543	103
	1 oz	35	7
roasted	½ breast (12.1 oz)	526	99
	1 oz	43	8

meat only

raw	½ breast (13.8 oz)	433	23
	1 oz	31	2
roasted	½ breast (10.8 oz)	413	20
	1 oz	38	2
Cutlet, braised	1 oz	45	8

Leg
meat and skin

raw	1 leg (12.3 oz)	412	112
	1 oz	33	9
roasted	1 leg (8.6 oz)	418	119
	1 oz	48	14

meat only

raw	1 leg (11.6 oz)	356	70
	1 oz	31	6

POULTRY

FOOD	AMOUNT	TOTAL CALORIES	FAT CALORIES
Leg (*cont.*)			
roasted	1 leg (7.9 oz)	355	76
	1 oz	45	10
Wing			
meat and skin			
raw	1 wing (4.5 oz)	203	89
	1 oz	45	20
roasted	1 wing (3.2 oz)	186	80
	1 oz	59	25
meat only			
raw	1 wing (3.2 oz)	96	9
	1 oz	30	3
roasted	1 wing (2.1 oz)	98	19
	1 oz	46	9

SAUCES AND GRAVIES

FOOD	AMOUNT	TOTAL CALORIES	FAT CALORIES
Sauces			
Barbecue, ready-to-serve	½ cup	94	20
Béarnaise	1 tbsp	53	48
	½ cup	423	384
dehydrated, prepared with milk and butter	1 tbsp	44	38
	½ cup	352	304
Cheese sauce	1 tbsp	31	21
	½ cup	250	170
dehydrated, prepared with milk	1 tbsp	19	10
	½ cup	152	80
Curry, dehydrated, prepared with milk	1 tbsp	19	10
	½ cup	154	77
Curry Cream	1 tbsp	40	31
	½ cup	320	248
Hollandaise	1 tbsp	82	80
	½ cup	656	640
dehydrated, made with butterfat, prepared with water	1 tbsp	15	11
	½ cup	120	88

SAUCES AND GRAVIES

FOOD	AMOUNT	TOTAL CALORIES	FAT CALORIES
Mushroom, dehydrated, prepared			
with milk	1 tbsp	14	6
	½ cup	112	48
Mushroom Cream	½ cup	352	307
Sour cream, dehydrated, prepared			
with milk	1 tbsp	32	17
	½ cup	256	136
Soy, ready-to-serve	1 tbsp	11	0
Spaghetti sauce, dehydrated	1 serving (¼ pkt)	28	1
Spaghetti sauce with mushrooms,			
dehydrated	1 serving (¼ pkt)	30	8
Stroganoff, dehydrated, prepared			
with milk and water	1 tbsp	17	6
	½ cup	136	48
Sweet and sour, dehydrated, pre-			
pared with water and vinegar	1 tbsp	18	0
	½ cup	144	0
Teriyaki			
dehydrated, prepared with water	1 tbsp	8	trace
	½ cup	64	4
ready-to-serve	1 tbsp	15	0
White sauce	1 tbsp	24	17
	½ cup	195	136
dehydrated, prepared with milk	1 tbsp	15	8
	½ cup	120	64

Gravies

FOOD	AMOUNT	TOTAL CALORIES	FAT CALORIES
Au jus			
canned	½ cup	19	2
dehydrated, prepared with water	½ cup	10	4
Beef, canned	½ cup	62	25
Brown, dehydrated, prepared with			
water	½ cup	4	1
Chicken			
canned	½ cup	94	61
dehydrated, prepared with water	½ cup	42	8
Mushroom			
canned	½ cup	60	29
dehydrated, prepared with water	½ cup	35	4
Onion, dehydrated, prepared with			
water	½ cup	40	3

SAUCES AND GRAVIES

FOOD	AMOUNT	TOTAL CALORIES	FAT CALORIES
Pork, dehydrated, prepared with water	½ cup	38	9
Turkey, dehydrated, prepared with water	½ cup	44	8

SAUSAGES AND LUNCHEON MEATS

FOOD	AMOUNT	TOTAL CALORIES	FAT CALORIES
Barbecue loaf, pork, beef	1 oz	49	23
	1 slice (.8 oz)	40	18
Beef, chopped and pressed	1 oz	40	18
Beerwurst, beer salami			
beef	1 oz	92	75
	1 slice (.8 oz)	75	61
	1 slice (.25 oz)	19	16
pork	1 oz	68	48
	1 slice (.8 oz)	55	39
	1 slice (.25 oz)	14	10
Berliner, pork, beef	1 oz	65	44
	1 slice (.8 oz)	53	36
Blood sausage	1 oz	107	88
	1 slice (.8 oz)	95	78
Bockwurst, raw	1 oz	87	70
	1 link (2.3 oz)	200	161
Bologna			
beef	1 oz = 1 slice	89	72
	1 slice (.8 oz)	72	59
beef and pork	1 oz = 1 slice	89	72
	1 slice (.8 oz)	73	58
pork	1 oz = 1 slice	70	51
	1 slice (.8 oz)	57	41
turkey	1 oz = 1 slice	57	39
Bratwurst, pork, beef	1 oz	92	71
	1 link (2.5 oz)	226	175
pork, cooked	1 oz	85	66
	1 link (3 oz)	256	198
Braunschweiger, pork	1 oz	102	82
	1 slice (.6 oz)	65	52

SAUSAGES AND LUNCHEON MEATS

FOOD	AMOUNT	TOTAL CALORIES	FAT CALORIES
Breakfast strips, beef, cured			
raw or unheated	1 slice (.8 oz)	92	79
cooked	1 slice (.4 oz)	51	35
Cheesefurter, cheese smokie, pork,			
beef	1 oz	93	74
	1 frank (1.5 oz)	141	112
Chicken roll, light meat	1 oz = 1 slice	45	19
Corned beef			
brisket			
raw	1 oz	56	38
cooked	1 oz	71	48
canned	1 oz	71	38
	1 slice (.74 oz)	53	28
loaf, jellied	1 oz = 1 slice	43	16
Dried beef, cured	1 oz	47	10
Dutch brand loaf, pork, beef	1 oz = 1 slice	68	45
Frankfurter			
beef	1 oz	91	75
	1 frank (1.6 oz)	145	119
	1 frank (2 oz)	184	151
beef and pork	1 oz	91	74
	1 frank (1.6 oz)	144	118
	1 frank (2 oz)	183	149
chicken	1 oz	73	50
	1 frank (1.6 oz)	116	79
turkey	1 oz	64	45
	1 frank (1.6 oz)	102	72
Ham			
chopped	1 oz	68	48
	1 slice (.74 oz)	50	36
minced	1 oz	75	53
	1 slice (.74 oz)	55	39
sliced			
extra lean	1 oz = 1 slice	37	13
regular	1 oz = 1 slice	52	27
Ham and cheese loaf or roll	1 oz = 1 slice	73	52
Ham and cheese spread	1 oz	69	47
	1 tbsp	37	25
Ham salad spread	1 oz	61	40
	1 tbsp	32	21
Headcheese, pork	1 oz = 1 slice	60	40
Honeyloaf, pork, beef	1 oz = 1 slice	36	11

SAUSAGES AND LUNCHEON MEATS

FOOD	AMOUNT	TOTAL CALORIES	FAT CALORIES
Honey roll sausage, beef	1 oz	52	27
	1 slice (.8 oz)	42	22
Italian sausage, cooked, pork	1 oz	92	66
	1 link (5/lb)	216	155
	1 link (4/lb)	268	192
Kielbasa, kolbassy, pork, beef	1 oz	88	69
	1 slice (.9 oz)	81	64
Knackwurst, knockwurst, pork, beef	1 oz	87	71
	1 link (2.4 oz)	209	170
Lebanon bologna, beef	1 oz	64	38
	1 slice (.8 oz)	52	31
Liver cheese, pork	1 oz	86	65
	1 slice (1.3 oz)	115	87
Liver sausage, liverwurst, pork	1 oz	93	73
	1 slice (.6 oz)	59	46
Luncheon meat			
beef			
loaved	1 oz = 1 slice	87	67
thin sliced	1 oz	35	8
	5 slices (.74 oz)	26	6
pork, beef	1 oz = 1 slice	100	82
pork, canned	1 oz	95	77
	1 slice (.74 oz)	70	57
Luncheon sausage, pork and beef	1 oz	74	53
	1 slice (.8 oz)	60	43
Luxury loaf, pork	1 oz = 1 slice	40	12
Mortadella, beef, pork	1 oz	88	65
	1 slice (.5 oz)	47	34
Mother's loaf, pork	1 oz	80	57
	1 slice (.74 oz)	59	42
New England brand sausage, pork, beef	1 oz	46	19
	1 slice (.8 oz)	37	16
Olive loaf, pork	1 oz = 1 slice	67	42
Pastrami			
beef	1 oz = 1 slice	99	74
turkey	1 oz = 1 slice	40	16
Pâté			
chicken liver	1 oz	57	33
	1 tbsp	26	15
goose liver	1 oz	131	112
	1 tbsp	60	51

SAUSAGES AND LUNCHEON MEATS

FOOD	AMOUNT	TOTAL CALORIES	FAT CALORIES
Peppered loaf, pork, beef	1 oz = 1 slice	42	16
Pepperoni, pork, beef	1 oz	141	112
	1 slice (.2 oz)	27	22
	1 sausage (9 oz)	1248	993
Pickle and pimento loaf, pork	1 oz = 1 slice	74	54
Picnic loaf, pork, beef	1 oz = 1 slice	66	42
Polish sausage, pork	1 oz	92	73
	1 sausage (8 oz)	739	587
Pork and beef sausage, cooked	1 oz = 1 patty	112	92
	1 link (.46 oz)	52	33
Pork sausage, cooked	1 oz = 1 patty	105	76
	1 link (.46 oz)	48	36
Poultry salad sandwich spread	1 oz	57	34
	1 tbsp	26	16
Roast beef, sliced	1 oz	60	22
Salami			
beef	1 oz	72	51
	1 slice (.8 oz)	58	42
beef and pork	1 oz	71	51
	1 slice (.8 oz)	57	42
pork, dry or hard	1 oz	115	86
	1 slice (.35 oz)	41	30
Sandwich spread, pork, beef	1 oz	67	44
	1 tbsp	35	23
Smoked link sausage			
pork	1 oz	110	81
	1 link (2.4 oz)	265	194
	1 link (.56 oz)	62	46
pork and beef	1 oz	95	77
	1 link (2.4 oz)	229	53
	1 link (.56)	54	44
Summer sausage, beef, cured	1 oz	95	75
	1 slice (.8 oz)	77	61
Thuringer, cervelat, summer sausage, beef, pork	1 oz	98	76
	1 slice (.8 oz)	78	62
Tongue, beef			
raw	1 oz	63	41
cooked, simmered	1 oz	80	53
Tripe, beef, raw	1 oz	28	10
Turkey breast, processed	1 oz	31	4
	1 slice (.74 oz)	23	3
Turkey, chopped and pressed	1 oz	50	27

SAUSAGES AND LUNCHEON MEATS

FOOD	AMOUNT	TOTAL CALORIES	FAT CALORIES
Turkey ham, cured turkey thigh meat	1 oz = 1 slice	36	13
Turkey roll			
light and dark meat	1 oz = 1 slice	42	18
light meat	1 oz = 1 slice	42	18
Vienna sausage, beef and pork, canned	1 oz	79	64
	1 sausage (.56 oz)	45	36

SOUPS

All the creamed soups are made with whole milk or water. If your soup is made with cream, add 65 fat calories per cup of soup.

FOOD	AMOUNT	TOTAL CALORIES	FAT CALORIES
Canned			
Asparagus, cream of			
prepared with milk	1 cup	161	74
prepared with water	1 cup	87	37
Bean, black, condensed, prepared with water	1 cup	116	14
Bean with bacon, condensed, prepared with water	1 cup	173	54
Bean with franks, condensed, prepared with water	1 cup	187	63
Bean with ham, chunky, ready-to-serve	1 cup	231	77
Beef broth or bouillon, ready-to-serve	1 cup	16	5
Beef, chunky, ready-to-serve	1 cup	171	46
Beef noodle, condensed, prepared with water	1 cup	84	28
Celery, cream of, condensed			
prepared with milk	1 cup	165	87
prepared with water	1 cup	90	50
Cheese, condensed			
prepared with milk	1 cup	230	131
prepared with water	1 cup	155	94
Chicken and dumplings, condensed, prepared with water	1 cup	97	50

SOUPS

FOOD	AMOUNT	TOTAL CALORIES	FAT CALORIES
Chicken broth			
condensed	1 cup	78	23
prepared with water	1 cup	39	13
Chicken, chunky, ready-to-serve	1 cup	178	60
Chicken, cream of, condensed			
prepared with milk	1 cup	191	103
prepared with water	1 cup	116	66
Chicken gumbo, condensed, pre-			
pared with water	1 cup	56	13
Chicken noodle, condensed, pre-			
pared with water	1 cup	75	22
Chicken noodle with meatballs,			
ready-to-serve	1 cup	99	32
Chicken rice			
chunky, ready-to-serve	1 cup	127	29
condensed, prepared with water	1 cup	60	17
Chicken vegetable			
chunky, ready-to-serve	1 cup	167	43
condensed, prepared with water	1 cup	74	26
Chili beef, condensed, prepared			
with water	1 cup	169	59
Clam chowder			
Manhattan			
chunky, ready-to-serve	1 cup	133	30
condensed, prepared with			
water	1 cup	78	21
New England			
condensed, prepared with milk	1 cup	163	59
condensed, prepared with			
water	1 cup	95	26
Consommé, with gelatin added,			
condensed, prepared with water	1 cup	29	0
Crab, ready-to-serve	1 cup	76	14
Gazpacho, ready-to-serve	1 cup	57	20
Lentil with ham, ready-to-serve	1 cup	140	25
Minestrone			
chunky, ready-to-serve	1 cup	127	25
condensed, prepared with water	1 cup	83	23
Mushroom, cream of, condensed	1 cup	170	155
prepared with milk	1 cup	203	122
prepared with water	1 cup	129	81
Mushroom with beef stock, con-			
densed, prepared with water	1 cup	85	36

SOUPS

FOOD	AMOUNT	TOTAL CALORIES	FAT CALORIES
Onion, condensed, prepared with water	1 cup	57	16
Oyster stew, condensed			
prepared with milk	1 cup	134	71
prepared with water	1 cup	59	34
Pea, green, condensed			
prepared with milk	1 cup	239	63
prepared with water	1 cup	164	26
Pea, split, with ham			
chunky, ready-to-serve	1 cup	184	36
condensed, prepared with water	1 cup	189	40
Pepperpot, condensed, prepared with water	1 cup	103	42
Potato, cream of, condensed			
prepared with milk	1 cup	148	58
prepared with water	1 cup	73	21
Scotch broth, condensed, prepared with water	1 cup	80	24
Shrimp, cream of, condensed			
prepared with milk	1 cup	165	84
prepared with water	1 cup	90	47
Stockpot, condensed, prepared with water	1 cup	100	35
Tomato, condensed			
prepared with milk	1 cup	160	54
prepared with water	1 cup	86	17
Tomato beef with noodle, condensed, prepared with water	1 cup	140	39
Tomato bisque, condensed			
prepared with milk	1 cup	198	59
prepared with water	1 cup	123	23
Tomato rice, condensed, prepared with water	1 cup	120	24
Turkey, chunky, ready-to-serve	1 cup	136	40
Turkey noodle, condensed, prepared with water	1 cup	69	18
Turkey vegetable, condensed, prepared with water	1 cup	74	27
Vegetable, chunky, ready-to-serve	1 cup	122	33
Vegetable, vegetarian, condensed, prepared with water	1 cup	72	17
Vegetable with beef, condensed, prepared with water	1 cup	79	17

SOUPS

FOOD	AMOUNT	TOTAL CALORIES	FAT CALORIES
Vegetable with beef broth, condensed, prepared with water	1 cup	81	17

Dehydrated

FOOD	AMOUNT	TOTAL CALORIES	FAT CALORIES
Asparagus, cream of, prepared with water	1 cup	59	16
Bean with bacon, prepared with water	1 cup	105	19
Beef broth or bouillon, prepared with water	1 cup	19	6
Beef broth, cubes, prepared with water	1 cup	8	2
Beef noodle, prepared with water	1 cup	41	7
Cauliflower, prepared with water	1 cup	68	15
Celery, cream of, prepared with water	1 cup	63	15
Chicken broth or bouillon, prepared with water	1 cup	21	10
Chicken broth, cubes, prepared with water	1 cup	13	3
Chicken, cream of, prepared with water	1 cup	107	48
Chicken noodle, prepared with water	1 cup	53	11
Chicken rice, prepared with water	1 cup	60	13
Chicken vegetable, prepared with water	1 cup	49	7
Clam chowder			
Manhattan	1 cup	65	14
New England	1 cup	95	33
Consommé, with gelatin added, prepared with water	1 cup	17	0
Leek, prepared with water	1 cup	71	18
Minestrone, prepared with water	1 cup	79	16
Mushroom, prepared with water	1 cup	96	44
Onion, prepared with water	1 cup	28	5
Oxtail, prepared with water	1 cup	71	23
Pea, green or split, prepared with water	1 cup	133	14
Tomato, prepared with water	1 cup	102	21
Tomato vegetable, prepared with water	1 cup	55	8

SOUPS

FOOD	AMOUNT	TOTAL CALORIES	FAT CALORIES
Vegetable beef, prepared with water	1 cup	53	10
Vegetable, cream of, prepared with water	1 cup	105	51

Homemade or Restaurant

FOOD	AMOUNT	TOTAL CALORIES	FAT CALORIES
Cream of mushroom soup	1 cup	170	155
French onion soup	1 cup	350	125
Gazpacho	1 cup	110	80
New England clam chowder	1 cup	230	145
Vichyssoise	1 cup	315	210

SWEETS

FOOD	AMOUNT	TOTAL CALORIES	FAT CALORIES
Cakes from Mixes			
Coffee, crumb (7¾ × 5⅝ × 1¼ inches)	⅙ cake	230	63
Devil's food, with chocolate frosting (9-inch round)	1/16 cake	235	72
Gingerbread (8-inch square)	⅑ cake	175	36
Yellow, with chocolate frosting (9-inch round)	1/16 cake	235	72
Pillsbury			
Fudge Brownie	2-inch square	150	63
Rocky Road Fudge Brownie Mix	2-inch square	170	72
Streusel Swirl	1/16 cake	260	99
Pillsbury Plus Butter Recipes			
Yellow Cake	1/12 cake	260	108
Lemon Cake	1/12 cake	250	99
Cakes from Scratch			
Angelfood (9¾-inch round)	1/12 cake	125	trace
Carrot, with cream cheese frosting (10-inch tube cake)	1/16 cake	385	190
Fruitcake, dark (7½-inch round)	1/32 cake	165	63
Pound (8½ × 3½ × 3¼ inches)	1/17 cake	120	45
Sheet (9-inch square), with un-cooked white frosting	⅑ cake	445	126

SWEETS

FOOD	AMOUNT	TOTAL CALORIES	FAT CALORIES
Cakes, Commercial and Restaurant			
Baked Alaska	1/12 cake	263	112
Cheesecake	1/12 cake	280	162
Devil's food, with cream filling	1 small cake	105	36
German chocolate cake	1/16 cake	521	277
Hazelnut torte	1/16 torte	315	187
Pound	1/12 cake	318	157
Sponge, with cream filling	1 small cake	155	45
White, with white frosting (9-inch round)	1/16 cake	260	81
Yellow, with chocolate frosting (9-inch round)	1/16 cake	260	130
Cakes and Pastries, Frozen (See also **FROZEN AND MICROWAVE FOODS)**			
Cheese Cake, Strawberry French (Sara Lee)	1 slice (2.6 oz)	200	99
Chocolate Éclairs (Rich's)	1 éclair (2 oz)	210	90
Chocolate Fudge layer cake (Pepperidge Farm)	1/10 cake (1.6 oz)	180	90
Chocolate Mousse (Sara Lee)	1 slice (1/10 cake)	200	126
Coconut layer cake (Pepperidge Farm)	1/10 cake (1.6 oz)	180	72
Pound All Butter (Sara Lee)	1 slice (1 oz)	130	63
Pound Cholesterol Free (Pepperidge Farm)	1 slice (1 oz)	110	54
Cake Frosting			
Pillsbury Milk Chocolate Frosting Supreme	for 1 piece (12/cake)	150	54
Candy			
Caramels, plain or chocolate	1 oz	115	27
Carob chips	1 oz (2⅔ tbsp)	140	63
Chocolate			
chips	1 oz	140	72
Hershey bar with almonds	1 oz	160	90
milk, plain	1 oz	145	81
milk, with almonds	1 oz	150	90
milk, with peanuts	1 oz	155	99
semisweet	1/4 cup	215	137

SWEETS

FOOD	AMOUNT	TOTAL CALORIES	FAT CALORIES
Chocolate (cont.)			
sweet, dark	1 oz	150	90
Kit Kat	1.625 oz	250	117
Mr. Goodbar	1.85 oz	300	180
Reese's Peanut Butter Cups (2)	1.8 oz	280	153
Fondant (mints, candy corn, other)	1 oz	105	0
Fudge, chocolate	1 oz	115	27
Gumdrops	1 oz	100	trace
Hard candies	1 oz	110	0
Jellybeans	1 oz	105	trace
Marshmallows	1 large	23	0
Peanut brittle	1 oz	120	27
Raisins, chocolate-coated	10 small	24	9
Cookies and Bars, Commercial			
Almond Supreme (Pepperidge Farm)	2 (1 oz)	140	90
Apple Newtons (Nabisco)	1½ (1 oz)	110	18
Apple Pastry (Stella D'oro Dietetic)	2 pieces (1.5 oz)	180	63
Apricot-Raspberry (Pepperidge Farm)	3 (1 oz)	150	54
Assorted Creme Filled Wafers (Estée)	5 (1.2 oz)	150	90
Barnum's Animal Crackers (Nabisco)	11 (1 oz)	130	36
Baronet Creme Sandwich (Nabisco)	3 (1 oz)	140	54
Biscos Sugar Wafers (Nabisco)	8 (1 oz)	150	63
Blueberry Newtons (Nabisco)	1½ (1 oz)	110	18
Bordeaux (Pepperidge Farm)	4 (1 oz)	150	45
Brown Edge Wafers (Nabisco)	5 (1 oz)	140	54
Brownie, frozen (Rachel's Double Chocolate with Walnuts)	2 oz	280	153
Brownie Chocolate Nut (Pepperidge Farm)	3 (1 oz)	160	90
Brussels (Pepperidge Farm)	3 (1 oz)	170	81
Brussels Mint (Pepperidge Farm)	3 (1 oz)	200	90
Butter Flavored (Nabisco)	6 (1 oz)	130	45
Cameo Creme Sandwich (Nabisco)	2 (1 oz)	140	45
Cappucino (Pepperidge Farm)	3 (1 oz)	160	81
Capri (Pepperidge Farm)	2 (1 oz)	160	81
Champagne (Pepperidge Farm)	3 (1 oz)	170	81

SWEETS

FOOD	AMOUNT	TOTAL CALORIES	FAT CALORIES
Chessmen (Pepperidge Farm)	3 (1 oz)	130	54
Chewy Chips Ahoy! (Nabisco)	2 (1 oz)	130	54
Chip-A-Roos (Sunshine)	2 (1 oz)	130	63
Chip Chip (Rippin'Good)	3 (1 oz)	140	45
Chips Ahoy! (Nabisco)	3 (1 oz)	140	63
Chips Chocolate (Lu)	2 (1 oz)	170	81
Chips Deluxe with Peanut Butter Chips (Keebler)	2 (1 oz)	160	72
Chips 'n Middles Fudge (Sunshine)	2 (1 oz)	140	54
Chips 'n Middles Peanut Butter (Sunshine)	2 (1 oz)	140	54
Chipsies (Keebler)	2 (1 oz)	160	72
Chocolate Chip (Estée)	4 (1 oz)	120	36
Chocolate Chip (Keebler Soft Batch)	2 (1 oz)	160	72
Chocolate Chip (Pepperidge Farm)	3 (1 oz)	150	72
Chocolate Chocolate Chip (Pepperidge Farm)	3 (1 oz)	160	81
Chocolate Chunk Pecan (Pepperidge Farm)	2 (1 oz)	130	63
Chocolate Creme Filled Wafers (Estée)	6 (.9 oz)	120	54
Chocolate Fudge Sandwich (Keebler)	2 (1 oz)	160	72
Chocolate Lace Pirouettes (Pepperidge Farm)	2 (1 oz)	110	54
Coconut (Estée)	4 (1 oz)	120	36
Coconut Bars (Rippin'Good)	3 (1 oz)	140	54
Cookie Break Vanilla Flavored Creme Sandwich (Nabisco)	3 (1 oz)	140	54
Cookie Jar Assortment (Rippin' Good)	2 (1 oz)	130	36
Country Style Oatmeal (Sunshine)	2 (1 oz)	110	45
Date Pecan (Pepperidge Farm)	3 (1 oz)	170	72
Deluxe Fudge Covered Grahams (Keebler)	4 (1 oz)	160	72
Devil's Food Cakes (Nabisco)	1 (1.3 oz)	110	9
Devil's Food Trolley Cakes (F.F.V.)	2 (1.2 oz)	120	18
Dutch Windmill (Rippin' Good)	3 (1 oz)	140	54
Egg Biscuits (Stella D'oro, Dietetic)	3 pieces (.9 oz)	120	27
E.L. Fudge (Keebler)	4 (1 oz)	140	54
Fig Bars (Sunshine)	2 (1 oz)	90	18

SWEETS

FOOD	AMOUNT	TOTAL CALORIES	FAT CALORIES
Fig Newtons (Nabisco)	2 (1 oz)	100	18
Fudge Stripes (Keebler)	2 (.7 oz)	100	54
Gaufrettes (Lu)	3 (.8 oz)	130	63
Giggles Chocolate Sandwich (Nabisco)	2 (1 oz)	140	54
Giggles Vanilla Sandwich (Nabisco)	2 (1 oz)	140	54
Ginger Man (Pepperidge Farm)	4 (1 oz)	130	45
Ginger Snaps (Sunshine)	5 (1 oz)	100	27
Golden Fruit (Sunshine)	2 small segments (1 oz)	150	27
Granola bars			
Chocolate Chip (Quaker)	1 (1 oz)	100	45
Peanut Butter and Chocolate Chip (Quaker)	1 (1 oz)	130	45
Raisin and Cinnamon (Quaker)	1 (1 oz)	130	45
Rice Krispies Chocolate Chip (Kellogg's)	1 (1 oz)	120	36
Granola Peanut Butter Sandwich (Rippin'Good)	2 (1 oz)	130	45
Hazelnut (Pepperidge Farm)	3 (1 oz)	170	81
Honey Maid Raisin Grahams (Nabisco)	2 whole (8 small segments)	120	18
Hydrox Chocolate Sandwich Cremes (Sunshine)	3 (1 oz)	160	63
Hydrox Double Chocolate (Sunshine)	3 (1 oz)	160	63
Ideal Chocolate Peanut Bars (Nabisco)	2 (1 oz)	150	72
Kettle (Nabisco)	4 (1 oz)	130	45
Kichel (Stella D'oro, Dietetic)	20 pieces (1 oz)	160	90
Le Petit Beurre (Lu)	3 (.9 oz)	120	27
Lemon Coolers (Sunshine)	5 (1 oz)	140	54
Lemon Crisp (Rippin'Good)	2 (1 oz)	130	36
Lemon Nut Crunch (Pepperidge Farm)	3 (1 oz)	170	90
Lemon Thins (Estée)	4 (1 oz)	120	36
Lido (Pepperidge Farm)	2 (1.2 oz)	190	99
Lorna Doone Shortbread (Nabisco)	4 (1 oz)	140	63
Macaroons (Rippin'Good)	2 (1 oz)	140	54

SWEETS

FOOD	AMOUNT	TOTAL CALORIES	FAT CALORIES
Marshmallow Twirls Fudge Cakes (Nabisco)	1 (1 oz)	130	45
Milano (Pepperidge Farm)	3 (1.2 oz)	180	90
Milk Chocolate Macadamia (Pepperidge Farm)	2 (1 oz)	140	72
Milk Lunch (Lu)	3 (.8 oz)	110	27
Mint Milano (Pepperidge Farm)	3 (1 oz)	230	117
Molasses Crisps (Pepperidge Farm)	5 (1 oz)	170	63
Mystic Mint Sandwich (Nabisco)	2 (1 oz)	150	72
National Arrowroot Biscuit (Nabisco)	6 (1 oz)	130	36
Nilla Wafers (Nabisco)	7 (1 oz)	130	36
Nutter Butter Peanut Butter Sandwich (Nabisco)	2 (1 oz)	140	54
Oatmeal (Sunshine)	2	110	45
Oatmeal Cremes Sandwich (Keebler)	2 (1 oz)	160	54
Oatmeal Peanut Sandwich (Sunshine)	2 (1 oz)	140	54
Oatmeal Raisin (Nabisco Almost Home)	2 (1 oz)	130	45
Oatmeal Raisin (Estée)	4 (1 oz)	120	36
Oatmeal Raisin (Keebler Soft Batch)	2 (1 oz)	140	54
Oatmeal Raisin (Rippin'Good)	2 (1 oz)	140	45
Orange Milano (Pepperidge Farm)	3 (1.4 oz)	230	117
Oreo Big Stuf Chocolate Sandwich (Nabisco)	1 (1.8 oz)	260	108
Oreo Double Stuf Chocolate Sandwich (Nabisco)	2 (1 oz)	140	63
Orleans Sandwich (Pepperidge Farm)	3 (1 oz)	180	108
Palmito (Lu)	3 (1 oz)	150	72
Party Grahams (Nabisco)	3 (1 oz)	140	63
Peach Apricot Pastry (Stella D'oro, Dietetic)	2 pieces (1.5 oz)	180	72
Peanut Butter (Keebler Soft Batch)	2 (1 oz)	160	72
Peanut Butter Chocolate Chip (Keebler Soft Batch)	2 (1 oz)	180	90
Peanut Butter Fudge (Nabisco Almost Home)	2 (1 oz)	140	63

SWEETS

FOOD	AMOUNT	TOTAL CALORIES	FAT CALORIES
Peanut Butter Wafers (Sunshine)	3 (1 oz)	120	54
Raisin Bran (Pepperidge Farm)	3 (1 oz)	160	72
Real Chocolate Chip (Nabisco Almost Home)	2 (1 oz)	130	45
Seville (Pepperidge Farm)	2 (1 oz)	100	45
Shortbread (Pepperidge Farm)	3 (1 oz)	130	63
Social Tea Biscuit (Nabisco)	6 (1 oz)	130	36
Southport (Pepperidge Farm)	2 (1 oz)	170	90
Strawberry (Pepperidge Farm)	3 (1 oz)	160	54
Strawberry Newtons (Nabisco)	1½ (1 oz)	110	18
Striped Chips Ahoy (Nabisco)	2 (1 oz)	150	72
Striped Chocolate Chip (Nabisco)	3 (1 oz)	150	72
Striped Dainties (Rippin' Good)	3 (1 oz)	150	72
Sugar (Pepperidge Farm)	3 (1 oz)	150	72
Sugar (Rippin' Good)	2 (1 oz)	140	54
Sugar Wafers (Sunshine)	3 (1 oz)	130	54
TC Rounds (FFV)	2 (1.1 oz)	160	72
Teddy Party Grahams (Nabisco)	3 (1 oz)	140	63
Toy (Sunshine)	5 (1 oz)	60	18
Vanilla Creme Filled Wafers (Estée)	6 (.9 oz)	120	54
Vanilla Sandwich (Rippin' Good)	3 (1 oz)	130	45
Vanilla Thins (Estée)	4 (1 oz)	120	36
Vanilla Wafers (Sunshine)	6 (1 oz)	130	54
Vienna Fingers (Sunshine)	2 (1 oz)	140	54
Walnut Chocolate Chip (Nabisco Almost Home)	2 (1 oz)	140	63
Walnut Chocolate Chip (Keebler Soft Batch)	2 (1 oz)	160	72

Frozen Novelties

FOOD	AMOUNT	TOTAL CALORIES	FAT CALORIES
Carnation			
Berry Swirl	1 bar	70	27
Vanilla Fudge Heaven Sundae	1 bar	170	99
Crystal Light			
Lemonade Fruit Punch	1 bar (1.8 fl oz)	14	0
Strawbery Cherry	1 bar (1.8 fl oz)	14	0
Dole Fruit 'n Cream Bars	1	90	9
Fruit 'n Juice Bars	1	70	<9
Sorbet, strawberry	½ cup	110	1
Dove Bar, vanilla	1 (6 oz)	497	335
Eskimo Pie, vanilla	3 oz	170	108

SWEETS

FOOD	AMOUNT	TOTAL CALORIES	FAT CALORIES
Häagen-Dazs			
Chocolate Dark Chocolate	1 bar	360	225
Vanilla Dark Chocolate	1 bar	330	225
Vanilla Milk Chocolate	1 bar	330	225
Jell-O			
Fruit and Cream Bar,			
Mixed Berry	1	70	27
Fruit Bar, Medley	1	45	0
Gelatin Pops	1	35	0
Pudding Pops			
Chocolate	1	80	18
Vanilla	1	70	18
Klondike			
Chocolate	1 bar (5 fl oz)	300	207
Krispy	1 bar (5 fl oz)	280	243
Lite	1 bar (2.5 fl oz)	140	90
Plain	1 bar (5 fl oz)	270	198
Vanilla Nuggets	1 nugget (1 fl oz)	70	54
Minute Maid Fruit Juices	2.25 oz	60	0
Nabisco Oreo Cookies 'n Cream			
Sandwich	1 cookie	60	27
	1 bar	220	135
Popsicle	1	70	0
Sealtest Light n' Lively ice milk,			
vanilla	½ cup	100	27
Tofutti Chocolate Supreme	4 fl oz	210	117
Weight Watchers			
Chocolate Dip	1 bar	110	63
Chocolate Mousse	1 bar	45	<9
Chocolate Treat	1 bar	100	9
Double Fudge	1 bar	60	9
Orange Vanilla Treat	1 bar	60	9
Vanilla Sandwich Bar	1 bar	150	27
Yoplait soft frozen yogurt bar,			
strawberry	1 bar	90	27

Pies, Commercial

FOOD	AMOUNT	TOTAL CALORIES	FAT CALORIES
Apple	⅙ pie	405	162
Blueberry	⅙ pie	380	153
Boston cream	⅙ pie	416	117
Cherry	⅙ pie	410	162
Cream	⅙ pie	455	207

SWEETS

FOOD	AMOUNT	TOTAL CALORIES	FAT CALORIES
Custard	⅙ pie	330	153
Lemon meringue	⅙ pie	355	126
Peach	⅙ pie	405	153
Pecan	⅙ pie	575	288
Pumpkin	⅙ pie	320	153
Puddings			
Caramel Bavarian cream	½ cup	246	128
Chocolate mousse	½ cup	324	199
Creme caramel	1 cup	303	125
Custard, baked	1 cup	305	61
Canned			
Chocolate	5 oz	205	99
Tapioca	5 oz	160	45
Vanilla	5 oz	220	90
Dry Mix			
Prepared with whole milk			
Chocolate	½ cup	155	36
Rice	½ cup	155	36
Tapioca	½ cup	145	36
Vanilla	½ cup	145	36
Snack Cakes and Pies			
Devil's food, with cream filling	1 small cake	105	36
Ho Hos (Hostess)	1 cake	120	54
King Don (Hostess)	1 cake	170	81
Pound Cake, All Butter (Sara Lee)	1 snack cake	200	99
Other Sweets			
Chocolate éclairs	1	239	122
Custard cream puffs	1	303	163
Danish pastry			
round	1	220	108
fruit	1	235	117
Doughnuts			
cake-type, plain	1	210	108
yeast, glazed	1	235	117
Gelatin dessert	½ cup	70	0
Honey	1 tbsp	65	0
Jams and preserves	1 tbsp	55	0
Jellies	1 tbsp	50	0

SWEETS

FOOD	AMOUNT	TOTAL CALORIES	FAT CALORIES
Molasses	1 tbsp	43	0
Sugar			
brown, firmly packed	1 cup	820	0
	1 tbsp	51	0
white			
granulated	1 cup	770	0
	1 tbsp	45	0
	1 pkt	25	0
powdered, sifted	1 cup	385	0
Syrups			
chocolate	1 tbsp	43	trace
table (corn or maple)	1 tbsp	50	0

VEGETABLES AND VEGETABLE PRODUCTS

FOOD	AMOUNT	TOTAL CALORIES	FAT CALORIES
Alfalfa seeds, sprouted, raw	1 cup	10	trace
Artichokes			
raw	1 medium	65	trace
	1 large	83	trace
cooked	1 medium	53	trace
	½ cup hearts	37	trace
Asparagus			
raw	½ cup	15	trace
	4 spears	13	trace
cooked	½ cup	22	trace
	4 spears	15	trace
Baked beans, canned			
plain or vegetarian	1 cup	235	10
with beef	1 cup	321	83
with franks	1 cup	366	152
with pork	1 cup	268	35
with pork and sweet sauce	1 cup	282	33
with pork and tomato sauce	1 cup	247	23
Baked Barbecue (Hanover)	1 cup	280	36
Baked Brown Sugar and Bacon (Hanover)	1 cup	240	18
Baked Vegetarian (Hanover)	1 cup	200	0
Pork 'n Beans (Heinz)	3.5 oz	122	16
Bamboo shoots			
raw	1 cup	41	trace

VEGETABLES AND VEGETABLE PRODUCTS

FOOD	AMOUNT	TOTAL CALORIES	FAT CALORIES
Bamboo shoots (*cont.*)			
cooked	1 cup	15	trace
canned	1 cup	25	trace
Beans			
black			
raw	1 cup	661	25
boiled	1 cup	227	8
great northern			
raw	1 cup	621	19
boiled	1 cup	210	7
canned	1 cup	300	9
kidney			
raw	1 cup	613	14
boiled	1 cup	225	8
canned	1 cup	208	7
kidney, California red			
raw	1 cup	607	trace
boiled	1 cup	219	trace
kidney, red			
raw	1 cup	619	18
boiled	1 cup	225	8
canned	1 cup	216	8
kidney, royal red			
raw	1 cup	605	7
boiled	1 cup	218	3
lima, baby			
raw	1 cup	677	17
boiled	1 cup	229	6
lima, large			
raw	1 cup	602	11
boiled	1 cup	217	6
canned	1 cup	191	4
mung			
raw	1 cup	719	22
boiled	1 cup	213	7
navy			
raw	1 cup	697	24
boiled	1 cup	259	9
canned	1 cup	296	10
pink			
raw	1 cup	721	21
boiled	1 cup	252	7

VEGETABLES AND VEGETABLE PRODUCTS

FOOD	AMOUNT	TOTAL CALORIES	FAT CALORIES
Beans (*cont.*)			
pinto			
raw	1 cup	656	20
boiled	1 cup	235	8
canned	1 cup	186	7
refried (Del Monte)	1 cup	260	32
shellie, canned	1 cup	75	4
small white			
raw	1 cup	723	23
boiled	1 cup	253	10
snap			
raw	1 cup	34	trace
cooked	1 cup	44	trace
canned	1 cup	36	trace
white			
raw	1 cup	674	15
boiled	1 cup	249	6
canned	1 cup	306	7
yardlong			
raw	1 cup	580	20
boiled	1 cup	202	7
yellow			
raw	1 cup	676	46
boiled	1 cup	254	17
Beets			
raw	1 cup slices	60	trace
	2 beets	71	trace
cooked	1 cup slices	52	trace
	2 beets	31	0
canned, drained	1 cup	54	trace
Black-eyed peas, cooked	1 cup	190	trace
Broadbeans			
raw	1 cup	511	21
boiled	1 cup	186	6
canned	1 cup	183	5
Broccoli			
raw	1 cup chopped	24	trace
	1 spear	42	trace
cooked	1 cup chopped	46	trace
	1 spear	53	trace
Brussels sprouts, cooked	1 cup	60	7
	1 sprout	8	trace

VEGETABLES AND VEGETABLE PRODUCTS

FOOD	AMOUNT	TOTAL CALORIES	FAT CALORIES
Cabbage			
raw	1 cup shredded	16	trace
	1 head	215	15
cooked	1 cup shredded	32	trace
	1 head	270	28
Cabbage, Chinese			
raw	1 cup shredded	9	trace
cooked	1 cup shredded	20	trace
Cabbage, red			
raw	1 cup shredded	19	trace
cooked	1 cup shredded	32	trace
Cabbage, Savoy			
raw	1 cup shredded	19	trace
cooked	1 cup shredded	35	trace
Carob flour	1 tbsp	14	trace
	1 cup	185	6
Carrots			
raw	1	31	trace
	1 cup shredded	48	trace
cooked	1 cup sliced	70	trace
Carrot juice	1 cup	98	trace
Cauliflower, cooked or raw	3 flowerets	13	trace
	1 cup pieces	24	trace
Celery, raw	1 stalk	6	trace
	1 cup diced	18	trace
Chard, Swiss			
raw	1 cup chopped	6	trace
	1 leaf	9	trace
cooked	1 cup chopped	35	trace
Chickpeas or garbanzos			
raw	1 cup	729	109
boiled	1 cup	269	38
canned	1 cup	285	25
Chili with beans, canned	1 cup	286	126
Coleslaw (made with light cream)	½ cup	42	14
Collard greens, cooked	1 cup chopped	27	trace
Corn			
cooked	1 ear	85	9
	1 cup kernels	178	19
canned, cream style	1 cup	186	10
popcorn (see **GRAIN PRODUCTS, SNACK FOODS**)			
Cowpeas			
raw	1 cup	562	19

VEGETABLES AND VEGETABLE PRODUCTS

FOOD	AMOUNT	TOTAL CALORIES	FAT CALORIES
Cowpeas (*cont.*)			
boiled	1 cup	198	8
canned	1 cup	184	12
canned with pork	1 cup	199	34
Cucumber, raw	1 cucumber	39	trace
	1 cup slices	14	trace
Dandelion greens			
raw	1 cup chopped	25	trace
cooked	1 cup chopped	35	6
Eggplant			
raw	3.6 oz	27	trace
cooked	1 cup cubes	27	trace
Endive, raw	1 cup chopped	8	trace
	1 head	86	9
Falafel	1 patty	57	27
Garlic, raw	1 clove	4	0
Hummus	⅓ cup	140	62
Hyacinth beans			
raw	1 cup	723	32
boiled	1 cup	228	10
Kale			
raw	1 cup chopped	33	trace
cooked	1 cup chopped	41	5
Leeks			
raw	1	76	trace
	¼ cup chopped	16	trace
cooked	1	38	trace
	¼ cup chopped	8	trace
Lentils			
raw	1 cup	649	17
boiled	1 cup	231	7
Lettuce, raw			
butterhead, Boston	1 head (5-inch)	21	trace
	1 outer or 2 inner leaves	2	0
crisphead, iceberg	1 head (6-inch)	70	trace
	1 wedge (¼ head)	20	0
	1 cup shredded	5	0
looseleaf, romaine	1 cup shredded	10	0
Mushrooms			
raw, sliced, chopped	1 cup pieces	20	0
	1 lb	127	13
cooked	1 cup pieces	42	7

VEGETABLES AND VEGETABLE PRODUCTS

FOOD	AMOUNT	TOTAL CALORIES	FAT CALORIES
Mushrooms (*cont.*)			
canned	1 cup pieces	38	trace
Mushrooms, shiitake			
dried	4 mushrooms	44	trace
cooked	4 mushrooms	40	trace
	1 cup pieces	80	trace
Okra			
raw	8 pods	36	trace
	1 cup slices	38	trace
cooked	8 pods	27	trace
	1 cup slices	50	trace
Onion rings, frozen, prepared (breaded and pan-fried in vegetable oil), heated	7 rings	285	168
Onions			
raw	1 cup chopped	54	trace
cooked	1 cup chopped	58	trace
Onions, green, raw	1 cup chopped	26	trace
Parsley, raw	10 sprigs	3	0
Parsnips			
raw	1 cup slices	100	trace
cooked	1 cup slices	126	trace
Peas, green			
raw	1 cup	118	trace
cooked	1 cup	134	trace
Peas, split			
raw	1 cup	671	21
boiled	1 cup	231	7
Peas and carrots, canned	1 cup	96	6
Peas and onions, canned	1 cup	122	8
Peppers			
hot chili, raw	1	18	trace
	½ cup chopped	30	trace
jalapeño	½ cup chopped	17	trace
sweet, raw	1	18	trace
	½ cup chopped	12	trace
sweet, cooked	1	13	trace
	½ cup chopped	12	trace
Potatoes			
baked in skin	1 (2⅓ × 4¾-inch, about 2/lb raw)	145	trace
	1 lb	325	trace

VEGETABLES AND VEGETABLE PRODUCTS

FOOD	AMOUNT	TOTAL CALORIES	FAT CALORIES
Potatoes (*cont.*)			
boiled in skin	1 (2⅓ × 4¾–inch)	173	trace
	1 (2½-inch diam, about 3/lb raw)	104	trace
	1 cup diced or sliced	118	trace
	1 lb	345	trace
boiled, pared before cooking	1 (2⅓ × 4¾–inch, 2/lb)	146	trace
	1 (2½-inch diam, 3/lb)	88	trace
	1 cup diced or sliced	101	trace
	1 lb	295	trace
au gratin, dry mix, prepared	1 cup	230	90
French fries (see also **FAST FOODS**)			
frozen, oven-heated	10 strips	111	39
fried in oil (prepared in restaurant)	10 strips	158	75
hashed brown, frozen, prepared	½ cup	170	81
mashed			
with whole milk	½ cup	81	6
with whole milk and butter or margarine	½ cup	111	40
potato chips	10	105	64
Pringle's	1 oz	170	117
Pringle's Light	1 oz	150	72
Utz	1 oz	150	90
	1 cup	125	75
potato pancakes, made with eggs and margarine	1 pancake	495	113
potato puffs, frozen, par-fried in vegetable oil	1	16	7
	½ cup	138	60
potato salad	½ cup	180	92
potato sticks	1 oz pkg	148	88
scalloped, from dry mix	1 cup	230	99
Pumpkin, cooked	1 cup mashed	49	trace
Pumpkin pie mix, canned	1 cup	282	trace

VEGETABLES AND VEGETABLE PRODUCTS

FOOD	AMOUNT	TOTAL CALORIES	FAT CALORIES
Radishes, raw	10	7	trace
	½ cup slices	10	trace
Sauerkraut, canned	1 cup	44	trace
Shallots, raw	1 tbsp chopped	7	trace
Soybeans			
raw	1 cup	774	334
boiled	1 cup	298	139
Soy products			
miso	1 cup	565	150
tofu	1 piece (2½ × 2¾ × 1–inch)	88	50
Spinach			
raw	1 cup chopped	6	trace
	10 oz pkg	46	trace
cooked	1 cup	41	trace
Spinach soufflé, made with whole milk, eggs, cheese, butter	1 cup	218	165
Squash			
summer (crookneck, zucchini)			
raw	1 cup slices	26	trace
cooked	1 cup slices	36	trace
winter (acorn, butternut)			
raw	1 squash	172	trace
	1 cup cubes	43	trace
cooked	1 cup cubes	79	trace
Succotash, cooked	1 cup	222	14
Sweet potatoes			
baked in skin	1 (5 × 2–inch diam)	118	trace
	½ cup mashed	103	trace
boiled without skin	1 cup mashed	344	trace
cooked, candied (with butter)	1 piece (2½ × 2–inch diam)	144	31
Tomatoes			
raw	1	24	trace
	1 cup chopped	35	trace
cooked	1 cup	60	trace
canned in tomato juice	1 cup	67	trace
Tomato juice, canned	1 cup	42	trace
Tomato products, canned			
marinara sauce	1 cup	171	75
paste	1 cup	220	21

VEGETABLES AND VEGETABLE PRODUCTS

FOOD	AMOUNT	TOTAL CALORIES	FAT CALORIES
Tomato products, canned (*cont.*)			
purée	1 cup	102	trace
sauce	1 cup	74	trace
spaghetti sauce (Prego, no salt added)	1 cup	200	108
Turnips, cooked	1 cup cubes	28	trace
Vegetable juice cocktail, canned	1 cup	44	trace
Water chestnuts, canned	1 cup slices	70	trace
Yam, cooked	1 cup cubes	158	trace
Zucchini			
raw	1 cup slices	26	trace
cooked	1 cup slices	36	trace

MISCELLANEOUS

FOOD	AMOUNT	TOTAL CALORIES	FAT CALORIES
Carob flour	1 tbsp	14	trace
Cocoa powder	1 tsp	5	trace
Gelatin, dry	1 envelope	25	trace
Ketchup	1 tbsp	15	0
Mustard	1 tsp	5	trace
Olives, green	4 medium	15	15
Olives, ripe	3 small or 2 large	15	15
Pickles			
dill	1 medium	5	trace
sweet	1	20	trace
gherkin	1	20	trace
Vinegar	1 tbsp	trace	0

Food Tables Index

This index was designed to help you find some of the harder-to-locate foods in these tables, as well as those foods that appear in several different categories.

GLOSSARY

TABLE OF
EQUIVALENT
MEASURES

APPENDIXES

REFERENCES

INDEX

Glossary

Adipose tissue. Tissue in which fat is stored.

Aerobic exercise. Steady, repetitive exercise that uses the large muscles and requires a steady supply of oxygen — in contrast to exercise that requires bursts of activity separated by periods of rest. Examples of aerobic exercises include walking, swimming, running, and biking. Aerobic exercise burns more fat than active sports, which burn more carbohydrate.

Basal metabolic rate (BMR). The rate at which energy is used when the body is completely at rest to maintain such vital functions as breathing, heartbeat, and digestion.

Burning or oxidation. The chemical process of combining substances (carbohydrates, fats, proteins in foods) with oxygen, resulting in the release of stored energy.

Calorie. A unit of heat or energy produced by burning (oxidizing) nutrients. Carbohydrates and proteins contain 4 calories per gram; fats, 9 calories per gram; and alcohol, 7 calories per gram.

Carbohydrate. One of the three major energy-containing nutrients in foods; the others are protein and fat. Carbohydrates are simple (sugars) or complex (starches); each type contains 4 calories per gram.

Cholesterol. A fatlike substance found in the cell membranes of all animals, including humans. Cholesterol is transported in the bloodstream. Some of it is manufactured by the body and some comes from the foods of animal origin that we eat. A healthy level of cholesterol for adults is below 200 mg/dL. A higher level is often associated with increased risk of heart disease.

Complex carbohydrate. One of the two major types of carbohydrates, which include starches. They are found in whole-grain and cereal products and fruits and vegetables. In their natural state complex carbohydrates are accompanied by dietary fiber.

Dietetic. A term used to describe a food that has been nutritionally altered in some way. "Dietetic" can mean less sodium, less fat, less sugar, or fewer calories. If a food is intended for weight loss, it must meet requirements for low-calorie or reduced-calorie claims. If not for weight loss, its label must state its special dietary purpose.

Energy. Power to do work. The energy in foods is measured in calories. A high-

295

energy food is a high-calorie food. Energy expenditure, as in exercise, is quantified in terms of calories expended or burned.

Fat. One of the three major energy-containing nutrients in foods; the others are carbohydrates and proteins. Fat is an oily substance that is found in many foods, especially oils, dairy products, and meat products. Fat is the major form of storing energy in the body. Fat stores in the adipose tissue total 140,000 or more calories. Fat contains 9 calories per gram.

Fat budget. The number of calories from ingested fat that are allowed per day to maintain a person's ideal weight. Fat budget is based on a percentage of desirable total calorie intake.

Fattening. A term commonly used to describe any substance that contributes to making a person fat. Many foods (often starchy ones) have been mislabeled "fattening." Truly, the most fattening substance is fat.

Fiber, dietary. A nondigestible substance found in plant products. It can be insoluble, like wheat fiber, or soluble, like oat bran, pectin (in fruits), and guar gum (in beans). Both types of fiber provide bulk and moderate the absorption of nutrients. Insoluble fibers help regularity, whereas soluble fibers reduce blood cholesterol.

Glucose. A simple carbohydrate or sugar found in foods and in the body; the preferred fuel for quick energy and the only fuel used by the brain.

Glycogen. The storage form of carbohydrate in the body; long chains of glucose linked end to end. Glycogen stores, which total about 800 calories, occur in liver, muscle, and other tissues.

Gram. A metric measure of weight. One ounce equals 28.35 grams. Nutrients are listed in grams on food labels: a gram of fat contains 9 calories; a gram of protein or carbohydrate contains 4 calories.

Hidden fat. Fat in foods that is not visible. Hidden fats include oils used in frying or baking and fat naturally present in foods, such as butterfat in cheese and whole milk, fat marbled throughout beef, or fat in the skin of poultry.

Ideal or desirable weight. Weight associated with general good health and lowest mortality rates.

Lean body mass. The metabolically active tissue in the body, primarily composed of muscle. The greater a person's lean body mass, the higher the metabolic rate and the greater protection against weight gain.

Lite or light. A term used to describe certain foods with the implication that they are lower in calories. In fact, lite or light may refer to color, texture, total calories, content of fat, alcohol, carbohydrate, sodium, or even portion size (light breads). The nutrition information on the label should be used to determine how much fat the product contains and thus how it can be fit into your fat budget.

Low-fat. A term used to imply that a food is acceptable for a weight reduction diet. Since there is no consistent definition of low-fat, foods labeled low-fat may actually contain substantial amounts of fat. To be sure a product can fit in your fat budget, check the fat content on the food label.

Metabolism. The sum of the chemical changes that occur to substances in the body. Much of metabolism is the conversion of food into living tissue and energy.

Monounsaturated fat. One of the three types of fat commonly found in foods. Monounsaturated fats help to reduce blood cholesterol levels. The richest source of monounsaturated fat is olive oil. Like all other fats, monounsaturated fat has 9 calories per gram.

Nitrites. Substances used to preserve, color, and flavor meat products. In the body, nitrites can be converted into nitrosamines, which have been shown to cause cancer.

Nondairy. A term commonly used for imitation dairy foods that contain no dairy products, such as imitation creamers, sour creams, and whipped toppings. While these products do not contain cholesterol, they do contain fat, often highly saturated fat like coconut oil. Check the nutrition information on labels to determine how much fat is present.

Nutrients. Substances in foods (carbohydrates, proteins, and fats) that contain energy and are building blocks for making living tissue. Also includes substances needed for normal bodily functioning, such as minerals and vitamins.

Obesity. Excess accumulation of body fat. Obese is defined as 20 percent to 40 percent over ideal weight, massively obese as greater than 40 percent over ideal weight.

Oxidation. See burning.

Polyunsaturated fat. One of the three types of fat commonly found in foods. Polyunsaturated fat helps to lower blood cholesterol, but in excess can lower the "good" cholesterol in the blood and has been associated with an increased risk of cancer. The most common sources of polyunsaturated fats are corn, sunflower, and safflower oils. Like all other fats, polyunsaturated fat has 9 calories per gram.

Protein. One of the nutrients in foods that provides energy and building blocks for making essential body constituents such as muscle, enzymes, and cell membranes.

Reduced-calorie. A term regulated by the Food and Drug Administration that means a product is at least one-third lower in calories than the food with which it is being compared. It does not necessarily mean that the product is low in fat. Consult the nutrition information on labels for fat content.

Saturated fat. One of the three types of fat commonly found in foods, saturated fat has a powerful effect on raising blood cholesterol levels. The most common sources of saturated fats are butterfat; beef, veal, lamb, and chicken fat; cocoa butter; hydrogenated vegetable oil; and the tropical oils (coconut, palm kernel, and palm). Like all other fats, saturated fat has 9 calories per gram.

Simple carbohydrate. One of the two major types of carbohydrate, also known as sugar. In contrast to complex carbohydrates, simple carbohydrates are not usually associated with any nutritionally beneficial substances and are often said to contain empty calories.

Sugar. Any carbohydrate with a sweet taste.

Thermogenesis or thermogenic effect of food. The process of producing heat. Carbohydrates in foods we eat increase the metabolic rate and produce a thermogenic effect.

Vegetable oil. The fat from plant products. Some vegetable oils are mostly unsaturated and are liquid at room temperature (olive, corn, sunflower) and some are mostly saturated and are solid at room temperature (coconut, palm kernel, palm). All vegetable oils are 100 percent fat and have 9 calories per gram.

Table of Equivalent Measures

Volume Measures

1 gallon	4 quarts
1 quart	4 cups 2 pints
1 pint	2 cups
1 cup	8 fluid ounces 16 tablespoons
½ cup	4 fluid ounces 8 tablespoons
⅓ cup	5 tablespoons + 1 teaspoon
¼ cup	2 fluid ounces 4 tablespoons
2 tablespoons	1 fluid ounce
1 tablespoon	3 teaspoons ½ fluid ounce

Weight Measures

1 pound	16 ounces 454 grams
3.5 ounces	100 grams
1 ounce	28.35 grams

Appendix A:
How to Keep a Food Record

A DIARY OF MY TRUE EATING HABITS

Now you are ready to get started on the road to leanness. Your first activity is to discover which foods have been making you fat. If you are like most people who want to lose weight, you know that you are eating some fattening foods. What you don't know is exactly how much fat is in the foods you eat or which foods are loaded with fat. That is why you are going to keep a food record, an activity you will find rewarding, insightful, and even a bit of fun.

HOW TO KEEP YOUR FOOD RECORD

Write down everything you eat for three days including one weekend day. Your diary is between you and yourself. No one else will look at it, so be completely honest. Eat normally. Do not refrain from eating something because you will have to write it down. Don't put that hand-ful of peanuts back in the dish because you will have to write it down. This record is a baseline. If you are too perfect (better than you usually are), you won't learn anything about yourself. It will appear that you have no baggage to discard.

Details Count
1. Record What You Eat When You Eat It: Write down what you eat when you eat it. Don't go back at the end of the day and fill in your record. You're bound to forget what you don't want to remember. Re-cording the time helps you see patterns in your eating. The fact that there are ten hours between your first and second entry may give you a clue as to why you are famished for dinner.

299

2. List All Foods Separately and List Amounts Accurately: Measure everything. Be accurate. Don't just write down peanut butter. Write down the amount you ate — peanut butter, 2 tablespoons. Don't simply write down chicken breast. Write down chicken breast with skin, batter-fried. Don't merely write down roast beef sub. Ask the sandwich maker how much roast beef and how much mayonnaise he gave you. (He'll know — his boss makes sure he gives everyone an exact amount.) Write down 6-inch sub roll, 4 ounces roast beef, 1 tablespoon mayonnaise. These details are important. If you eat out, ask the waiter what's in the cream sauce and how much butter was melted on the swordfish, the potato, vegetables, or toast.

Sample Food Record Listings

TIME	FOOD	AMOUNT		
9 A.M.	Peanut butter	2 tbsp		
1 P.M.	Chicken breast with skin, batter-fried	1 breast		
1 P.M.	Roast beef	4 oz		
	6″ sub roll	1		
	Mayonnaise	1 tbsp		

HINTS ON MEASURING AND RECORDING WHAT YOU MEASURED

Liquids

Measure: Use measuring cups to measure liquids. In addition, you might fill the glasses, mugs, or cups you normally use with liquid to measure the amount each holds.

Record: Milk products, coffee whiteners, and cooking oils should be recorded in measuring cup and spoon amounts.

Most other liquids should be recorded in fluid ounce amounts.

Sample Food Record Listings

TIME	FOOD	AMOUNT		
8 A.M.	2% milk	1 cup		
8 A.M.	Half-and-half	1 tbsp		
8 A.M.	Orange juice	6 fl oz		
1 P.M.	Eggnog	8 fl oz		

This table of equivalent measures should help you record liquids.

1 cup = 8 fluid ounces
½ cup = 4 fluid ounces
¼ cup = 2 fluid ounces
2 tablespoons = 1 fluid ounce

Solid Food

Meat, poultry, and fish: Read package labels or use a scale to measure the weight, in ounces, of beef, lamb, pork, veal, poultry, and fish. Record the number of ounces, indicating whether the meat was raw or cooked when weighed and if fat is included, or has been trimmed.

If necessary, use the following estimates:

¼ cup meat = 1 ounce meat
Chicken breast half = 3 ounces
4 ounces raw meat without bone = 3 ounces cooked
6 ounces raw meat with bone = 3 ounces cooked

Candy, cheese,* cold cuts, nuts, yogurt, frozen yogurt: Read the label on the package or use a scale to measure the weight in ounces. Save packages with nutrition labeling for use later. Record weight of food in ounces.

Sample Food Record Listings

TIME	FOOD	AMOUNT		
1 P.M.	Flank steak, meat and fat, raw	5 oz		
6 P.M.	Salmon, baked	6 oz		
9 P.M.	Swiss cheese	2 oz		
9 P.M.	Salami, beef	0.8 oz (1 slice)		
9 P.M.	Yogurt, Whitney's lemon	6 fl oz		

Fast foods: Fast foods should be recorded by unit, piece, serving, order, or slice, except for shakes, which are measured in fluid ounces.

---

*Note: cottage cheese and ricotta are exceptions; they should be measured in a measuring cup.

Sample Food Record Listings

TIME	FOOD	AMOUNT		
1 P.M.	McDonald's Quarter Pounder	1		
1 P.M.	Kentucky Fried Chicken breast	1 piece		
1 P.M.	Jack-in-the-Box onion fries	1 serving		?
1 P.M.	Long John Silver's breaded shrimp	1 order		
9 P.M.	Domino's pizza	2 slices		
9 P.M.	Roy Rogers chocolate shake	11.25 fl oz		

Cereals,* cottage cheese, creams, fats, frozen desserts, canned fish, sliced fruit, grains, milks, nuts,** pasta, puddings (not canned), rice, salad dressings, sauces and gravies, snacks, soups, vegetables: Use measuring cups and spoons to measure and record these foods.

Sample Food Record Listings

TIME	FOOD	AMOUNT		
8 A.M.	Cream of Wheat, cooked	1 cup		
8 A.M.	Bran Chex	1 oz or ⅔ cup		
Noon	Sour cream	3 tbsp		
Noon	Noodles, egg, cooked	¾ c		
1 P.M.	Tomato soup, prepared with milk	1½ c		
9 P.M.	Cashews	12 nuts		

Bread: Record by slice.

Cakes and pies: Record by a fraction of the whole dessert, for example, ¹⁄₁₀ cake.

Crackers and cookies: Record by unit, that is, 5 crackers.

Frozen food: Record by package or fraction of package you eat. Save packages with labels for future reference.

---

*You may also weigh and record cereal in ounces.
**You may also weigh and record nuts in ounces or count and record the number of nuts you eat.

Sample Food Record Listings

TIME	FOOD	AMOUNT		
8 A.M.	Oatmeal bread	2 sl		
Noon	Cheesecake	1/12 cake		
Noon	Blueberry Newtons	4 cookies		
1 P.M.	Lean Cuisine, Chicken à l'Orange	1 package		

Summary Chart

The following table lists foods and the units used to measure them.

FOOD/BEVERAGE	UNIT	EXAMPLES
Dairy/Eggs		
Butter	pat, teaspoon, tablespoon	
Cheese, hard, soft	ounce	2 oz Cheddar
Cheese, curd type	cup	1/2 c cottage cheese
Cream	tablespoon	1 tbsp light cream
Milk	cup	1 c buttermilk
Yogurt	fluid ounce	8 fl oz nonfat strawberry yogurt
	cup	1 c nonfat plain yogurt
Egg	1 egg	
	1 egg white	
	1 egg yolk	
Fast Foods	number	1 cheeseburger
	order	1 order shrimp
	ounce	8 oz shake
	piece	1 chicken breast
	serving	1 serving coleslaw
	slice or fraction of whole*	2 slices, 10-inch pepperoni pizza
Fats and Oils		
Margarine	teaspoon, tablespoon	2 tsp Promise
Oils	teaspoon, tablespoon	1 tbsp olive
Salad dressings	teaspoon, tablespoon	1 tbsp Russian
Fish and Seafood	ounce	4 oz flounder

*Specify diameter of whole (i.e., pizza, 14-inch diameter).

FOOD/BEVERAGE	UNIT	EXAMPLES
Frozen and Microwave	Depends on product	Use information on food labels
Fruits and Fruit Juices	piece cup	1 apple ½ c applesauce
Grain Products Bagel Bread Cereal Cracker Pasta/rice Popcorn Roll	 number slice cup ounce number cup cup number	 1 bagel 1 slice rye ¾ c Wheatena 1 oz Cheerios 3 Wheat Thins 2 c macaroni 5½ cups air-popped 1 poppy seed
Meats	ounce	5 oz round steak, with fat
Nuts and Seeds	ounce tablespoon number of kernels cup	3 oz pecans 2 tbsp peanut butter 12 peanuts ¼ c pumpkin seeds
Poultry	piece ounce	½ chicken breast 3 ounces white meat turkey
Sauces and Gravies	tablespoon cup	3 tbsp mushroom gravy ¼ c cream sauce
Sausages and Luncheon Meats	ounce slice link	2 oz turkey bologna 2 slices salami 1 link smoked sausage
Soups	cup	1½ c tomato soup
Sweets Cakes Cookies, bars Pie Sugar, jelly	 fraction of whole number fraction of whole teaspoon, tablespoon	 1/12 chocolate cake 1 sugar cookie ⅙ pumpkin pie 1 tsp grape jam
Vegetables and Vegetable Products	cup number	½ c spinach 1 carrot

Remember to record every detail of what you eat so that you have enough information to determine the fat calories later.

Use the forms on the following page to keep your food record. You may wish to order a pocket-size "Passbook," which includes abbreviated *Choose to Lose* food tables, and a balance book to keep a two-week record of the total and fat calories you consume. See the last page of the book for details.

Go to It!

When you have completed your food record, return to Chapter 3. If you are too impatient to wait three or four days before you pick up *Choose to Lose* again and are sure that knowing a lot about fat in food will not influence what you record, continue reading Chapter 3 and complete your food record. Be sure that you are completely honest about your entries. They don't have to look good. They are for your eyes only.

Food Record

Date: Day:

TIME	FOOD	AMOUNT		

Food Record

Date: Day:

TIME	FOOD	AMOUNT		

Food Record

Date: Day:

TIME	FOOD	AMOUNT		

Food Record

Date: Day:

TIME	FOOD	AMOUNT		

Appendix B: Fat Calories of *Eater's Choice* Recipes

The fat calories of the *Eater's Choice* recipes given below are from the 1989 revised edition, third and subsequent printings.* They do not include the recipes adapted and used in *Choose to Lose*.

RECALCULATING FAT CALORIES

If you wish to further reduce the fat content of these recipes, the following directions will help you determine the new lower number of fat calories.

1. Figure out how many fat calories you are eliminating from the recipe.

   > 1 tablespoon of olive oil contains 119 fat calories;
   > 1 tablespoon of margarine contains 90 fat calories.**

   For example, the recipe for *Gazpacho I* calls for 3 tablespoons of olive oil. You decide to use only 2 tablespoons of olive oil instead. You are eliminating 1 tablespoon of olive oil (119 fat calories).

2. Look at the following list to find the fat calories per serving in Gazpacho I — 60 fat calories in each serving. To figure out the fat calories for the entire recipe, multiply the number of servings (6) by the number of fat calories in each serving (60).

   $$6 \times 60 = 360 \text{ fat calories}$$

3. Subtract the fat calories you eliminated (119) from the total fat calories of the recipe (360).

   $$360 - 119 = 241$$

*To determine the printing of your book, turn to the copyright page. You will see a list at the bottom — Q 10 9 8 7 6 5 4 3 . The last number is the printing number. In this example, the book is in its third printing.
**These recipes were made with Promise margarine, which contains 90 calories of fat per tablespoon.

The fat calories for the entire recipe of *Gazpacho* with 1 tablespoon of olive oil eliminated are 241. To get the new fat calories per serving, divide 241 by the number of servings (6).

$$241 \div 6 = {\sim}40$$

The *Gazpacho* with reduced fat has about 40 fat calories per serving.

FAT CONTENT OF *EATER'S CHOICE* RECIPES

RECIPE	FAT CALORIES PER SERVING
Soups	
Avgolemono	6
Matzo Ball	26
Mushroom	18
Potato with Leeks and Broccoli	25
Peanut Butter	107
Apple Squash	23
Green Tomato	28
Sweet Cabbage	1
Broccoli	31
Corn Chowder	38
Watercress	18
Gazpacho I without croutons	60
with croutons	62
Gazpacho II without croutons	60
with croutons	61
Hot and Sour	22
Mulligatawny	31
Monhegan Island Fish Chowder	28
Mild Fish Chowder	20
Minestrone	18
Vegetable Soup Provençal	17
Green Pesto	39
Lentil and Everything . . .	13
Chilled Strawberry	0
Cuban Black Bean	32
Chicken	
Lime-Peanut-Ginger	99
Chicken Kiev	108
Indonesian Peanut	120
Tandoori	13
Chicken with Apples and Onions	48
Chicken Smothered in Vegetables	44
Peppery Chicken	43

FAT CONTENT OF *EATER'S CHOICE* RECIPES

RECIPE	FAT CALORIES PER SERVING
Chicken (*cont.*)	
Ma-Po Bean Curd	57
Chicken Couscous	53
Grilled Apricot-Ginger Chicken	38
Sesame Chicken Brochettes	70
Baghdad	63
Chinese	
breast	13
thigh	24
drumstick	19
Phyllo Chicken with Rice, Artichokes, and Cream	
Sauce	79
Cuban	64
Lemon-Mustard	73
Coq au Vin	
breast	97
drumstick	103
thigh	108
Pineapple	30
Creamy Chicken Pie	126
Kung Pao Chicken with Broccoli	76
Chicken Paprikash	69
Chicken with Apricots, Sweet Potatoes, and Prunes	74
Singapore	62
Tortillas con Pollo	50
Chicken Curry	68
Mongolian Hot Pot	
peanut sauce (per tablespoon)	70
chicken, scallops, tofu, and vegetables	40
Sate Ajam	93
Keema Matar	90
Ginger Chicken with Green Onions	51
Orange-Soy	29
Chicken Verde	73
Vegetables, Chicken, and Cellophane Noodles	44
Chicken Nuggets Chez Goor	73
Shepherd's Chicken Chili Pie	54
Turkey	
Basic Turkey Cutlet	75
Turkey Scaloppine Limone	98
Turkey Scaloppine Marsala	98
Turkey Cutlets with Artichoke-Cream Sauce	102

FAT CONTENT OF *EATER'S CHOICE* RECIPES

RECIPE	FAT CALORIES PER SERVING
Turkey (cont.)	
Turkey Véronique	70
Turkey Roll-ups Firenze	32
Breaded Turkey Cutlet	137
Turkey Sautéed with Onions and Almonds	93
Broccoli Baked Turkey	32
Creamy Turkey Casserole	49
Turkey with Snow Peas	6
Fish and Seafood	
Broiled Monkfish with Orange Sauce	52
Marinated Fish Steaks	
with monkfish	46
with swordfish	90
Salmon with Cucumber-Grape Sauce (3 oz steaks)	
with Atlantic salmon	82
with chinook salmon	114
with pink salmon	60
with sockeye salmon	99
Curry Fish	
without condiments	52
with condiments	65
Dill Fish	12
Flounder Fillets Stuffed with Fennel Rice	44
Phyllo-wrapped Fish and Mushroom Sauce	
with mushroom sauce	118
without mushroom sauce	61
Fish with Mushroom Sauce	84
Oriental Fish Kebabs	51
Shanghai Fish	12
Fish with Peppercorns, Thyme, and Mustard	23
Salmon Soufflé	32
Scallops Provençal	79
Scallops or Shrimp Caribbean	
with shrimp	35
with scallops	26
Spicy Shrimp Louisiana	55
Vegetables	
Sweet Vegetable Mélange	30
Vegetable Soufflé with Tahini Sauce	22
tahini sauce (per tablespoon)	27
Muriel's Chinese Vegetables	40

FAT CONTENT OF *EATER'S CHOICE* RECIPES

RECIPE	FAT CALORIES PER SERVING
Vegetables (*cont.*)	
Italian Mixed Vegetables	45
Ratatouille	36
Artichoke	0
with margarine (per tablespoon)	90
Curried Beans	25
Chickpeas with Lemon and Herbs	46
Green Beans Basilico	16
Broccoli and Mushrooms	21
Sesame Broccoli	20
Caraway Carrots	15
Carrots and Leeks	30
Cauliflower Sauté	40
Celery-Mushrooms	30
Keema Eggplant	24
Eggplant with a Greek Influence	35
Lentils and Potatoes	23
Braised Mushrooms Oriental	55
Potatoes Lyonnaise	37
Fluffy Sweet Potatoes	38
Spinach and Tomatoes	44
Spinach Oriental	30
Acorn Squash	15
Glazed Acorn Squash	0
Afghan Squash	30
Curried Zucchini	22
Pizza, Chili, Quiche, and Tortillas	
Pizza, whole	578
each slice	36
Calzone	46
Pissaladière, slice	92
Spinach Quiche, slice	70
Tomato Quiche, slice	108
Craig Lefebvre's Pawtucket Chili	21
Tortillas	20
Pasta, Rice, and Other Grains	
Creamy Fettuccine with Vegetables	9
Peasant Pasta	68
Pasta Mexacali	19
Pasta with Pesto	106
Spaghetti Touraine	149

FAT CONTENT OF *EATER'S CHOICE* RECIPES

RECIPE	FAT CALORIES PER SERVING

Pasta, Rice, and Other Grains (*cont.*)

Olive-Artichoke Rice	36
Rice Pilau with Apricots and Raisins	21
Lemon Rice with Spinach and Red Pepper	15
Fried Rice	46
Bulgur with Tomatoes and Olives	23
Barley Plus	30

Salads

Tarragon-Raisin Chicken Salad	36
Coriander Chicken Salad	21
Chicken Salad with Shallots and Mushrooms	48
Oriental Chicken Salad	145
Salade Niçoise	105
Indonesian Vegetable Salad	59
Tabbouli	31
Eastern Spinach Salad	35

Sandwiches and Dips

Tofu (Mock Egg Salad) Sandwich, per sandwich	54
Eggplant Appetizer	56

	FAT CALORIES	
FOOD	PER LOAF	PER SLICE OR PIECE

Breads

Shaker Daily Loaf	117	7
French	104	10
Buttermilk Herb	338	20
Ginger-Orange	221	13
Challah	317	13
Peanut Butter	263	15
Pumpernickel	243	10
Honey Whole-Wheat	342	17
Oatmeal	167	10
Whole-Wheat Bagels		23
Mother's Oat Bran Muffins		
with walnuts		49
without walnuts		36
Orange Oat Muffins		34
Banana-Carrot Muffins		
with walnuts		64
without walnuts		37
modified with walnuts		51
modified without walnuts		24

FAT CONTENT OF *EATER'S CHOICE* RECIPES

FOOD	FAT CALORIES PER SLICE OR PIECE
Breads (*cont.*)	
Gingerbread Muffins	59
Buttermilk Pancakes	19
Desserts	
Applesauce Cake	89
Apple Cake	114
Banana Cake	110
Lemon Loaf	
with walnuts	142
without walnuts	76
Carrot Cake Sans Oeufs	40
Ginger Cake with Pear Sauce	63
Orange Cake	74
Peach Pound Cake	74
Cocoa Angel Food Cake	<1
Marble Cake	75
Divine Buttermilk Pound Cake	66
with mocha frosting	81
with walnut glaze	71
Spice Cake	96
with frosting	118
Chocolatey-Chocolate Cocoa Cake	71
Mocha Cake	
with icing	61
without icing	50
Strawberry Tart	57
Strawberry-Rhubarb Pie	63
Apple Pandowdy	74
Deep-Dish Pear Pie	61
Cocoa Brownies	54
Marvelous Cookies	39
Apple-Nut Cookies	25
Pears Hélène	23
Strawberry Mousse	0

Appendix C: Progress Chart

WEEK	FAT BUDGET	AVERAGE DAILY FAT INTAKE*	AVERAGE DAILY EXERCISE**	WEIGHT
1				
2				
3				
4				
5				
6				
7				
8				
9				
10				
11				
12				

*To calculate your average daily fat intake for each week, add up the total fat calories you consumed each day of the week and divide by 7.
**To calculate your average daily exercise for each week, add up the minutes of sustained aerobic exercise you did each day of the week and divide by 7.

References

Chapter 1

Acheson, K. J., Y. Schutz, T. Bessard, K. Anantharaman, J. P. Flatt, and E. Jequier. "Glycogen Storage Capacity and de Novo Lipogenesis During Massive Carbohydrate Overfeeding in Man." *American Journal of Clinical Nutrition* 48 (1988):240–247.

Barrows, K., and J. T. Snook. "Effect of a High-Protein, Very-Low-Calorie Diet on Resting Metabolism, Thyroid Hormones, and Energy Expenditure in Obese Middle-Aged Women." *American Journal of Clinical Nutrition* 45 (1987):391–398.

Bray, G. A. "Obesity — A Disease of Nutrient or Energy Balance?" *Nutrition Reviews* 45 (1987):33–43.

"Can Eating the 'Right' Food Cut Your Risk of Cancer?" *Tufts University Diet and Nutrition Letter* 6 (1988):2–6.

Donato, K., and D. M. Hegsted. "Efficiency of Utilization of Various Sources of Energy for Growth." *Proceedings of the National Academy of Sciences* 82 (1985):4866–4870.

Dougherty, R. M., A. K. H. Fong, and J. M. Iacono. "Nutrient Content of the Diet When the Fat Is Reduced." *American Journal of Clinical Nutrition* 48 (1988):970–979.

Dreon, D. M., B. Frey-Hewitt, N. Ellsworth, et al. "Dietary Fat: Carbohydrate Ratio and Obesity in Middle-Aged Men." *American Journal of Clinical Nutrition* 47 (1988):995–1000.

Elliot, D. L., L. Goldberg, K. S. Kuehl, and W. M. Bennett. "Sustained Depressions of the Resting Metabolic Rate after Massive Weight Loss." *American Journal of Clinical Nutrition* 49 (1989):93–96.

Flatt, J. P. "Dietary Fat, Carbohydrate Balance, and Weight Maintenance: Effects of Exercise." *American Journal of Clinical Nutrition* 45 (1987):296–306.

———. "Effect of Carbohydrate and Fat Intake on Postprandial Substrate Oxidation and Storage." *Topics in Clinical Nutrition* 2(2) (1987):15–27.

———. "Metabolic Feedback on Food Intake Among ad Libitum Fed Mice." *International Journal of Obesity* 9 (1985):A33.

Gray, D. S., J. S. Fisler, and G. A. Bray. "Effects of Repeated Weight Loss and

Regain on Body Composition in Obese Rats." *American Journal of Clinical Nutrition* 47 (1988):393–399.

Hammer, R. L., C. A. Barrier, E. S. Roundy, J. M. Bradford, and A. G. Fisher. "Calorie Restricted Low-Fat Diet and Exercise in Obese Women." *American Journal of Clinical Nutrition* 49 (1989):77–85.

Katch, F., and W. D. McArdle. *Nutrition, Weight Control, and Exercise.* Philadelphia: Lea & Febiger, 1988.

Lissner, L., D. A. Levitsky, B. J. Strupp, et al. "Dietary Fat and the Regulation of Energy Intake in Human Subjects." *American Journal of Clinical Nutrition* 46 (1987):886–892.

Manson, J. E., M. J. Stampfer, C. H. Hennekens, and W. C. Willett. "Body Weight and Longevity." *Journal of the American Medical Association* 257 (1987):353–358.

Mattes, R. D., C. B. Pierce, and M. I. Friedman. "Daily Caloric Intake of Normal-Weight Adults: Response to Changes in Dietary Energy Density of a Luncheon Meal." *American Journal of Clinical Nutrition* 48 (1988):214–219.

Romieu, I., W. C. Willett, M. J. Stampfer, G. A. Colditz, et al. "Energy Intake and Other Determinants of Relative Weight." *American Journal of Clinical Nutrition* 47 (1988):406–412.

Schutz, Y., J. P. Flatt, and Eric Jequier. "Failure of dietary fat intake to promote fat oxidation: a factor favoring the development of obesity." *American Journal of Clinical Nutrition* (1989) 50:307–14.

Steen, S. N., R. A. Oppliger, and K. D. Brownell. "Metabolic Effects of Repeated Weight Loss and Regain in Adolescent Wrestlers." *Journal of the American Medical Association* 260 (1988):47–50.

Chapter 2

Dennison, D. *The DINE System: The Nutritional Plan for Better Health.* St. Louis: C. V. Mosby, 1982.

Chapter 3

National Center for Health Statistics. *Anthropometric Reference Data and Prevalence of Overweight, United States 1976–1980.* DHHS Publication No. 87-1688. Washington, D.C.: Government Printing Office, 1987.

U.S. Department of Health and Human Services. "Health Implications of Obesity." *National Institutes of Health Consensus Development Conference Statement.* vol. 5, No. 9, 1985. National Institutes of Health, Office of Medical Applications of Research, Building 1, Room 216, Bethesda, MD 20205.

U.S. Department of Health and Human Services. *The Surgeon General's Report on Nutrition and Health.* DHHS (PHS) Publication No. 88-50210. Washington, D.C.: Government Printing Office, 1988.

The fat tables are based on data from the following sources:

U.S. Department of Agriculture. *Composition of Foods.* Agriculture Handbook No. 8. Washington, D.C.: Government Printing Office, sec. 1–16, rev. 1976–1989.

U.S. Department of Agriculture. *Nutritive Value of American Foods in Common Units.* Agriculture Handbook No. 456. Washington, D.C.: Government Printing Office, November 1975.

Chapter 8

Stunkard, A. J., and H. C. Berthold. "What Is Behavior Therapy? A Very Short Description of Behavioral Weight Control." *American Journal of Clinical Nutrition* 41 (1985):821–823.

Stunkard, A. J., T. T. Foch, and Z. Hrubec. "A Twin Study of Human Obesity." *Journal of the American Medical Association* 256 (1986):51–54.

Stunkard, A. J., T. I. A. Sorenson, C. Hanis, et al. "An Adoption Study of Human Obesity." *New England Journal of Medicine* 314 (1986):193–198.

Chapter 9

Ballor, D. L., V. L. Katch, M. D. Becque, and C. R. Marks. "Resistance Weight Training during Calorie Restriction Enhances Lean Body Weight Maintenance." *American Journal of Clinical Nutrition* 47 (1988):19–25.

Cooper, Kenneth. *The New Aerobics.* New York: Bantam Books, 1983.

Cooper, Kenneth, and Mildred Cooper. *The New Aerobics for Women.* New York: Bantam Books, 1988.

Hammer, R. L., and C. A. Barrier, E. S. Roundy, J. M. Bradford, and A. G. Fisher. "Calorie Restricted Low-Fat Diet and Exercise in Obese Women." *American Journal of Clinical Nutrition* 49 (1989):77–85.

Hill, J. O., P. B. Sparling, T. W. Shields, and P. A. Heller. "Effects of Exercise and Food Restriction on Body Composition and Metabolic Rate in Obese Women." *American Journal of Clinical Nutrition* 46 (1987):622–630.

Katch, F., and W. D. McArdle. *Nutrition, Weight Control, and Exercise.* Philadelphia: Lea & Febiger, 1988.

Rippe, J. M., A. Ward, J. P. Porcari, and P. S. Freedson. "Walking for Health and Fitness." *Journal of the American Medical Association* 259 (1988):2720–2724.

U.S. Department of Health and Human Services, Public Health Service. *Exercise and Your Heart.* National Institutes of Health Publication No. 18-1677, 1981.

Chapter 10

Dougherty, R. M., A. K. H. Fong, and J. M. Iacono. "Nutrient Content of the Diet When the Fat Is Reduced." *American Journal of Clinical Nutrition* 48 (1988):970–979.

Goor, R., and N. Goor. *Eater's Choice: A Food Lover's Guide to Lower Cholesterol,* rev. ed. Boston: Houghton Mifflin, 1989.

James, W. P. T., M. E. J. Lean, and G. McNeill. "Dietary Recommendations after Weight Loss: How to Avoid Relapse of Obesity." *American Journal of Clinical Nutrition* 45 (1987):1135–1141.

Index

CHOOSE TO L♥SE
POCKET COMPANIONS

CHOOSE TO LOSE PASSBOOK

The key to losing weight is to stay within your Fat Budget. This convenient, pocket-sized passbook with a handsome vinyl cover contains everything you need to keep track of your fat intake:

- ABBREVIATED FOOD TABLES, which list the total calories and fat calories of hundreds of foods and have space for your favorites.
- BALANCE BOOK for keeping a two-week record of the fat calories and total calories of the food you eat as well as the time you spend exercising.

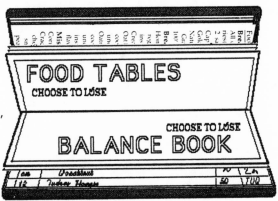

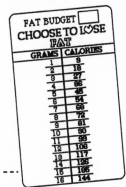

CHOOSE TO LOSE FAT GRAM/CALORIE CONVERTER

The ingredient label shows 17 grams of fat per ice cream bar. To determine the number of fat calories quickly, just reach for your durable plastic Choose to Lose FAT GRAM/ CALORIE CONVERTER to see that 17 grams of fat equals 153 fat calories — an indispensable aid (the size of a credit card) to help you make intelligent food choices. *Included with the Passbook or available separately.*

ORDER FORM

SHIP TO:

Name _____

Address _____

City _____ State _____ Zip _____

ITEM	QUANTITY	PRICE EACH	TOTAL PRICE
Passbook with Gram/Calorie Converter		$4.50	$
Gram/Calorie Converter		.50	
Balance book refills		.75	
The Choose to Lose Diet (hardcover)		17.95	
Eater's Choice (softcover)		11.95	
	5% tax (MD residents)		
Send check or money order to:	Handling		.50
	TOTAL ORDER		$

Send check or money order to:
   Choose to Lose
   P.O. Box 2053
   Rockville, MD 20852